ISBN 978-1-331-72639-5
PIBN 10226712

1 MONTH OF
FREE
READING

at

www.ForgottenBooks.com

By purchasing this book you are eligible for one month membership to ForgottenBooks.com, giving you unlimited access to our entire collection of over 700,000 titles via our web site and mobile apps.

To claim your free month visit:

www.forgottenbooks.com/free226712

Geo, C, Hodges   4°⁰

Greenwood

S.C.

, 1908

---

rs. Hodges and myself
ended this meeting from
gunning toward. G.C.H.

EXECUTIVE COMMITTEE LAYMEN'S MISSIONARY MOVEMENT.

Begin at top, and read from left to right

G. W. CAIN, W. R. LAMBUTH, F. M. DANIEL, GEN. JULIAN S. CARR, JOHN R. PEPPER, W. G. M. THOMAS, C. H. IRELAND, T. S. DE ARMAN, D. H. ABERNATHY, E. D. NEWMAN.

THE

CALL OF GOD TO MEN

PAPERS AND ADDRESSES

OF THE CONFERENCE OF THE LAYMEN'S MISSION-ARY MOVEMENT OF THE METHODIST EPISCOPAL CHURCH, SOUTH

————

Held at Chattanooga, Tenn., April 21–23, 1908

————

PUBLISHED FOR THE LAYMEN'S MISSIONARY MOVEMENT OF
THE METHODIST EPISCOPAL CHURCH, SOUTH
G. W. CAIN, SEC., NASHVILLE, TENN.

OFFICERS AND COMMITTEES.

___

(ii)

NOTE.

IN producing this report of the Laymen's Missionary Conference, held in Chattanooga April 21-23, 1908, it was the earnest desire of all the leaders of the Movement, and those most nearly related to the preparation of the book, that it should be a very helpful campaign volume. For this reason it was necessary that some one should be found who might carefully arrange and edit the matter and bring it out in the best, most attractive, and useful manner. By common consent Rev. W. W. Pinson, D.D., one of our Missionary Secretaries, was invited to take charge of the work, including the preparation of the initial chapters and historical statement which would properly introduce that which was to follow, and at the same time give an adequate setting to the whole. We acknowledge with pleasure our debt of obligation for the valuable service thus rendered the Movement.

JOHN R. PEPPER, *President;*
Laymen's Missionary Movement
of the M. E. Church, South.

(iii)

MISSIONARY STATISTICS, MAY 21, 1907.

Men and women employed...................................... 14,915
Native helpers... 91,967
Increase in missionaries..................................... 1,632
Increase in native laborers.................................. 5,449
Stations and out-stations.................................... 31,504
Increase in stations and out-stations........................ 8,745
Schools 27,000
Pupils 1,231,492
Communicants 1,640,234
Increase 24,023
Professing Christians.. 3,564,326
Added last year.. 129,608
Total income... 21,719,101
Increase 3,452,853

These figures are taken from the latest and most reliable sources and include the societies of the United States, Great Britain, Ireland, Scotland, the British Colonies, and the countries of Continental Europe.

Significant Facts from the Statistics of the M. E. Church, South, for 1908.

1. We raised for all purposes $10,829,940.
2. The General Board and the Woman's Board of Foreign Missions raised $715,120.
3. Of this amount, we spent in the United States $67,857.
4. This left for missions in foreign countries $647,263.
5. The whole amount of missionary money expended in the United States, including Church Extension, was $528,861.
6. Of the whole amount raised for all purposes, we expended for the conversion of the heathen six per cent.
7. We contribute for our own work at home an average per member of $6.
8. We contribute for the conversion of the heathen an average per member of forty-two cents.
9. On each of the 8,000,000 souls to whom we minister in the United States we expended $1.28.
10. On each of the 40,000,000 of heathen for whom we are responsible we expended one and a half cent.
11. The proportion was eighty-five times as much at home as abroad.
12. On each one of the six million unsaved of our own population we expended in missionary money alone nine cents.
13. On each of the 40,000,000 heathen for whom we are responsible we expended one and a half cent.
14. Those at home had $10,000,000 already to their credit, the heathen nothing; those at home Christian light and civilization, those abroad a heathen environment.
15. If it requires $10,000,000 annually to keep 8,000,000 evangelized, how long will it take a little over a half million annually to evangelize 40,000,-000?
16. If it is necessary to expend $528,861 missionary money on 8,000,000 in a Christian land, is the sum of $647,263 a reasonable response to the needs of 40,000,000 in heathen lands?

(iv)

CONTENTS.

Page

HISTORICAL STATEMENT vii

I. THE AWAKENING.

I. A Conference That Counts................... 3
II. Purposes and Plans......................... 13
III. Addresses: Welcome and Response............. 27
    Mayor Crabtree and General Julian S. Carr.
IV. The Laymen's Missionary Movement—Why and
    How.. 35
    Hon. Samuel B. Capen, LL.D.
V. A World Campaign for Missions................ 55
    J. Campbell White.
VI. The One Great Mission of the Church.......... 73
    Bishop A. W. Wilson.

II. THE OBLIGATION.

VII. The Duty of the Stronger to the Weaker Races.... 87
    Hon. James Bryce.
VIII. The Supreme Obligation of the Hour........... 101
    Bishop E. R. Hendrix.
IX. The Challenge of the City.................... 113
    Rev. Josiah Strong, D.D.
X. The Call to Go Forward...................... 131
    Bishop W. A. Candler.

III. THE OPPORTUNITY.

XI. The Supreme Opportunity of the Hour.......... 151
    William T. Ellis.
XII. China: The Gibraltar of Missions.............. 169
    Rev. D. L. Anderson, D.D.
XIII. Korea: A Great Religious Awakening........... 181
    Rev. J. L. Gerdine.

(v)

Page

XIV. The Christian Conquest of Japan................ 191
Rev. S. H. Wainright, D.D.

XV. Brazil: A Bugle Call to Victory................. 201
Rev. E. A. Tilly.

XVI. Cuba: On the Firing Line..................... 209
Rev. W. G. Fletcher.

XVII. Medical Work in the Orient................... 221
Dr. T. F. Staley.

IV. Mobilizing the Forces.

XVIII. The Educational Movement in Missions........... 231
Rev. Ed F. Cook.

XIX. Protestant Literature in Spanish................ 241
Rev. P. A. Rodriguez.

XX. The Work of the Conference Lay Leader......... 247
Thomas B. King.

XXI. The Work of the District Lay Leader............ 255
A. Trieschmann.

XXII. Work of a Lay Leader in the Congregation....... 263
L. M. Pennington.

Appendix 271

HISTORICAL STATEMENT.

THE history of the Laymen's Missionary Movement is an inspiring chapter in the progress of the kingdom. It began, like many another great movement, in a prayer meeting; and yet the Spirit was moving on a wider scale than that one meeting. Once the few men who were gathered there had declared their mind and purpose, it was discovered that far and wide there was a quick and hearty response that indicated the unformulated presence of the same impulse among the laymen of all sections and of all denominations. Sooner than any one dreamed the whole Church was alive with the stir and bustle of expectation and preparation. Almost suddenly the pillar of cloud had lifted, and the signal for advance had flashed along the line. There was the feeling everywhere that the hour had struck for an unusual forward movement. Laymen who had shown little interest in foreign missions and only a moderate devotion to the Church awoke to the realization that something worth their while was going on. They found themselves appealed to by a cause greater than ever stirred the blood of a mere king of finance, and more noble than ever drenched earth's battlefields with the blood of heroes.

A movement must be harnessed to make it permanently useful. Like any other force, it must be delivered upon machinery in order to practical results. In order that this movement might not waste itself in mere enthusiasm, it was necessary for it to find or form a channel for itself. Wisely it was thought by the leaders that the Churches did not need a new organization, but rather a broader vision and a quickened conscience in the organizations already existing. The laymen at the head of this movement therefore disclaimed the intention of adding a new society and declared it to be their purpose to arouse the laymen of all Churches to a sense of duty to the heathen, and set about devising ways and means of evangelizing the whole world in this generation. To this great purpose the laymen of all Churches were entreated to rally under the existing organizations of their own denominations. The Laymen's Missionary Movement did not go forth as a society seeking members, but as an advocate of a great cause. It came as a voice crying in the wilderness of commerce and politics and secular toil that the kingdom of heaven is at hand.

(vii)

THE MOVEMENT DEFINED.

1. The Laymen's Missionary Movement is a lineal descendant of the famous haystack prayer meeting. It was born in a missionary prayer service, and was suggested by the indifference of laymen to foreign missions.

2. Its aim is missionary and not general, except as it stands for the most universal and all-embracing idea of Christian service. Since the modern Church is seeking to banish the artificial words "home" and "foreign" from the vocabulary of missions, this Movement embraces our own as well as all other lands.

3. It is more a movement than an organization, and its methods are educational and inspirational rather than administrative. It does not so much aim to add machinery as to generate power and accelerate motion.

4. It does not aim to supplant or absorb other organizations, but to work with and through them. It has no excuse for existence for its own sake and has no ends to carry on its own account; but exists to aid the Churches and Boards in carrying out the Great Commission. In this it is analogous to the Student Volunteer and Young People's Missionary Movements. They stand in sympathetic and coöperative relation to all forms of young people's organizations for missionary agitation, yet remain distinct. This Movement holds a like relation to all laymen's denominational and local organizations. Whether the general awakening among laymen is cause, consequence, or coincidence of this Movement does not alter the fact of its distinctness and singularity of purpose.

5. It can accomplish its great work only by adhering to its providential task and maintaining its integrity as a missionary movement. Since students, young people, and women have furnished a fruitful and growing constituency for this same great aim, as was to be expected, the laymen are not proving an exception.

6. It is interdenominational, and owes much of its power to inspire and its strength of appeal to this fact. This gives it scope, catholicity, and the inspiration of numbers, and puts it in line with the broader views of the laymen of our time.

7. The movements that are making and circulating an inspiring and enlightening literature and commanding an enthusiastic following of vast numbers are broadly catholic and stand for one great idea and aim. This is emphatically true of missions. No single denomination, no organization with a variety of objects could

even hope to approach in these respects the Student Volunteer and Young People's Missionary Movements, and, in possibility for such achievements, the Laymen's Missionary Movement.

It remained for the laymen of each denomination to harness this Movement within their denominational machinery. Accordingly at the Annual Meeting of the Board of Missions of the Methodist Episcopal Church, South, in May, 1907, a paper was offered by a committee consisting of E. R. Hendrix, J. B. Greene, and A. F. Watkins, which had been appointed to report on the subject. This paper, which was unanimously adopted, is as follows:

"We look with favor upon the inauguration of this movement among the laymen of the Church, and recommend that our Missionary Secretaries be instructed to arrange for a Laymen's Missionary Convention, to be held next winter in some centrally located city. We recommend also that the Secretaries be authorized to make arrangements for a conference, in the near future, of about fifty influential laymen, to consider plans for the promotion of the work among our laymen and to organize a Laymen's Committee, which, together with the Secretaries, shall make preparation for the Laymen's Convention."

Following this instruction, a few leading laymen met in Nashville at the call of the Secretaries on August 7, 1907, and effected a temporary organization preliminary to the meeting of fifty as suggested above, and laid out plans for that meeting. Mr. John R. Pepper, of Memphis, Tenn., was chosen Chairman, and Mr. C. H. Ireland, Greensboro, N. C., Secretary. A committee of five was appointed to arrange for the meeting of fifty, consisting of John R. Pepper, C. H. Ireland, Thomas S. Weaver, John R. Nelson, and W. W. Pinson. Knoxville, Tenn., was selected as the place of meeting. A General Committee was chosen, consisting of John R. Pepper, C. H. Ireland, T. S. Weaver, W. M. Sloan, F. A. Critz, T. T. Fishburne, E. P. Peabody, A. D. Reynolds, J. B. Greene, H. N. Snyder, John P. Pettijohn, J. H. Hinamon, G. D. Shands, A. E. Bonnell, and J. C. Hindman.

The meeting of fifty was held as arranged on September 17, 18, 1907, at Knoxville, Tenn. Fifty-three leading laymen representing almost the entire territory of the Church came together, and in a meeting characterized by great zeal and earnestness discussed the Movement and devised plans for its further organization and for the gathering of a great Conference of laymen later.

Mr. John R. Pepper presided. Addresses were delivered by Hon. T. B. King, of Memphis, Bishop E. R. Hendrix, Mr. J. Campbell White, of New York, General Secretary of the Movement, C. H. Ireland, Bishop E. E. Hoss, H. W. Baker, Havana, Cuba, Bishop W. A. Candler, and others. The officers elected were: John R. Pepper, of Memphis, Tenn., President; C. H. Ireland, Greensboro, N. C., Vice President; G. W. Cain, Nashville, Tenn., Secretary; and F. M. Daniel, Mammoth Springs, Ark., Treasurer. These officers, together with D. H. Abernathy, Julian S. Carr, and W. G. M. Thomas, were made the Executive Committee. The suggestion made in the opening address of Chairman Pepper that there should be ten thousand laymen in our Church willing to enroll themselves as "emergency men," pledged to give financial aid to the emergencies that might arise from time to time in the progress of the Church, met with an enthusiastic reception. A spontaneous, not to say hilarious beginning was made on the spot. Gen. Julian S. Carr, of North Carolina, in an eloquent speech put his State at the head of the volunteer column by offering to pledge five thousand dollars to the emergency fund. Others followed in like tenor.

The following "Call" was issued to be sent to the laymen of the whole Church:

A Call to the Laymen.

Less than one year ago the Laymen's Missionary Movement had its beginning in a prayer meeting in New York City. It has already become not only interdenominational but international in extent. Its growth has heartened the Church, cheered the missionaries, and awakened the laymen. It is spreading missionary intelligence, gathering missionary facts, and swelling the missionary income. It is harnessing the hitherto unused resources of the laity and transforming duty into enthusiasm. It proceeds on the assumption that the obligation of the Church is the duty of the whole membership; hence the great command is not only for those who go to the front, but equally for those who tarry by the stuff.

Already the Movement has invaded one denomination after another, and is taking its place in the forefront of denominational forces. It is not a society, nor a brotherhood, nor an independent movement, but a movement within established ecclesiastical limits. It is not meant to form new missions nor send out missionaries, nor in any way act independently of mission boards, but to arouse the laymen and bring to their consciences the duty and to their hearts the joy of sharing in the great work the Churches are doing for a lost world.

The women, the children, and the young people have found their place in the missionary ranks, but hitherto the men who run the world's business and hold the world's purse strings have had but little interest in missions. The time has come and the call has gone forth for the men to arouse themselves to action.

The student volunteers from the colleges and universities have sounded a trumpet call to their fathers and brothers to furnish the sinews of war while they go to the front. The first of the student volunteers, Samuel J. Mills, said at the famous Haystack Prayer Meeting, in 1806: "We can do it if we will." Samuel B. Capen, first President of the Laymen's Missionary Movement, said in 1906: "We can do it, *and* we will." It is for the laymen of Southern Methodism to help make good this inspiring challenge of the twentieth century.

The coming of more than a million of foreigners to our shores annually, many of whom are turning their steps to our Southland, the commercial conditions which are drawing large numbers of people together in mining and manufacturing districts, the rapid drift of the rural population to the cities, constitute problems that demand immediate, wise, and liberal treatment. And since the gospel of Christ is the only answer to the unrest of the times and the only solution for the vexing problems, of our complex civilization, the Church must not be found wanting in the face of these conditions.

The amazing transition in heathen and Roman Catholic lands, the turning to the West for light, the decay of ancient religions, the pathetic drift from the moorings of ages, and the search for some anchor for faith, constitute a challenge to the Church which she cannot deny and be true to her commission. Before our own Church lie white harvests of opportunity such as never confronted us before, and our missionaries stand at open doors and plead in vain for the means and equipment to enter them. In order that the nine hundred millions of unevangelized heathen may be reached in this generation, it is estimated that our Church must send the gospel to forty millions. This is a task that calls for the business intelligence, united prayers, and combined resources of our lay-

men. To slight this obligation and allow the hearts of our missionaries to break while we live in luxury and lay up for ourselves
treasures on earth is to live under condemnation and die in disgrace.

There are at least five hundred thousand laymen in our Church.
It is safe to say that very few of these contribute regularly to missions; hence this cause is not receiving even a fraction of its legitimate share of the thought, prayer, and growing wealth of our
laymen. This is an age of great enterprises and of great wealth,
and in no section is this more emphatically true than in the South.
Providence never misadjusts its movements. When the doors of
heathenism are thrown wide open, the Church is providentially
equipped to enter.

It was Maxwell, a Methodist layman, who opened the eyes of
Mr. Wesley to the power of the laity, and Methodism owes much
of her success to this discovery. That noble layman of England,
Mr. Perks, in his recent visit to our country, startled us with the
statement that over four-fifths of the sermons preached in Methodist pulpits in England on a given Sunday were preached by unor-
dained men. Methodist laymen of America must show themselves
true to the traditions of their Church and prove themselves worthy
of their fathers.

We, therefore, call upon our fellow-laymen to keep pace with
the laymen of other Churches, and follow the brave prophetic
souls who are pressing the battle for the world's evangelization in
this generation. Let us join the lengthening ranks of this modern
movement for "A Campaign of Education," "A Plan for Evangelization," and a thorough "Investigation of the Fields" from the
layman's standpoint. The South's peerless soldier, Robert E. Lee,
said truly in a letter to his son: " 'Duty' is the sublimest word in any
language." Shall soldiers of the great Leader of Galilee think to
do less than their duty? It is his to command and ours to obey.
Our duty is measured by our capacity. What we can do, we ought
to do. Let us line up for great things under the motto: "Do Your
Best, and Do It Now."

The time and place of holding the Greater Laymen's Conference
were left in the hands of the Executive Committee, as were also the
programme and other arrangements.

The work of organizing and arousing the laymen of the Church
was pushed forward successfully during the preparations for the

CHATTANOOGA COMMITTEE ON ARRANGEMENTS.

T. O. TROTTER.   CREED F. BATES.

L. F. FOUST, CHAIRMAN.

J. N. TRIGG.   B. F. FRITTS.

great Conference. At the fall sessions of the Annual Conferences the laymen met and organized for an active campaign. Everywhere the Movement met with a reception that gave abundant promise of the great results already realized.

The Executive Committee selected Chattanooga as the place most suitable for holding the great Conference, and April 21-23, 1908, as the time. This meeting is now a matter of history, the larger part of which is contained in this volume, as far as the mere facts can be printed. But the larger, nobler, and by far truer history will never be written. It is recorded in the indelible characters of quickened lives, broadened visions, intensified devotion, enlarged liberality, and the deep, steady, ever-widening impulse that stirs the hearts and consciences of our laymen.

The Conference was preceded by much prayer. A Prayer Calendar was sent out, and it was known that a multitude throughout the Church were lifting up their hearts in prayer for the blessing of God upon the occasion. The two days preceding the Convention were days of prayer. At noon each day a large body of men gathered to pray for the Conference about to convene. From the first hour it was manifest these prayers were answered. During the Conference the noon hour was observed as a time of heart searching and earnest prayer.

The Committee of Arrangements provided an excursion up the beautiful Tennessee River by steamer, which was free to the delegates and greatly enjoyed by them. This was one of numberless courtesies by the citizens of Chattanooga.

Too much praise cannot be given the local committees of Chattanooga, whose names will be found in the Appendix, for their wise and untiring efforts in behalf of the Conference. Much of the success of the meeting was due to their work. Their thorough organization and businesslike methods left nothing to be desired. Their liberal provisions for the Conference, made possible by the generosity of the citizens, will not soon be forgotten. The Reception Committee brought the whole Conference under obligations. Mr. W. T. Ellis paid them this high compliment: "May I add, on behalf of those of us who were so favored as to be guests of the Convention, that the Convention Committee and the city of Chattanooga created a new definition of convention hospitality? I think that all of us, from the Ambassador down to myself, are henceforth 'yours to command.'"

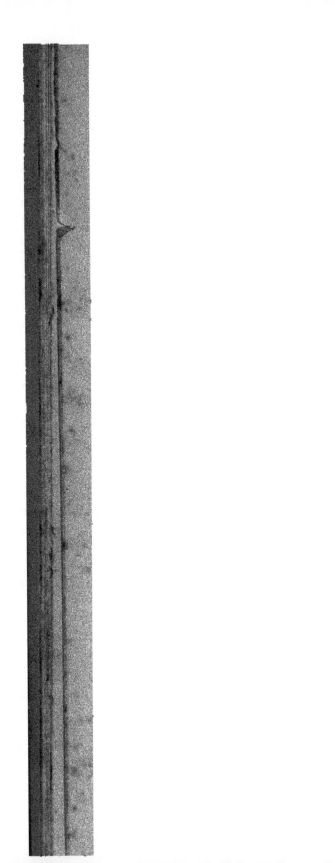

THE CALL OF GOD TO MEN.

OUR MISSIONARY CONFESSION.

1. The world is our parish.

2. It is the mission of the whole Church to give the gospel to the whole world.

3. "We desire a league, offensive and defensive," with all who are striving to fulfill this mission.

4. Our entire Church is a missionary society, and each member is under pledge, as well as under command, to help give the gospel to every creature.

5. It is as much the duty of every member to help to support a parish abroad as a parish at home.

6. Our giving should be an act of worship (Prov. iii. 9), cheerful (2 Cor. ix. 7), and according to the rule of three (1 Cor. xvi. 2):

INDIVIDUALLY	"Let every one of you
SYSTEMATICALLY	Lay by him in store on the First day of the week
PROPORTIONATELY	As God hath prospered him."

(xvi)

I.

THE AWAKENING.

I. A CONFERENCE THAT COUNTS.

II. Purposes and Plans.

III. Welcome and Response.

IV. The Plan, Purpose, and Need.

V. A World Campaign for Missions.

VI. The One Great Mission of the Church.

(1)

I hope it will hurt no speaker's sensibilities if I register as my outstanding "impression" of the Convention the conviction that the gathering was so great in itself that the personality of the delegates completely overmastered every utterance from the platform. Those strong, genial, levelheaded, purposeful men so filled my thought that I am still talking about them on every occasion. They are what made the Convention great; they are of the men who have made the New South; they are the men who will make new and adequate the missionary enterprise of Southern Methodism.—*William T. Ellis, Philadelphia, Pa.*

It was a great Missionary Conference because of the splendid preparation covering several months; for the emphasis laid upon prayer before the gathering; for the large number of splendid representative men from all over the South; for their enthusiasm; for their vision of what they ought to do; for their faith in what the blessing of God would do; for their plan to reach every man in the whole Church with a message of his personal obligation; for the setting up of the machinery to do this and providing the funds. It was a serious hour and great with future possibilities.—*Samuel B. Capen, LL.D., Boston, Mass.*

(2)

A CONFERENCE THAT COUNTS.

The Laymen's Missionary Conference at Chattanooga is now a matter of history. A thousand laymen, of the best and brainiest of the South and West, took counsel together. The programme of two full days was carried through without a break. Every speaker, from Ambassador Bryce on Tuesday evening, April 21, to Bishop E. R. Hendrix on Thursday evening, April 23, was present ready to take his place on the programme. The themes covered the salient phases of mission work abroad and at home, and rarely has such an array of splendid addresses ever been uttered on any American platform.

The spirit of the Conference was up to a high level. The whole tone of it was earnest and reverent. The atmosphere was athrill with high purpose. There was no lightness nor anything to indicate a want of the deepest seriousness, and through the whole occasion vibrated the spirit of prayer and religious joy. No one could fail to feel that these men, gathered from the four quarters of the land and from all the walks of life, were dominated by one high and ennobling purpose. One could not fail to be struck with the fact that those sentiments most earnestly and unanimously applauded were those most nobly altruistic and most broadly and truly Christian. Nothing trifling or narrow or sectional or unbrotherly could have found welcome. And when the reports which expressed the consensus of the body were adopted, they were in keeping with this lofty spirit. The plans emanating from this gathering are prophetic of the mightiest advance in missions our great Church has ever known. They ring clear and strong a challenge to the faith and consecration of the Church that ought to stir the heart of the most apathetic.

Let one only think a moment of the character and ability of these thousand men, the Christian chivalry of the Southland, the sons and grandsons of men who did deeds about Chattanooga in the sixties to make the pages of history glow, and who themselves

(3)

have done and are doing things in all the lines of noble achievement worthy of their fathers and of their country. Such a body, composed of men who direct the affairs of commerce and government, whose counsels any cause would covet, sitting at the feet of Christ to receive anew the Great Commission and to put their abilities at the command of the Church, is a scene as inspiring as it is unusual. When their counsels have resulted in a well-defined plan of campaign for missionary effort for the 500,000 laymen of whom they form the advance guard, no mind can calculate the greatness of the outcome. They form the reserve corps of that "far-flung battle line" on whose ranks the sun never sets. If, as Phillips Brooks said, "the heroic in a cause is measured by the ideality, magnanimity, and the bravery of that cause," then no men ever met in a cause representing such heroism as that which brought these men together. This missionary army has set before it a task no less than the saving of a lost world, a motive no meaner than the love of God and man, a spirit to give and to toil without the hope of earthly recompense. The sharer of the vision and spirit of the missionary is a sharer of his heroism. These men gathered to clasp hands with the missionaries in a fellowship of service and to pledge the thought and energy that make the age splendid with material enterprises to the greater enterprise of a world's enlightenment. That pledge will thrill the hearts of the missionaries with the assurance that the commissary department shall not fail, nor the equipment for the campaign be wanting.

Such a purpose pitches the psalm of life to a high key. It glorifies toil with the splendor of a high ideal and transfigures the drudgery of business with the beauty of a sublime motive. It sets the hammers of industry ringing a jubilate and the machinery humming in harmony with the angels' song of peace. It gives to the countinghouse a new sacredness and to money the stamp of a new value. The money made and managed for the cause of missions may be fitly inscribed, "In God We Trust," although it needs no such sign of its untainted worthiness. No more do these men need the touch of ecclesiastical hands to set them apart to sacred service. The hand of God has been laid upon them. The call of Providence is in their ears and a strange, sweet impulse in their hearts. The nations stretching out their hands, shackled with superstition, have called not in vain, and these, God's freemen, make haste to set them free also.

No longer is the cause of missions relegated to the category of sentimentalism. It is no longer the theme of visionaries and religious enthusiasts. It has got itself mixed up with the practical, doable, rational matters of the men of affairs. Statesmen, diplomats, kings of commerce, literary men, the men who build railroads, develop mines, dig canals, and guide nations, are found planning, writing, speaking, giving, praying for missions. It is a far cry to the time when William Carey, the consecrated cobbler, was not able to get himself heard on the subject. A hundred years, fruitful with missionary achievements, have passed since Samuel J. Mills made the Haystack Prayer Meeting famous with the declaration: "We can do it *if* we will." We enter upon a new century with an aroused laity whose motto is: "We can do it *and* we will." Surely we have seen the tokens of a mighty change and the sure pledge of greater changes yet to be.

> "Through the harsh noises of our day
> A low, sweet prelude finds its way;
> Through clouds of doubt and nights of fear
> A light is breaking calm and clear.
>
> That song of love, now low and far,
> Ere long shall swell from star to star
> That light the dawning day which tips
> The Golden-Spired Apocalypse."

It has been said that England conquered half the world in a fit of absent-mindedness. These men are not facing the great undertaking of the world's evangelization in any absent-minded mood. They are animated by a definite purpose, which they are following with clear-sighted vision and alert intelligence.

The plan of organization adopted is not cumbersome nor complicated. It is neither hampered by constitution nor distressed with by-laws. Recognizing this uprising as more a movement than an organization, as more the furnishing of new force than the access of new machinery, they set about simply and efficiently harnessing it and giving it articulate connection with existing machinery. A glance at the "Plan" will convince any one that this has been successfully done without displacing a cog or adding an ounce to the weight of the machine. They have wisely planned to deliver this new force on the common task through our splendid polity, and to mobilize this reënforcement. No polity except our own could possibly have lent itself so easily to such a movement without friction or danger to any existing office or institution.

The laymen have accepted the challenge of the Student Volunteers for the evangelization of the world in this generation, and have gone farther, for they have counted the cost, surveyed the task, and set the machinery in motion for its accomplishment. The Methodist laymen of the South have lined up with the other forces of Christendom and accepted as their proportion of the common responsibility the evangelization of 40,000,000 of people in the six fields in which our Church is represented. On the basis that has been widely agreed upon, they estimate that the cost of this enterprise will be three million dollars a year to sustain and equip the sixteen hundred missionaries necessary to do the work. They unanimously resolve to make this their aim and call upon the whole Church to join them in the purpose to reach it. This they declare is neither an unreasonable nor an impracticable task when our wealth and providential opportunity are considered. Realizing that to quadruple our present income for foreign missions is not the work of a day, they set before themselves the task of increasing the offerings to the foreign boards to $1,000,000 the coming year. Thus they have shown a commendable courage, sagacity, and moderation.

To meet special emergencies that may arise from time to time incident to the opening of new fields and the progress of the work, they resolved to form an Emergency Corps. This is to be a body of volunteers who pledge themselves as minutemen to respond, with such a sum as may by each one be indicated in his pledge, to any reasonable call for funds to meet the demands of an emergency when it has been recommended by the Executive Committee. This is to enable the Boards to advance wherever and whenever Providence may open the way, and it will save many a strategic opening, such as is now lost for lack of funds to meet it.

An intelligent and well-digested campaign of education was projected. This is so planned as to make possible the enlightenment and enlistment of the whole Church, and is based on the wise hypothesis that all inspiration is based on information. It indicates fixed and patient determination to carry the situation by siege rather than by assault.

The presence of a great number of physicians was providential, and it was an inspiration of incalculable meaning that brought about the inauguration of the Medical Missionary Society of the Methodist Episcopal Church, South. This society will enlist the thousands of doctors of our Church in the study and furtherance of our medical work in foreign fields and in hospitals also at home. Thus they will be put in touch with that branch of service in which they are most interested.

The text of important papers adopted will be found in the next chapter of this volume. These should be read. The addresses represent the views of the speakers; these papers represent the consensus of the great body of laymen themselves. No one who reads them can fail to be impressed with the breadth of vision, the optimism, faith, and courage they indicate; nor will he wonder that one widely familiar with the field and highly connected with the Laymen's Missionary Movement of the world said of this Conference: "You have sounded a note that will ring high and clear all over this land, and the action of this body will be a stirring example to other bodies."

That we might be able to see ourselves as others see us, we have gathered a few of the many expressions of those who saw the Conference from various angles and whose judgment is to be valued.

Mr. Samuel B. Capen, LL.D., Boston, Mass., Chairman of the Laymen's Missionary Movement, whose address before the Conference made a most profound impression, says: "It was a *great* Missionary Conference because of the splendid preparation covering several months; for the emphasis laid upon prayer before the gathering; for the large number of splendid representative men from all over the South; for their enthusiasm; for their vision of what they ought to do; for their faith in what with the blessing of God they would do; for their plan to reach every man in the whole Church with a message of his personal obligation; for the setting up of the machinery to do this and providing the funds. It was a serious hour and great with future possibilities."

Mr. J. Campbell White, of New York, General Secretary of the Movement, who spoke a message of great power, declares: "The Chattanooga meeting was the greatest Men's Missionary Convention ever yet held in the South, and one of the greatest ever held anywhere. Its deliberate action puts the whole Methodist Church, South, abreast of the most progressive denominations in their effort to evangelize their fair share of the world field in this genera-

tion. The raising of $15,000 on the spot to provide working ex-
penses for the Movement for two years was eminently wise and
businesslike. In the carrying out of the policy adopted thousands
of capable lay leaders will probably be discovered and developed.
Every department of the Church's activities will be quickened.
And the effort to evangelize forty millions of non-Christians
abroad will be the means of the largest possible expansion and
usefulness of the Church in America."

Mr. William T. Ellis, of Philadelphia, the missionary of the
secular press, a widely read and much-quoted man of the day,
writes: "I hope it will hurt no speaker's sensibilities if I register
as my outstanding 'impression' of the Convention the conviction
that the gathering was so great in itself that the personality of the
delegates completely overmastered every utterance from the platform. Those strong, genial, level-headed, purposeful men so filled
my thought that I am still talking about them on every occasion.
They are what made the Convention great; they are of the men
who have made the New South; they are the men who will make
new and adequate the missionary enterprise of Southern Methodism. May I add, on behalf of those of us who were so favored
as to be guests of the Convention, that the Convention Committee
and the city of Chattanooga created a new definition of Convention
hospitality? I think that all of us, from the Ambassador down to
myself, are henceforth 'yours to command.' "

Mr. J. Harry Tyler, of Baltimore, Md., Secretary of the Laymen's Missionary Movement of the Northern Baptist Church,
says: "I congratulate you upon the spirit and result of the Laymen's Missionary Movement Conference at Chattanooga. The
large and representative attendance evidenced deep and widespread
interest among the laymen, which augurs well for the future. The
educational exhibit was particularly impressive and instructive.
Give the people facts. Money and service will follow. I see danger in a tendency in some sections to embrace too many objects in
the Movement. Limitation is vital to its success. The idea of
emergency men is good. The Conference did wisely not to set the
financial aim too high. Leave no stone unturned to reach your
mark. To follow up systematically and thoroughly such a Conference, thus making effective and permanent its *enthusiasm*, is
all-important."

Senator J. L. Foust, one of Chattanooga's leading citizens, gives his opinion as follows: "The recent Laymen's Conference held in Chattanooga has been of inestimable benefit to Chattanooga in a spiritual way. Christianity and its duties, responsibilities, and opportunities, and the duties, responsibilities, and capabilities of the newly discovered asset of the Church, the laymen, were greatly impressed upon, not only Southern Methodism here, but upon all the Christian people of the city. The importance of missions has been placed more forcibly before the people of Chattanooga, and the cause of missions generally has been given a great uplift."

The Chattanooga *Star,* one of the papers which gave its space liberally, said in an editorial: "Now that the Laymen's Conference has passed into history, the people of Chattanooga can pause to take stock and see what was accomplished. It was a representative body of men, and these men began a great work for the cause of missions. Their presence here was an inspiration to this community, and they set in motion certain currents of thought that are sure to run through the life of this people for a long time to come. The programme was of an unusually high order, and every speaker invited was here and carried out his part. Some of the speakers were men of eminence in their several lines of endeavor, and a few of them have world-wide fame."

The following is from Mr. Charles A. Rowland, Athens, Ga., Chairman Laymen's Missionary Movement, Presbyterian Church in the United States: "I considered myself fortunate in being permitted to attend the Laymen's Missionary Conference of the Southern Methodist Church at Chattanooga. One look at that vast audience was enough to satisfy any one that business men are rapidly beginning to realize that missions is a man's business. The fact, too, that they had left their business for three days to consider their individual world-wide responsibility indicates that a new element has entered into the missionary enterprise, which is going to be a tremendous force in enabling the Church of Christ to give the gospel to the world in the next twenty-five years."

Two of our chief shepherds have given expression to their estimates of the Conference in strong words. Bishop Candler says: "The Laymen's Missionary Movement promises much good for the cause of Christ on both sides of the world—a speedier carrying of the gospel to the pagan world and a more rapid growth in grace among the laymen of our own country. The recent meeting at Chattanooga showed that the movement has taken strong hold of a large number of the best and wisest laymen in the Church. The attendance on that meeting, in both quantity and quality, gives assurance that the strong men of the Church are going to take hold of the cause of missions as never before in our history. Evidently they propose to lift this greatest work of the Church above the support of occasional collections taken to meet minimum assessments, and place it upon the high plane of a great business enterprise conducted under the convictions of Christian consecration."

Bishop Hendrix says: "The Laymen's Convention in Chattanooga takes rank in importance and power with the Ecumenical Missionary Conference in New York City in 1900, and with the New Orleans Missionary Conference of 1901. It is the child of the New Orleans meeting, as that was of the New York gathering. It could not have taken place seven years ago, because our laymen are just now beginning to realize that they are 'members in particular' of the body of Christ. While the laymen, jointly with the Missionary Secretaries, prepared the programme, they modestly refrained from filling all the hours, but sought the help of some visiting missionaries and of a few specialists in missions, like Bishops Wilson and Candler and the great specialist in missionary work in America, Dr. Josiah Strong. There was unity of sentiment, a calm recognition of personal duty, a heroic desire to advance. By their own vote they recognized that of the 500,000,000 unevangelized heathen that fell to America our Church's proportion was not less than 40,000,000, and that we should have 1,600 missionaries in the field and furnish $3,000,000 a year to sustain them. This will mean $2 a year, or less than four cents a week, from each of our 1,725,000 preachers and members. Some devout laymen will give thousands of dollars hereafter who have hitherto been giving only their share of a small assessment. But best of all, many will give their lives as well, either in person or by having a personal representative on the field. The Church discovers herself rich in undeveloped resources of lives and treasure now ready for consecrated use. Hitherto we have hardly dared call on the Reserves, lest there be no response; now the thousands of Reserves are asking to be called on for money or service. It is God speaking in the awakened and willing hearts of our laymen."

II.

PURPOSES AND PLANS.

DECLARATION.

We, laymen of the Methodist Episcopal Church, South, with a sense of gratitude to God for a part in the work of his Church, and keenly realizing our obligation to him for the right use of our light and opportunities, hereby declare:

1. That we accept the estimate of our secretaries that 40,000,000 is our just share of the unevangelized peoples for whose evangelization we, as a Church, are in the providence of God responsible. We now employ one missionary for every 158,000 of these people, and we contribute one and a half cents toward the evangelization of each person of the 40,000,000 souls.

2. That at our present rate it would require two hundred years to evangelize this number. To accomplish it in this generation will require the employment of 1,600 missionaries and the outlay of $3,000,000 annually. This means four times the money and missionaries we now supply, and yet it is less than one missionary to every one thousand of our membership and less than two dollars annually on an average for each member of our Church.

3. In view of our wealth and opportunity, together with the urgency and sacredness of the obligation, this is neither an unreasonable nor impracticable task. We therefore hereby resolve on our part to set about reaching this goal, and call upon our leaders to set this aim before the Church.

4. As a step in the direction of this achievement, we urge upon our fellow-laymen to join us in the purpose to increase our missionary contribution to our Boards of Foreign Missions to $1,000,000 during the coming year. This means an increase of a little more than $200,000 above what we are now paying. We hereby request our bishops, secretaries, presiding elders, and pastors to make the watchword for the year "A Million Dollars for Foreign Missions."

5. Since prayer is our mightiest human agency, we urge on our brethren, in common with other bodies, to join in the use of the noon hour of each day as a time of prayer for the awakening of the Church to a sense of its obligation and for the speedy evangelization of the world.

(12)

II.

PURPOSES AND PLANS.

AFTER what has been said already, no one will be surprised that the papers adopted by the Conference are considered of sufficient importance to form a separate chapter. We are sure the reader will agree with us. A movement is to be measured not only by the loftiness of its intentions, but also by the intelligence of its methods. It was not the courage and patriotism of Japan alone that won in her war against Russia. It was also and chiefly the high intelligence with which she planned her campaign and the skill with which she pushed it. It must be so always. Even a sacred cause gains nothing by bungling methods. These papers demonstrate the thoroughness and intelligence with which the laymen's campaign has been planned, and make it clear that this is no burst of enthusiasm that is to waste itself in mere sentiments.

We have not here included everything that was adopted for obvions reasons. It is sufficient that those papers which expressed the mind of the body on things fundamental should be embodied in this permanent form. Others will be found in the appendix.

The Declaration, printed on the opposite page, states the issues of this laymen's campaign clearly and strongly. It was adopted with unanimity, except on one item, and even with applause. The only dissent from its terms was on the financial side. The figure of a million dollars the first year was considered by many as entirely too low, and an effort was made to amend that part of the paper, making it read "one million eight hundred thousand dollars," an increase of one million the first year. This motion was received with applause. It was only after a breezy discussion and a conservative speech from Dr. Lambuth, Missionary Secretary, that a majority voted to set the figure as low as a million dollars for the first year.

Dr. Lambuth said:

"I rise simply to make an explanation. It is hardly necessary to discuss the resolution which has been presented to you by your committee, inasmuch as the resolution immediately follows the

magnificent presentation of the demands which you have heard
are made to-day upon the Churches of Christendom. [Applause.]

"I would divide the 40,000,000 up about as follows: For the
Island of Cuba we are responsible for 1,000,000; for there are already in our Church one-third of the Protestant membership on
that island, the population being 1,500,000. For Mexico, 4,000,-
000. We are the strongest Church in Mexico, and the population
is 12,000,000. That makes one-third of the population. In Brazil,
with a population of 18,000,000, I put the figure at 6,000,000, or
one-third of the population of Brazil. For Japan, with 47,000,000,
we put it down to the very small number of 6,000,000, and really
it ought to be 10,000,000 for our section of Japan. Then there's
Korea, with a population, at a minimum, of 10,000,000, and many
place it at 12,000,000. I put our responsibility at 2,000,000. In
China we occupy one-half of a province, which has a population
of 30,000,000 souls, and about one-half of another province, with
a population of about 25,000,000 souls; so I'll put it at about 21,-
000,000 for those provinces in the Chinese Empire. This makes a
total of 40,000,000. This has been based upon a careful and conservative study of the field by our Board for fifty years.

"We now have 252 missionaries, including the missionaries of
the Woman's Board, 175 of these being under the General Board,
and nearly half of the latter number being the wives of missionaries; splendid workers many of them are, and yet not all of them,
on account of domestic duties, are able to go out from their homes
and do active work. Therefore we ought to have 1,600 able-
bodied men and women engaged in these six fields in order to
reach the 40,000,000 souls within our generation, which we can do
if we employ this force; and an outlay of $3,000,000 annually in
order to maintain the force of 1,600 missionaries, with their equipment of schools and hospitals, and for evangelistic funds and other
equipment essential for the carrying on of this work. This means
four times the money and missionaries we now supply; and yet
it is less than one missionary to every 1,000 of our membership,
and less than two dollars annually for each member of our great
Church.

"I will say nothing about what the Northern Presbyterian
Church makes itself responsible for—100,000,000 souls, and the
resolve by its laymen to raise the $6,000,000 required to reach this
100,000,000 souls—but I wish to refer for a moment to the South-

ern Presbyterian Church, that plucky little Church that works with us, side by side, here in these Southern States, with a membership of 250,000. It raises now for foreign missions $275,000 annually, which is more than one dollar per member. [Applause.] And we, the great Methodist Episcopal Church, South, with a membership of 1,700,000, are giving forty cents each—forty cents each!—and that by the side of the Presbyterian Church, which puts down a dollar. "Not content with this, the General Assembly of the Southern Presbyterian Church last year resolved, inasmuch as it was responsible for 25,000,000 souls, to raise $1,000,000 a year, which makes four dollars apiece for the Southern Presbyterian Church. [Applause.] We raised as a Church this last year $715,000 for foreign missions under the Parent and the Woman's Boards, which would bring it up to about $750,000; so that there would be left about $250,000 to raise under these two Boards before you reach the million line.

"Your Secretaries having consulted this morning in regard to the matter, it is in their judgment far better for us, with the objective of 1,600 missionaries, and with the amount of $3,000,000, that we set ourselves during the next twelve months to undertake the thing that we can do, raising a call for $1,000,000 and bring up the $250,000. Then next year raise a call for $2,000,000, and so on until we reach the $3,000,000. In this way we can put our force on the field and maintain it! [Applause.]

"In consideration of our being in the midst of the fiscal year of our Annual Conferences, and in view of the financial stringency which we have had during the past year, we deem it wise that you confine this part of the paper to the sum mentioned—that is, two hundred or two hundred and fifty thousand dollars—in order to make the round $1,000,000 for missions, not losing sight of the fact that your goal is $3,000,000, or two dollars per member, for the Methodist Episcopal Church, South."

It was indeed a rare sight to see a Missionary Secretary stand before laymen and caution them against a radical advance in missionary finance.

The following amendment offered by Mr. John P. Pettijohn was adopted:

Resolved: 1. That, in order to meet the great demands now upon our Church looking to the complete occupation of the foreign fields now open to us, we proceed at once to increase our contributions to foreign missions up to the sum of $1,000,000.

2. That, when this shall have been done by the end of the fiscal year of the General Board of Missions, March 31, 1909, our Executive Committee shall request the General Board of Missions to make a call for a million and a half dollars for foreign missions, which would be about a dollar a member for the Methodist Episcopal Church, South.

The stewardship of the body of laymen is, in its last analysis, dependent on the stewardship of individuals. And when all has been said and resolved, the final outcome will be determined by the response of the units that make up this army. Realizing this, the Conference unanimously adopted the following as their measure of personal financial obligation:

Whereas our Southland has been blessed with great increase of wealth; and whereas riches will be a curse to us unless we recognize our stewardship for God; and whereas the only safe financial basis for the individual Christian and the Church is that set forth in God's word—viz., for each to lay by in store as God has prospered him a portion of his income which he recognizes as holy unto the Lord; and whereas such habit would settle our financial Church problems; therefore be it

Resolved: 1. That we urge each member of every Church to adopt the plan of paying not less than one-tenth of his income to God's cause.

2. That we request the Publishing House to furnish the literature and tracts on tithing, and especially Bishop Key's sermon in pamphlet form, and that our pastors aid and encourage all the lay leaders to begin a campaign of education and consecration on this subject.

3. That the pastors be urged to preach the gospel of money; and to the end that they be unhampered in so doing, we recommend that the stewards wherever practicable relieve our pastors of taking all collections.

4. We believe the mission work is one, and that the best available men should be sent to mission appointments, and we urge the bishops and their cabinets to send the most efficient men possible to our missions at home and abroad. To secure this, we pledge them our coöperation both in supporting the workers and in sacrificing our personal preferenees for particular men to serve our local Churches.

• 5. We call upon our young men to recognize that heroic service is needed in our mission work and to volunteer for service in the mission field at home and abroad.

6. That our Church papers publish these resolutions, and that the Executive Committee provide for putting a printed copy into the hands of all our laymen.

This was followed by a resolution expressing a desire to be helpful and share the work, and offering to pastors the service of the laymen in the raising of the annual collections, declaring: "Such a service, if asked from us, and such a duty, if placed in our hands, we will accept as a loving service for our Church and a sacred duty which we owe to our God."

No question elicited more interest than the proposition to form an Emergency Corps. Interest had been created in this matter by a pamphlet written by Mr. John R. Pepper on that subject, calling for ten thousand emergency men who would stand ready to respond in aid of such emergencies as might be properly presented from time to time. The resolution reads as follows:

Resolved, That an Emergency Corps, working under the auspices of and in coöperation with the General Board of Missions, is hereby established in the Methodist Episcopal Church, South, each member of which is pledged, according to his ability, to respond to any emergency call for money, provided that no such call shall be made except upon the indorsement of the Executive Committee of this Movement; provided, further, that membership in this Corps may be terminated upon notice.

All laymen are urged to join this company by sending to the Secretary of the Executive Committee their request for membership, and thus coöperate to make this Movement a powerful agency for good in our Church.

On this resolution Dr. Lambuth said, among other things:

"It is hardly necessary that I should speak to any of these resolutions, because they have already been adopted by you, and unanimously; but I make this apology for doing so: First of all, the great need of the home field in our rural districts, in our mining sections, in our cities, and among our foreign population (you have just heard the statement that 1,250,000 came to our shores last year; and, secondly, because a leaflet has been prepared by the Chairman, which he has been entirely too modest to say anything about. I therefore take the liberty of asking that I be given your permission to read part of this leaflet. The title of it is: 'War Is On! Ten Thousand Emergency Men Needed.'

"On the first two pages is shown the progress of the work from 1807 to 1907. Then your Chairman proceeds to show in this pamphlet that the forces and funds are inadequate. He then adds that emergency men and money are needed; and this, brethren, is without distinction of home and foreign missions. It includes in its needs these people who are at our doors, and for which need we have not otherwise provided. He suggests in this leaflet that out of the 500,000 mature men in our Church it is entirely reasonable

2

that we should find 10,000 laymen, genuine lovers of God, of the souls of men, and of the Church in which they have been reared and which has given them shelter all their lives, who will be willing to have their names and post office addresses recorded at headquarters, and who will pledge by God's blessing to respond one or more times a year or at frequent intervals, as the case may be, in certain definite sums, as each may elect for himself in the light of God's providence and in answer to his own enlightened conscience, such funds to be called for by the regular authorized methods of .the Church and to pass through the hands of the General Board of Missions.

"Now, there is where you will get funds for hospitals; there is where—more important still—you will get funds for your Italians (10,000 strong in Florida) pouring into the city of New Orleans; for your Hungarians in the State of Texas, where they have fairly taken up two whole counties, where the farmers have moved out and the American schoolhouses have been closed, where some of our churches have been closed because of this foreign population, and where we have had no missionary to speak to them in their own tongue.

"Your Chairman adds: 'What we do must be done quickly, as it is an actual fact that every time a watch ticks or your pulse beats it records the dropping off of an immortal heathen soul into eternity without even having heard the name of Jesus Christ, the only name "under heaven given among men, whereby we must be saved."'

"He closes by suggesting that the names and addresses of the emergency men shall be sent to the Board of Missions—or more properly to the Secretary, I should say, of your Executive Committee—indicating that, if they are willing to subscribe at any time there is an emergency call, at home or abroad, this call shall be in accordance with these resolutions which you have just adopted by unanimous vote. That insures your subscription being sent in as prescribed.

"I am glad to say that one layman, a member of this body, has already announced the fact that he will be an emergency man to the extent of $5,000 if needed. [Applause.] That being the case, I am sure there are others who will put themselves on that list, and let it grow until you have ten thousand emergency men who shall meet these great emergencies, and thus put this great work upon a solid basis at home and abroad, for which sometimes we make appeals in vain."

In keeping with the declaration already quoted, "Missions Is One," and in keeping also with the well-defined policy of our Church, the following paper was adopted:

Whereas the movement of the population is from the country to the cities, and thirty-nine of the one hundred largest cities of the United States are located in the territory occupied by the Methodist Episcopal Church, South (in recent years these cities have had a tremendous growth, owing to the marked industrial development of our Southland. Protestant Churches have not kept pace in their membership with the growth of the cities' population. Downtown and slum districts are rapidly congesting with churchless masses and perplexing problems); and whereas the unprecedented foreign immigration of more than a million and a quarter in 1907 has developed a distinct movement to the Southern States (foreign ships direct from Southern Europe now enter Gulf and South Atlantic ports loaded with raw immigrants who are distributed throughout the South and Southwest. These aliens are both a menace to our American institutions and a challenge to our Protestant Christianity); and whereas our mill operatives, mining population, and mountain people constitute peculiar situations which are difficult to reach with the gospel; and whereas the last General Conference organized the Home Department of the Board of Missions and authorized the Board to elect an assistant secretary to have charge of the same, with specific instructions to develop a system for the evangelization of the cities, the foreigners in our midst, and the mill, mining, and mountain populations, and unite our great Church in a concentrated effort to solve these problems; therefore be it

Resolved by the Laymen's Missionary Conference of the Methodist Episcopal Church, South, now assembled in Chattanooga, Tenn., That we very heartily indorse this connectional movement of the whole Church to evangelize the entire home land and pledge our hearty support to the Home Mission Department of the Board of Missions toward making effective whatever plans may be adopted.

The resolution which called forth the most universal and vociferous applause was the resolution on "Prohibition," a subject that never failed by its slightest mention to elicit the unqualified and enthusiastic indorsement of the body. There was no mistaking the side on which these representative Methodist laymen stood on this great question. The preamble and resolution, which were unanimously adopted, are as follows:

Whereas one of the greatest curses to the human race is the sale and use of intoxicating liquors and opiates; and whereas the evangelization of the world is seriously hindered by this traffic, at home and abroad, as Ambassador Bryce, from Great Britain, truthfully said in his address on this platform; and whereas the legalizing of the traffic is criminal partnership which besmirches the character of any nation and discredits our missionary operations; therefore be it

Resolved, That we favor the complete wiping out of the traffic, except for medicinal and scientific purposes.

The Plan of Organization, though simple, is thoroughly adjusted to our policy, and is sufficient to meet the needs of the Movement. It is as follows:

1. This Movement shall be called the Laymen's Missionary Movement of the Methodist Episcopal Church, South.

2. The officers shall consist of a President, three Vice Presidents, a Secretary, and a Treasurer. There shall be an Executive Committee of nine laymen and the Secretary of the Board of Missions, who shall be *ex officio* a member of this committee. This committee shall have full power to act in the interim of meetings of the Central Committee.

3. The Central Committee shall consist of the Conference Lay Leader from each Annual Conference, to be chosen by the lay delegates to the Annual Conference, together with a Vice Leader to act in the absence of the Leader, or, in case of no election, to be appointed by the Conference Board of Missions. They shall meet at the call of the Executive Committee.

4. There shall be held a delegated Conference every two years at such time and place and with such delegation as the Central Committee may determine. The officers and Executive Committee shall be chosen by the Central Committee at the time of each Biennial Conference. Vacancies may be filled by the Executive Committee.

5. There shall be a Conference Committee in each Annual Conference. It shall be composed of one Lay Leader from each presiding elder's district, who shall be elected annually by the lay delegates to the District Conference. The Leader of the Annual Conference shall be *ex officio* Chairman of this committee.

6. There shall be a District Committee to be composed of one Lay Leader from each congregation to be selected by the Quarterly Conference of the charge. The Lay Leader of the district shall be Chairman of this committee.

7. There shall be a Missionary Committee of five members or more in each individual Church, to be elected by the Church Conference of which the Lay Leader for that Church shall be Chairman.

8. All of these Leaders, together with all members of the Movement, shall be within the limits and subject to the directions and constituted authority of the Church, and shall work in coöperation with the Parent and Conference Boards of Missions.

The unit of administration in this Plan of Organization is the Leader. The Annual Conference, District, and Church Leaders are so related to each other that any instructions, plans, or literature can be sent down the line from the Central Committee to the last layman of the Church, information and coöperation being in this way swiftly secured from the remotest bounds of the Church. Full, alert, and prompt coöperation alone on the part of all these Leaders will make this Movement effective in securing its great ends. The failure *of any one* of them will break the force and render ineffective to that extent the work of all the rest.

The following paper was offered by the Committee on Organization and adopted:

We, your Committee on Permanent Organization, beg leave to submit the following supplemental report:

The report submitted yesterday set forth the missionary policy of the Laymen's Movement, but was not sufficiently comprehensive to take in all the interests that it contemplates.

Therefore, we declare the full purpose of the Laymen's Movement to be the enlistment of the laymen of the Church in all its varied activities, such as missions, home and foreign, city evangelization as outlined by the City Methodist Union, Church extension, education, Sunday schools, Epworth Leagues, personal work, philanthropy, reform, benevolence, fraternity, and such other work as may be necessary to the Church in carrying out her God-given mission.

The Educational Policy adopted is no less thorough and far-reaching than the Plan of Organization. It includes a basis, a policy, and a plan:

The basis of all permanent interest is information. The foundation of every deep conviction is knowledge. Recognizing these facts from the beginning, the Laymen's Missionary Movement announced as its first aim "to project a campaign of education among the laymen to be conducted under the direction of the various Mission Boards." In line, therefore, with this policy, it is needful that we should inaugurate a far-reaching campaign of missionary education.

THE POLICY.

As missionary education involves instruction first in principles, then in facts, and also the development of a sense of obligation, we would recommend, in order to establish these lines of educational influence, the following:

1. A prayerful and regular study of the Bible by the laymen of the Church, with a greater emphasis on its missionary interpretation and with more careful consideration of the doctrine of Christian stewardship.

2. The free distribution among all laymen of the Church of a well-selected leaflet literature touching every important phase of the great missionary enterprise.

3. A persistent effort to make great books on missions a necessary part of every intelligent layman's library and to select and circulate those missionary books specially adapted to interest and inspire laymen.

4. A vigorous effort to increase the list of subscribers to Go Forward, the missionary periodical of the Church, and to enlarge the circulation of Conference organs.

5. The frequent discussion of missions from the scriptural and business point of view by laymen in missionary meetings, rallies, and institutes.

The Plan of Execution.

Recognizing the fact that this Movement looks beyond the perpetuation of itself to the making of a great Missionary Church, we feel the need of well-laid plans for carrying into effect the policy above outlined. We therefore suggest,

I. As touching the text-book of missions:

1. A declaration of faith in the Bible as a missionary book.
2. A systematic effort to enlist men in daily Bible study and prayer.
3. The introduction of missions as a supplemental course of study in Sunday school classes composed of men.
4. The publication in booklet form, for free distribution, of a brief but strong discussion of "The Bible as a Missionary Book."

II. As touching the publication and circulation of a general missionary literature and the missionary literature of our own Church, we recommend:

1. The establishment of a Literature Department which shall adequately provide for the selection, creation, and circulation of a leaflet literature covering every phase of missions and adapted to our needs, and the selection and circulation, at the least possible cost, of such great missionary books as will appeal, in the subject treated or manner of treatment, to thoughtful men; also the prosecution of plans for increasing the circulation of our missionary periodicals.
2. That this Literature Department be located in Nashville, Tenn., in order that the Movement may avail itself of the best possible facilities for both publishing and circulating this literature.
3. Such an affiliation of this Movement with the great educational movements in missions will secure to us the best missionary books at the least possible cost and at the same time put us in constant touch with the best plans and materials for missionary education.

III. As touching wider lay activity in the agitation of missions, we recommend:

1. That the laymen who are studying the subject accept as often as possible invitations to discuss missionary topics at the various Conferences and other meetings of the Church.

2. That the experienced and successful laymen of the Church volunteer to aid the young preachers of the near-by country charges and small towns in their plans of missionary education.

3. That the representative business men of the Church recognize the spirit and purpose of the great commission and acknowledge the feasibility of its success by taking a stand for larger missionary activity and larger Christian liberality.

IV. As touching the controlling spirit and purpose of the great Laymen's Missionary Movement and our desire for the best results and for uniform loyalty in our own Church, we recommend:

That in all missionary agitation and education, and in every effort to enlarge the missionary activities of the Church, the Movement shall be careful to keep in thorough sympathy and close coöperation with the constituted authorities of the Church.

Thus were the lines definitely laid out on which the forces are to move. No body of men could have more clearly conceived what they were aiming at or more thoroughly planned to compass it. Truly in the language of the emergency call, "The war is on!" and the lines are getting in motion.

III.

ADDRESSES: WELCOME AND RESPONSE.

The power for good of an organization like this, composed of men animated by the sole purpose of doing good to others, is beyond estimate. I apprehend that the real business of the Convention will be to discuss and formulate plans for directing this great force into good works where the greatest results can be accomplished. I would not by the slightest suggestion disparage foreign missionary work nor by any word of mine discourage the devoted and consecrated men and women who contribute and labor in that field. But there is at our doors an opportunity that is so rich in possibilities and so promising of certain results that it appeals not only to our Christianity, to .our love of fellow-men, but to our patriotism as well. I refer to the youth and young manhood of the mountain sections and remote rural districts of this section of the South.—*Address of Welcome.*

The great Niagara for centuries has filled the eye of the tourist with wonder and admiration next akin to awe. It has been a world of wasted power. But this utilitarian age has laid the hand of availability upon those great and hitherto untamed forces, and has decreed that the world and mankind shall receive a recompense from this hitherto dormant power. Likewise, the Church has discovered in its laity a great Niagara, and our purpose in coming to your hospitable town is to launch a movement that plans to organize into a world power those hitherto untrained forces that mean so much for the Church and that have, like the waters of the great Niagara, remained in a large sense unbridled.—*Response.*

(26)

ADDRESSES: WELCOME AND RESPONSE.

ADDRESS OF WELCOME.

HON. W. R. CRABTREE, MAYOR OF CHATTANOOGA.

Mr. President, Ladies and Gentlemen: On behalf of the municipality and of all our people, I extend to you and to your distinguished guests a cordial welcome to Chattanooga.

In this convention city many meetings are held representing organized effort in commercial and industrial enterprise, in benevolence and fraternity, and in educational and religious work. But we have never entertained a body of men whose character and purposes command higher respect, or an organization whose possibilities for good are so great.

As Chief Executive of Chattanooga and as a Methodist layman, I wish to express my appreciation of your selection of Chattanooga as the place for this meeting. Your coming is a joy to us, and your stay will be a benediction to this community.

It is eminently fitting and proper that the first great representative Convention of the Laymen of the Methodist Episcopal Church, South, should be held in this city. Chattanooga's magic development and marvelous and well-balanced growth are typical of the success of this Movement, and should be an inspiration to its members.

In 1865 Chattanooga was a straggling village, whose only claim to distinction was that its commanding strategic position brought together here in conflict the brave soldiers of the North and the South, and that here were fought the sanguinary and spectacular battles of Chickamauga, Missionary Ridge, and Lookout Mountain. Within the past ten years our advancement has been startling and our growth so stupendous as to be almost beyond belief. During that period our population has grown 74

per cent, our investment in manufacturing 233 per cent, and the
value of our manufactured products 220 per cent. In the past
seven years our bank deposits have increased 181 per cent, and
the receipts of the Chattanooga post office 136 per cent. Our
remarkable financial strength and soundness during depression and
panic is shown by the fact that cashiers' checks have not been
circulating media here and clearing house certificates are unknown
in Chattanooga.

But best of all, the civic pride and moral and religious tone of
the community have increased to a corresponding extent. The
men's organizations of all our Churches are strong, effective, and
seeking more work to do in the cause of righteousness. I cannot
better express a wish for the greatest growth and usefulness for
the Laymen's Movement than by saying I hope your organization
will be animated by the potency, the virility, and the zeal of the
"Chattanooga spirit."

The power for good of an organization like this, composed of
men animated by the sole purpose of doing good to others, is
beyond estimate. I apprehend that the real business of the Convention will be to discuss and formulate plans for directing this
great force into good works where the greatest results can be
accomplished. I would not by the slightest suggestion disparage
foreign missionary work nor by any word of mine discourage the
devoted and consecrated men and women who contribute and
labor in that field. But there is at our doors an opportunity that
is so rich in possibilities and so promising of certain results that
it appeals not only to our Christianity, to our love of fellow-men,
but to our patriotism as well. I refer to the youth and young
manhood of the mountain sections and remote rural districts of
this section of the South. In the mountains of East Tennessee,
Georgia, and Alabama there are multiplied thousands of families
who are entirely without or have grossly inadequate religious
teaching and educational facilities. Their children are being
reared in ignorance; and yet these people are the descendants of
the English and Scotch-Irish who fought with Cromwell and who
came to these shores in search of religious and political freedom.
Their forefathers were the pioneers who endured hardship and
blazed the way for the white man's advance across the continent.
They descend from the men who followed Jackson to New Or-

GROUP OF CONFERENCE LAY LEADERS.

Begin at top, and read from left to right

J. B. CARLISLE, JUDGE R. D. HART, GEN. J. S. CARR, JUDGE F. A. CRITZ, JUDGE B. J. CASTEEL,
J. L. GAUGH, A. E. BONNELL.

leans and redeemed this country from a succession of humiliating defeats.

With just cause we boast of our great undeveloped resources of mineral and coal and timber, and we devote our best energies to their development. But the greatest undeveloped resource of the Central South is these young men and women, with their pure blood, their fine natural minds, and their inbred love of liberty and country. They respond to the teachings of religion and culture; they long for education and the opportunities it brings. No nobler work can engage your energies; you can confer no greater blessing upon our beloved country than by giving the religious teaching and educational facilities they need.

Chattanooga is delighted beyond measure that this Conference has brought within our gates, as an honored guest, one of the highest products of our Christian civilization in the person of the distinguished statesman and publicist who is to be the principal speaker of the evening—a man who at a time when he was a foremost member of the greatest legislative body in Europe gave to the world a work which has won the admiration and applause of every intelligent American citizen, and which yet stands as an unrivaled exposition and analysis of our American Constitution and system of government; a man whose broad, enlightened, and sympathetic comprehension of all that pertains to human society has given him world-wide honor and preëminence and made him a typical representative of the aspiration and spirit of this occasion and of those who are gathered here to plan and work for human betterment. [Applause.]

RESPONSE TO ADDRESS OF WELCOME.

GEN. JULIAN S. CARR, DURHAM, N. C.

Mr. Chairman, Your Honor the Mayor, Ladies and Gentlemen: I am profoundly grateful for the very handsome way in which your Honorable Mayor bade us welcome to this progressive, prosperons, and hospitable city. His beautiful words were like "apples of gold in pictures of silver;" and I feel prouder than Jason, returning victorious from his search for the golden fleece, because our lines have fallen in such pleasant places. Those of us who have enjoyed your refined hospitality, who have had our loves warmed and our hearts made glad by the many polite attentions showered on us on previous occasions were perhaps, in a manner, prepared; but the tokens are that even we will be amazed.

When Coleridge presented to Dorothy Wordsworth a work of his genius, she said to him: "It is a book to caress, peculiar, distinctive, individual. We will read it together in the gloaming, and when the gathering dusk doth film the page, we will sit with hearts too full for speech and think it over." So we, when we return to our several homes, will recall with a deep sense of appreciation the soul-stirring, charming, cordial welcome which has been spoken to us this evening, and "will sit in the gloaming, with hearts too full for speech, and think it over."

It has been wisely remarked that this Convention marks an epoch. I am reminded of an epoch that planned to fix the history of the world for a hundred years. At the little town of Tilsit, on the river Neimen, in Prussia, precisely at 1 o'clock on June 25, 1807, boats put off from opposite sides and rowed rapidly toward a raft in the middle of the stream. Out of each boat stepped a single individual, and the two met in a small wooden compartment in the middle of the raft, while cannon thundered salvos from both shores, and the shouts of great armies drawn up on both banks drowned the roar of artillery. The two persons were the Emperor Napoleon and Alexander, Emperor of Russia, and the history of the time tells us that they met to "arrange the destinies of mankind." The conference lasted but two hours. It was entirely private between the two emperors, and yet it was fraught with consequences momentous to millions. It was one of the greatest crises of human history, when the currents of power that govern nations take new directions and break over the bounds and barriers of ages. But the designs promulgated by Napoleon and Alexander were defeated.

We come to this epochal event without the flare of trumpets or the roar of cannon. We come in the name of the Prince of Peace to launch a Movement momentous to millions and rich in purposes pertaining to the destinies of mankind; a movement predicated upon success, and not, like the plans of the two emperors, doomed to failure; a movement as clear as the sun, as fair as the moon, and as terrible as an army with banners.

The great Niagara for centuries has filled the eye of the tourist with wonder and admiration next akin to awe. It has been a world of wasted power. But this utilitarian age has laid the hand of availability upon those great and hitherto untamed forces and has decreed that the world and mankind shall receive a recompense from this hitherto dormant power. Likewise, the Church has discovered in its laity a great Niagara, and our purpose in coming to your hospitable town is to launch a movement that plans to organize into a world power those hitherto untrained forces that mean so much for the Church and that have, like the waters of the great Niagara, remained in a large sense unbridled.

When we are properly organized we propose to hang our banner upon the outer walls, inscribed: "Ask of me, and I shall give thee the heathen for thine inheritance, and the uttermost parts of the earth for thy possession."

At the arsenal at Woolwich there is a huge magnet with double poles, which is in regular use for hoisting purposes. You look with amazement as it hoists and lowers shells and guns and enormous armor plates. Immense bodies weighing tons are raised easily and swung in place. This Movement launched to-night means to take hold of the great body of laity in the Methodist Episcopal Church, South, and swing them into place in this great work of evangelizing the world.

When the little "yellow men" who had won such renown at Port Arthur, fresh from the scenes of desolation and the impress of glory which their superb deeds had won, were being placed in line before the great battle of Mukden, with victorious voices they shouted: "Banzai! Banzai! Clear the way! Clear the way! We be from Arthur!"

Imbued with a somewhat similar spirit, we Methodist laymen want to spring to the work with the cry of "Banzai! Banzai! Clear the way and give us an opportunity of aiding in the great work of laying the world as a trophy at the foot of the cross and doing cheerfully and prayerfully our part to hasten the time when

> Every kindred and every tongue
> On this terrestrial ball
> Will bring forth the royal diadem
> And crown him Lord of all."

When Michael Angelo, the renowned sculptor of all ages, came to old age, he was stricken with blindness. He caused the lad who led him to carry him regularly every day to the statue of Torso Belvidere, where he would sit for hours while he studied those beautiful lines with his finger tips and while his sightless eyeballs could not feast upon its beauties. Ever and anon a smile as if born of heaven would play over his countenance. His explanation was that it was studying those beautiful lines in his young manhood that had created the love of art in his bosom. So will we whose faces are turned to the setting sun and whose heads are covered with the snows of winter that never melt find strength and comfort coming here in the evening tide of our lives to aid in launching a Movement that means so much to the Church and the world.

Away up in the Arctic country the nights are weeks or even months in length. When these long and weary nights are almost over, a beautiful custom prevails. The people will collect on a neighboring hill and wait for the longed-for rising of the sun. The multitudes grow as the stars fade away and the tokens of the coming dawn illumine the eastern horizon. When the first flood of golden sunlight sweeps across the icy plains, the assembled people join in welcome and a grand chorus of song.

Typifying this beautiful custom and mindful of the years in which the great power now being developed by this Laymen's Movement has, like the long Arctic night, slept unused and without profit to the world and the Church, we have hurried to this beautiful city as the first gray of the dawning betokens the coming of the glorious day—the first flash light of the golden sunlight that proclaims the birth of the new day in the life of the Church— and the stars of doubt and hesitancy are fading from the beautiful horizon, to raise our banners and shout:

> "Waft, waft, ye winds, the story,
>   And you, ye waters, roll,
> Till, like a sea of glory,
>   It spreads from pole to pole;
> Till o'er our ransomed nature,
>   The Lamb for sinners slain,
> Redeemer, King, Creator,
>   In bliss returns to reign."

In conclusion, my dear Mr. Mayor, in the name of the five hundred thousand laymen who constitute the grand Methodist Episcopal Church, South, I beg to assure you that we gratefully appreciate your beautiful and cordial welcome extended to this Laymen's Conference; and in the name of my brother laymen, through you, to devoutly thank the good people of lovely, hospitable Chattanooga. [Applause.]

IV.

THE LAYMEN'S MISSIONARY MOVEMENT
—WHY AND HOW.

3

A hundred years ago, under the haystack at Williamstown, five students held a prayer meeting, the result of which was the beginning of modern missionary work in this country. There were but seven societies in all the world. We have to-day over 400 societies interested in foreign missions, with over 15,000 trained missionaries, 92,000 native helpers, 36,000 stations and out-stations, nearly 100 colleges with 35,000 students, and 1,250,000 boys and girls in high and common schools. Christian hospitals and dispensaries have been opened among the non-Christian nations, and 2,500,000 patients were ministered to last year. In the various missionary presses there are nearly 400,000,000 pages printed every year. The United States gave last year nearly $10,000,000 for foreign missionary work, and the native Christians themselves $1,300,000. Inasmuch as a day's wage in the East is only 15 or 20 cents, this is equivalent in our currency to more than ten million dollars.

Considering the difficulties at the start, this wonderful success is one of the miracles of the centuries. Yet great as this work has been, we have to acknowledge that it has been done by a *small minority* of our Church members. It is believed that not more than one man in five makes any offering worthy of himself or of the cause. This is most evident when we look at the fact that the average gift per member is less than a dollar a year, or the value of a postage stamp a week! When we remember how many men there are in our Churches giving $50, $100, and many of them $1,000 a year, we see how many there must be who are doing absolutely nothing.

(34).

IV.

THE LAYMEN'S MISSIONARY MOVEMENT—WHY AND HOW.

SAMUEL B. CAPEN, LL.D.

Mr. President, I thank you for this very kind introduction, and I am very glad, men of the South, to look into your faces and discuss with you this great question. I'm sorry that I was late, but I was detained in New York, as some of you may know, by a great meeting in Carnegie Hall in the interests of the Laymen's Missionary Movement, where there were three thousand men present, and where we had an address by the Honorable Secretary Taft, who made a splendid talk, coming out squarely for the necessity of Christian missions to save the world. Therefore you will be glad to have me late, I am sure, bringing a message like this from the great meeting in New York.

May I say this word also? For I am profoundly persuaded that, year after year, in this great nation, we are more and more to depend on the God-fearing men and women, the home-loving people in this Southland, to give us strength and that help to carry us through the crises in our national life.

I want to reverse the order of my subject this morning, if I may do as the old Hebrew did, and read from right to left instead of left to right, and put "The Need" first and "The Plan" afterwards.

A hundred years ago, under the haystack at Williamstown, five students held a prayer meeting, the result of which was the beginning of modern missionary work in this country. There were but seven societies in all the world. We have to-day over 400 societies interested in foreign missions, with over 15,000 trained missionaries, 92,000 native helpers, 36,000 stations and

(35)

out-stations, nearly 100 colleges with 35,000 students, and 1,-
250,000 boys and girls in high and common schools. Christian
hospitals and dispensaries have been opened among the non-
Christian nations, and 2,500,000 patients were ministered to last
year. In the various missionary presses there are nearly 400,-
000,000 pages printed every year. The United States gave last
year nearly $10,000,000 for foreign missionary work, and the
native Christians themselves $1,300,000. Inasmuch as a day's
wage in the East is only 15 or 20 cents, this is an equivalent in
our currency to more than ten million dollars.

Considering the difficulties at the start, this wonderful success
is one of the miracles of the centuries. Yet great as this work
has been, we have to acknowledge that it has been done by a
small minority of our Church members. It is believed that not
more than one man in five makes any offering worthy of himself
or of the cause. This is most evident when we look at the fact
that the average gift per member is less than a dollar a year, or
the value of a postage stamp a week! When we remember how
many men there are in our Churches giving $50, $100, and many
of them $1,000 a year, we see how many there must be who are
doing absolutely nothing.

In the providence of God a new Movement has been started.
A little more than a year ago about fifty men met in a prayer
meeting in the city of New York. There were present some of
the leading merchants and professional men in that city. As
a result of that prayer meeting it was voted to organize this
Laymen's Missionary Movement, and it has been heartily ap-
proved by the representatives of the Foreign Mission Boards of
the United States and Canada. At the invitation of the British
Missionary Societies, six of our men went to London last May,
and there has been organized both in England and in Scotland
a Movement similar in every respect to our own. Among the
prominent men who coöperated to launch the Laymen's Movement in Great Britain were men like Lord Guthrie, Lord Kin-
naird, Lord Overtoun, and the Lord Mayors of various cities.
All over our country and Canada men have gathered together in
hearty response, and our Churches have been stirred upon this
subject as never before. The literature of the Movement has
been in great demand, over 75,000 copies of the original address

having been distributed.   But with all the multiplicity of organizations and societies in our modern life, it is a most natural question to ask: "Why is this new Movement started?   Is it necessary?"

I. Success Abroad.

My first answer is: It is needed because of the *success* of foreign missionary work.   A short time ago Carnegie Hall, New York, was filled to overflowing to hear a brave, modest man tell the story of his wonderful missionary work in Labrador. He is worthy of hearty support and of all the praise that can possibly be bestowed upon him.   But if he were here, he would be the first to ask us to recognize that he is but one of thousands of men and women all over the world who have given up quiet and comfortable homes and have gone into the dark and needy places of the world in doing this most Christlike missionary work.   I think it is Bishop Ridley who has said that it is not missions but missionaries that are the miracle of our age.

A few years ago we were thinking most often of Japan; before that, of India.   Now we are thinking of China, where changes more rapid than ever before have come to a great nation.   We must remember always that every third or fourth man in the world is a Chinaman; and China, therefore, is the greatest numerically of the non-Christian powers.   Let us note some of the changes that have taken place recently:

(*a*) August 1, 1901, the Empress Dowager passed a decree that, in future, examination papers of students should be upon Western learning instead of upon what Confucius taught.   Here are some of the questions:

Honan: What improvements are to be derived from the study of foreign agriculture, commerce, and postal systems?

Kiang-su and An-huei: What are the chief ideas underlying Austrian and German prosperity?   How do foreigners regulate the press, post office, commerce, railways, banks, bank notes, commercial schools, taxation? and how do they get faithful men?   Where is the Caucasus, and how does Russia rule it?

Kiang-si: How many sciences, theoretical and practical, are there?   In what order should they be studied?   Explain free trade and protection.   What are the military services of the world? What is the bearing of the Congress of Vienna, the Treaty of Berlin, and the Monroe Doctrine on the Far East? Wherein lies the naval supremacy of Great Britain? What is the bearing of the Siberian Railway and Nicaragua Canal on China?

Shan-tung: What is Herbert Spencer's philosophy of sociology? Define the relations of land, labor, and capital. How best to develop the resources of China by mines and railway? How best to modify our civil and criminal laws to regain authority over those now under extraterritoriality privileges? How best to guard land and sea frontiers from the advance of foreign powers?

Fu-kien: Which Western nations have paid most attention to education, and what is the result? State the leading features of the military systems of Great Britain, Germany, Russia, and France. Which are the best colonizers? How should tea and silk be properly cultivated? What are the government, industries, and education of Switzerland, which, though small, is independent of surrounding great powers?

Kwang-tung (Canton): What should be our best coinage— gold, silver, and copper like Western countries, or what? How could the workhouse system be started throughout China? How to fortify Kwang-tung Province? How to get funds and professors for the new education? How to promote Chinese international commerce, new industries, and savings banks versus the gambling houses of China? What is the policy of Japan— only following other nations or what? How to choose competent diplomatic men? Why does China feel its small national debt so heavy, while England and France with far greater debts do not feel it?

Hu-peh: State the educational systems of Sparta and Athens. What are the naval strategic points of Great Britain, and which should be those of China? Which nation has the best system of stamp duty? State briefly the geological ages of the earth, and the bronze and iron ages. Trace the origin of Egyptian, Babylonian, and Chinese writings.

(b) There are to-day one hundred and fifty-seven newspapers in China, one of them edited by a woman.

(c) Ten years ago there were no native post offices; now there are 1,800.

(d) The Viceroy of the great province of Chi-li has ordered the schools opened in their temples if necessary. He has said that the white man was in some ways superior to them, and he has felt that the difference must be because of his book, and therefore all through the schools of that great province the pupils are ordered to study the Bible.

(e) Officeholders have been forbidden to use opium. That we may understand what this means, it is as far-reaching in its influence as if President Roosevelt should forbid our officials to use liquor.

(f) There is an aroused interest in China with regard to the education of women, which has been one of the weakest points in the Chinese Empire.

We think of Turkey as the most difficult mission in the world because of Mohammedanism. Recently one of our great diplomats and a high government official told me that he wanted us to go on putting in our schools and our colleges, for, as he remarked, "there will be a break-up in Turkey before long, and you gentlemen then will be on top with the work you have done." This simply confirms what an officer of the Sultan said a few years ago: "What Dr. Hamlin is silently doing with his Robert College and the American missionary with his theological seminaries and schools and books, all the diplomats of Europe united cannot overbalance." As is well understood, Bulgaria was created by the graduates of Robert College.

Certainly the success of foreign missionary work during the last seventy-five years, under the leadership of these self-denying men and women, is one of the marvels of our day. They have helped to change the course of history and alter the map of the world. The success of this work across the sea has been so great that it has been impossible for our Mission Boards, with their present resources, to do what is waiting to be done. *This success has made this new Movement a necessity.*

II. Success at Home.

Success in many ways in the home field has made this new Movement both a possibility and a necessity.

(a) The Boards of all our denominations are splendidly organized and have the entire confidence of our Churches. They have a strong financial standing and their drafts have place equal with those of our best bankers in the markets of the world. Their officers are "dead in earnest," with the emphasis on the word *earnest* and not on the word *dead*.

(b) These Mission Boards have won to a large degree the moral support of our government. I can speak for the American Board, and I am sure it will be true of the other Boards, that the correspondence with the State Department at Washington is always sympathetic. At the time of the Chinese war Secretary Hay, in his correspondence with us, used the words "our missionaries in China," identifying our men with the government in that way. A short time ago twenty-three men visited Washington and had a conference with President Roosevelt and Secretary Hay with regard to the conditions of our work in Turkey, and I was able to say in behalf of the American Board that our missionaries have worked eighty years in Turkey, under the most trying circumstances, and all their work has been done within the law and no one has ever been found to be disloyal. All letters received from the Department show the same spirit of interest in our work.

(c) There is a new constituency here at home among our young people ready for greater things. Christian Endeavor Societies and Epworth Leagues have been training the young people to be interested in missions. The Student Volunteer Movement has been firing the young men and women in our colleges with a passion to do missionary work. The Young People's Missionary Movement in its educational work has been equally successful in arousing our young men and women to recognize the claims of this work upon them, and that if they cannot go to the front in person they must help support those who do. Yale and Oberlin both have their missions in China, Harvard has its work in India, the University of Pennsylvania has also its medical mission in China. There is an entirely new conception of missionary work in the current thought of to-day. These two quotations from President Endicott Peabody, at the head of the celebrated boys' school at Groton, illustrate what I mean: "The work of missions is the grandest in the world, and missionaries are the heroes of our times." And again: "Boys, I would rather you would be foreign missionaries than President of the United States."

III. The Opportunity.

A third reason for this new Movement is *the opportunity.*

(*a*) There has been a *practical shrinkage* in the size of the world during the past few years, and the world is wide open as never before. Steam and the cable have almost annihilated time and distance. Measured by the time required to reach various foreign missionary stations, the world is only about one-tenth as large as it was a hundred years ago. When the first missionaries went to Hawaii, by sailing vessel around Cape Horn, it was over a year before we heard in Boston of their safe arrival. Now, taking into account the five hours' difference in time, it is possible to get a message there before it starts.

(*b*) Recent years have brought a great change in the United States as a *world power.* The battle at Manila Bay, with the destruction of Cervera's fleet and all that has grown out of it, has changed the whole diplomatic power of this nation in the world. John Bright during our Civil War, over forty years ago, declared that if the United States of America should survive fifty years there would not be a gun fired in the world without the permission of this nation. This has not become literally true, but certainly when the nations of the world threatened to divide up China it was Mr. Hay who declared that there must be an "open door," and there was an "open door." It was the influence of this nation that brought to an end the war between Japan and Russia. It is the influence of this nation that has made the Hague Conferences a success.

It is Secretary Root whose visit to the South American republics with his splendid message of brotherhood has given new prestige to our republic. Gladstone declared that the United States was to be the great servant among the nations. And what higher honor could come to us than this? for the Master taught us nineteen centuries ago that greatness consists in service.

How have we obtained this proud position? More than anything else, I believe, because of our missionary work. Our representatives have gone into all the world. Many of them have

been statesmen as well as missionaries. Japan is an illustration
of the uplift that is to come to all nations when Christianity enters. Our missionaries have represented a nation that has treated others for the most part with absolute justice. We have not
wanted their territory. Our errand among them is of peace and
good will.

These men, going to and fro, have been like the web of the
weaver's shuttle, binding the nations together and giving our
nation prestige and honor everywhere. The splendid diplomacy
of the past few years and the golden rule policy of Secretary
Hay, carried on by Secretary Root, have been made possible by
the influences which were started by the men of the Haystack
and carried on by our Churches of every name.

(*c*) As a further thought in connection with the greatness of
the present opportunity, the great missionary movement that
started at the Haystack Prayer Meeting has done more than
anything to break down barriers among nations *and federate
the world together.* The missionary has gone everywhere with
his message of love and good will. He has not only planted
the Church, but the school and the press and the hospital. He
has taught the non-Christian nations not only of the one Father,
but of human brotherhood. Even what we call calamities have
enlarged the opportunity and made the cross stand out more
clearly.

The Armenian massacres called universal attention to the great
work going on in the Turkish Empire, and the fidelity of the
missionaries won the admiration of the world. The famine in
India helped to break down caste and show the people of India,
as we fed them, the infinite superiority of the religion of Christ.
The moral support which our people gave to Japan in her recent
war with Russia won the heart of that nation. But it was because the missionaries had entered these nations and had laid the
foundations of a Christian civilization that such work could be
done and such results follow.

Furthermore, as our Mission Boards have been planting everywhere the Christian schools and colleges, the *student world,*
through the Intercollegiate Y. M. C. A. and the Student Volunteer Movement, is being bound more and more closely together.
The English language, which at the time of the Haystack Prayer

Meeting was spoken by the comparatively few peoples of the United States and England, is now becoming the language of students everywhere. In most of the nations where our missionaries work there is very little printed in the native tongue, and the student necessarily looks for his highest thoughts to English books, permeated as they are with the spirit of Christianity. The English language is becoming more and more the language of the world. Old barriers are down in the student world, and there is a oneness in it as never before.

The steady sweep of the Anglo-Saxon race, with its love of freedom, and the growing universality of the English language, and the Christianity which is the basis of it all, are everywhere undermining false religions, breaking down barriers, and carrying everything before it. The world is becoming one around the Cross, which the men of the Haystack and their successors carried out and planted everywhere. *All this has given new prestige and opportunity to American missionaries.*

(*d*) We must also recognize the *accelerating power* in all our foreign missionary work. There has recently been held in the city of Shanghai, China, the centenary meeting recognizing the beginning of Morrison's labors in China. But it will be well for us to remember that Morrison labored twenty-five years in the Chinese Empire and then had less than half a dozen converts. In the first twenty years of the American Board's work in Bombay more than one missionary died for each convert. Now we know how the work is going on in these countries by leaps and bounds. The missionary converts in Korea have doubled nine times in seventeen years.

We have been doing in the first century the slowest part of the work, for we have been putting in the foundations. It is like erecting one of our great business buildings. You dig down till you get to solid rock, and it sometimes seems as though this foundation work never would get up to the street level; but by and by this point is reached, then the floor is laid, and then see how rapidly the rest of the work goes on. There is a gang of men on the rear, one on each side, and one on the front; and almost by magic it seems the building is being constructed. Our Mission Boards have been doing the slow part of the work, establishing the Churches, colleges, schools, hospitals, printing and

industrial plants; but that work is done now and we want to
build the superstructure at a far more rapid pace. We do not
want to pass this work over to others, certainly not to our children. But let *it be our piece of work and let us do it now.*

IV. INDIFFERENCE OF THE MANY.

A fourth necessity for this new Movement is the lack of interest of so many in our Churches commensurate with the importance of this work. Notwithstanding its great success, and
in the face of these wonderful opportunities everywhere, we have
to confess that the majority of our Church members are not yet
deeply interested in foreign missions, and, as has already been
said, the work is really being supported by a small proportion of
our Church members. When we remember that the total amount
of the gifts for foreign missions does not average one-third of
a cent per day for our members, there is no need of further
argument. This pitiable fact is its own argument.

Here, then, is an especial reason for this new Movement. We
want to reënforce the splendid work now being carried on by
this minority. We want to be a dynamo to give added force to
the existing machinery. We want to create, if possible, a tremendous energy which shall be felt throughout our Churches.
We believe it is possible to reach the majority of the men of
the Church and interest them as never before in this the greatest
work in the world. I am sure we must all admit that it is wrong
to have our foreign missionary work any longer represent the
work of the minority. The solemn obligation to evangelize the
world rests upon every Christian man alike to the extent of his
ability and opportunity. He is bound either to go in person or
to help send some one else. And we want to do this now. There
is money enough in the hands of the membership of our Churches to supply every need of men and buildings and equipment,
and with the blessing of God make it possible to evangelize the
world in this generation, if we only will.

V. THE PLACE OF THE GREATEST NEED.

Another reason for this new Movement is because of the fact
that the non-Christian nations are in the greatest need. It is a
reproach to the Protestant Christians of the United States that

they are giving, to help furnish the gospel to the 500,000,000 people for which they are responsible in non-Christian countries, only about nine million dollars annually, or less than two cents for each person. No wonder the man of the world smiles at the pitiably small expression of our interest in these people in comparison with what we spend upon ourselves. We want to help remove this reproach by centering our thoughts upon the nations who have hardly heard yet that there is a Christ, who are pleading for Christian education and Christian institutions, and who have had no fair chance. We are not unfamiliar with the greatness of the needs at home and of the problems which immigration especially is thrusting upon us. It seems to us that there is another cry across the sea which is much louder and more imperative. We hear the cry from India, with its one hundred and fifty millions of women (nearly twice the whole population of the United States) living in a nation which believes in the sacredness of the cow and the degradation of women. In that part of India where Mohammedanism has entered forty millions of women are shut up in the zenanas, bare and filthy; behind curtains they spend their whole lives; girls are despised when born, bartered away to some unknown husband, neglected in sickness, live without hope, and die in the darkest despair. Then there are the millions of Hindu widows, some of them only eight or ten years of age. The cry of distress is fearful. The following is an extract from a letter received a few days ago from one of my children in India: "I do wish the people at home could contrast a Christian girls' school in Madura with the heathen methods of bringing up the girls, and the contrast would seem nothing less than a miracle of miracles. A Christian girls' boarding school and the life of temple girls and child wives are as far apart and as different from each other as heaven and hell. If people at home could only see what it means to educate girls in this country, I am sure they would give money by the millions instead of by the coppers."

Then there is the cry of China. Never perhaps in the history of the world has there been such a revolution in a great nation; she has aroused from her slumber of centuries and is facing the light. Her demand for Christian teachers is not only insistent, but it is impossible to answer but a very small percentage of the calls that come. We can mold China now for Christ, for the people are receptive—ten years hence it may be too late.

We all rejoice in the wonderful progress of Japan, as she has taken her place now among the great nations of the earth. We rejoice in the progress that Christianity has made there during the past few years. But there is only one adult Christian as yet to every thousand of the population, and these are massed partially in evangelistic centers, while thirty millions of that nation have heard of Christianity only in the most general way. Every word that comes from Japan tells us how eager she is to hear the message of the truth.

For the 80,000,000 of people in the United States we have 150,122 Protestant ministers and 20,000,000 members of Protestant Churches. In the fields occupied by the missionaries of this country, containing 500,000,000 of people, how few as yet the missionaries and helpers are! Including the whole population of the United States, there is one ordained minister for every 546 persons, and in the non-Christian world one ordained minister for every 183,000 people. In the empire of China there is but one ordained pastor for every 267,000 persons.

To make this need still more clear, if possible, let us narrow our vision. Take the single State of Massachusetts, with its thousands of churches, its colleges and academies, and all its various institutions of philanthropy; yet it has a population of but little over three millions. In one American Board field in China we have two districts with 5,500,000 people, or nearly double the population of the State of Massachusetts, and with but nine white missionaries and a few native helpers.

But narrow it still more. Take the city of Boston, with its 600,000 people. What should we say if all the religious, educational, and hospital work were overlooked by four men with perhaps fifty helpers just out of heathenism? And yet that is a fair illustration of conditions as they exist, on an average, in our field across the sea.

In heathen lands at the present time there is one medical missionary to every 2,500,000 people. In the United States to the same number of people there are 4,000 physicians. On the basis that now exists in the non-Christian countries there would be two physicians for the whole of New England and thirty-two in the whole United States. There are over one hundred and fifty hospitals alone in the city of New York. When we remember the awful physical suffering which exists across the sea, is it not right for us to be in earnest to even up conditions and to see that the sufferers in non-Christian countries have a fairer chance?

And one of the best features of all this is that it will help the work at home. Jacob Riis's oft-quoted saying is absolutely true: "Every dollar contributed to foreign missions releases ten dollars' worth of energy for dealing with the tasks at our own doors." The history of the Church in Great Britain and in this country has proved universally true: that wherever there is a Church with a broad vision and interested in the work of foreign missions it is blessed in its own work at home. There is money and to spare for all the needs both at home and abroad. So long as our Church members, on the average, have been giving for real missionary work in their own Churches at home and abroad only about four cents a week, or the value of two postage stamps, there is no immediate danger of our Churches being impoverished by the appeal that is now being made for larger things.

VI. What the Plan Is Not.

Before explaining what we hope to do, and to prevent any possible misunderstanding, let me say that there will be no attempt on our part to duplicate what is already being done. We are not starting a new missionary board to collect funds or to administer them. It is not in our thought to raise up or to send out missionaries. It is not an interdenominational movement which plans to work outside the regular denominational lines and make a new missionary brotherhood independent of those already established.

VII. What the Plan Is.

What exactly do we hope to do?

First, we already have a General Committee of one hundred men, made up of representatives of various denominations in the United States and Canada. It is an interdenominational federation organized to do the greatest possible work and to do it quickly. It has an Executive Committee of fifteen men, two of them from Canada, with monthly meetings in New York.

Second. In coöperation with the Laymen's Missionary Movement it is urged that in all the great cities there should be organized at once interdenominational coöperating committees to promote an aggressive and adequate missionary policy in all the Churches in their district.

Third. This Interdenominational Coöperating Committee should plan to secure a group of key men in each local Church, who shall be pledged to care for foreign missionary interests, working always in harmony with pastors and Church committees.

Fourth. Let these key men, in parlor and dining room conferences, endeavor to reach all the men in their own local Churches. We want what has been called "applied personality."

Every Church should select a committee of from five to ten men, who would sit down together, look at this missionary work in the large, get fired with it, and then divide up the men of the Church, calling upon them or writing them letters and bringing the subject into the Church meetings for discussion. By so doing we could increase our gifts so much that we could revolutionize the world. Not only could we install new machinery, but the machinery that is now working at half time, and often creaking badly, would be oiled and hum with new life.

Fifth. In doing this personal work an endeavor should be made to secure as many men as possible to subscribe to the Declaration Card of the Laymen's Missionary Movement:

> Believing it to be the duty of the Church of Christ to preach the gospel to every creature, it is my purpose to pray, to give, to study, and to work, as God may give me opportunity, that the Church of this generation may obey this command.

Sixth. A further endeavor should be made to secure from all the men in all our Churches definite pledges of money worthy of the present-day opportunities and of the Master whom we serve.

Seventh. We believe that it will be possible to reach and utilize existing Church clubs, many of which are organized simply for social purposes. What the men need to-day is something that calls for service.

Eighth. We have already commissioned more than fifty business and professional men, who are visiting, at their own expense, the various mission stations of the world, seeing for themselves what is being done, and are reporting one by one their conclusions. We believe that such a report will do much to remove the skepticism which now so ignorantly exists with regard to foreign missionary work.

There is no lack of money, for whenever there is an appeal for humanity, a flood in Texas, a volcanic eruption in the West Indies, or an earthquake in San Francisco, the result is always the same—generous gifts from rich and poor alike. If we can only make real to our Churches at home the desperate need of our brothers across the sea, who are groping in the dark with no knowledge of the true God, then there will be money enough to properly support our missionary work. We believe the report of this commission will greatly help to set this great need before our people so that they will respond. Furthermore, the value to the Orient of the coming of our leading Christian men, as any one can see, will be very great.

VIII. Plan the Work and Work the Plan.

The whole plan, as you have already discovered I am sure, is the getting together of all our forces for this great work. We *want to plan the work and then work the plan.* We often say that we "have been playing at missions." But, as has been pointed out by General Weaver, we have not even been doing this, for we have not even done "team work." This is what we are hoping to do now. "Together" is the twentieth century word. We want to organize our Churches as never before for larger giving, to pour in the money and call out the reserves for the death grapple with false religions and superstitions.

IX. Movement Essential.

We are persuaded that this Movement is essential because we are to cover a ground which has not been adequately done before. We are not duplicating the work of others. The Student Volunteer Movement has to do with providing the *missionaries.* The Young People's Movement has to do with the missionary *education and training of the men and women.* The Mission

4

Boards are admirably equipped for the work of *administration.*
The purpose of this new Movement is to furnish more rapidly
the *money,* and thereby help to push the work all along the line.
This money can be transmuted into power and made to do its
work thousands of miles away. If I may be allowed to quote
a sentence from Mr. Speer, while we "cannot serve God *and*
mammon, we can serve God *with* mammon."

There are some who may remember Hon. Alpheus Hardy, one
of the leading merchants of Boston a generation ago, and for a
long time Chairman of the Prudential Committee of the American Board. When a young man he had it in mind to be a
minister; but, his eyes failing him, he was compelled to give up
his study. For a long time he was in trouble. Finally a vision
came to him: "I will go into business and make money and let
that be my missionary work." The story of what he did for
Joseph Neesima, the founder of the Doshisha, is one illustration
of what Mr. Hardy did with his money. What he did, others
perhaps in this audience are doing. But we want to increase the
number.

Years ago there was a young man in Boston who was so
stirred by a missionary address that he gave himself to missionary work. He had no ability to teach or to preach, but he
became a missionary all the same. He lived frugally, and out
of an income of $1,500 he gave away each year more than $1,000,
so that for many years he had his own missionary representing
him at the front. We may not include that man's name in the
missionary roll, but he had his partner there, and methinks the
Master will recognize the oneness of the work.

David Livingstone, the night before leaving home, talked far
into the night about the prospects of the kingdom. His father
and he agreed that "the time would come when rich men would
think it an honor to support whole stations of missionaries, instead of spending their money on hounds and horses." Has not
that time now come? We must lay this great work more and
more upon the consciences of our men of wealth and make it as
easy and natural for the many to give as some are doing now.
We must be equally in earnest to reach those who have less to
give that all may be partners together. Then there will be no
financial problems to vex and to hinder.

The Haystack Prayer Meeting a hundred years ago helped to save our nation from *narrow provincialism*. This new Movement, we believe, with the blessing of God, will help to save our nation from *materialism*.

For our own honor as Christian men, for the sake of the men and women who represent us at the front and who are breaking down under their burdens, for Christ's sake, whose we are and whom we serve, let us together enter upon this final struggle to conquer the world. Brother men, let us together help quickly to lift the cross higher and higher, that it may shine brighter and clearer in all the nations.

V.

A WORLD CAMPAIGN FOR MISSIONS.

I was reminded very vividly, as some of the Chattanooga Committee took me out through Chickamauga Park, over this historic battle ground, of a far greater sacrifice that was made by our States and our homes a generation ago. From the State of Illinois, one soldier out of every seven of the entire population went to the front; from the State of Kansas, one out of every six; from the State of South Carolina, one out of every five; from the State of Louisiana, one out of every four; from the State of North Carolina, 20,000 more soldiers went to the front than they had voters in the State. That is the kind of sacrifice that a nation will make when it is desperately in earnest. And do you mean to tell me that if the Church of Christ became in earnest about evangelizing the world it would not give one of its sons or daughters out of every 1,000 of its membership in order that the message of the Prince of Peace may be heralded around the world?

I was very much struck with the inscription on the Georgia monument this afternoon: "To the lasting memory of all her sons who fought on this field—those who fought and lived, and those who fought and died; those who gave much, and those who gave all—Georgia erects this monument." That's the kind of spirit with which we must confront this great world problem—those who are willing to give much and those who are willing to give all. The Senator who was with us this afternoon said: "There is not any recognition there of those who gave only a little." And in the last great rounding up that is coming yonder in the future there will be recognition that you and I will desire—only for those who have given much or who have given all. And I believe our reward and happiness, in the presence of our King, will be largely in proportion as we have given to his service and glory.

(54)

V.

A WORLD CAMPAIGN FOR MISSIONS.

J. CAMPBELL WHITE.

There are two theories of the Christian Church: One is that it is a fort, and its members guards, and their chief duty is to hold the fort and keep the forces of evil from making any fresh encroachments. The other theory is that the Church of Christ is an army of conquest that cannot be satisfied with present achievements, that will never rest satisfied until the orders of our Commander in Chief have been literally obeyed.

For thousands of years the highest civilization of the world centered around the Mediterranean Sea. During the last two or three centuries the chief events of world history have occurred around the Atlantic Ocean. The next and most extensive development of the human race seems destined to be around the borders of the Pacific. The presence of the American fleet in Pacific waters is only one of many indications that the drift of civilization is irresistibly westward, until it involves the Orient, where live more than half the entire population of the earth.

The awakening of the Orient means the adding of thousands of millions of dollars annually to the commerce of the nations. It involves vast and complex problems of statesmanship, and it presents an unprecedented and imperative challenge to the Church of Christ, which has grown to be the dominating constructive factor in all human progress and history. It may be that vast armies and ironclad battle ships can do something, in a negative kind of way, to prevent war; but the only thing that can guarantee universal peace is the message and

(55)

the spirit of the Prince of Peace filling the world. It might be a very serious question whether Christian governments themselves would not insure universal peace more economically, more quickly, and more certainly by maintaining a standing army of missionaries rather than a floating navy of battle ships.

We do well to realize the very close relationships of commerce, statesmanship, and the missionary enterprise. The fact is that they are all so closely interrelated that we could not separate them one from the other if we would; and I do not believe we would care to do it if we could. Missionaries are the pioneers of civilization and of commerce, and by their presence and influence in lands where they are at work have so multiplied the volume of business that the entire cost of the foreign missionary enterprise might be paid out of a fraction of the profits from the business which has resulted from their presence in these countries.

We do well also to realize how closely our missionaries have been related to the great problems of international statesmanship. In many cases they have actually been the agents of the governments, and in other cases the official interpreters of the governments in important diplomatic negotiations. They have been out much farther into the heart of these great non-Christian nations than the diplomats have been, and through the missionaries the most authentic information from the frontiers has come.

The fact is that the missionaries foresaw and foretold the Boxer uprising long before the diplomats believed it was coming; and had it not been for the courage and the character and the consummate skill of the missionary force, and the loyalty and faithfulness of the native Christian Chinese, the entire foreign community would have been obliterated in the siege of Peking. So we need to realize that missions are interlaced so closely with all the progress of civilization that they are really fundamental to it. Secretary Taft, who spoke to a great audience of men (the greatest and most representative that has ever been held on the subject of foreign missions on this continent, if not in the world) last Monday night in Carnegie Hall, in New York, stated that the presence and work of the missionaries in the Orient is the absolutely indispensable condition of extending civilization to that part of the world. We expect to have his address printed, so that you can have it in detail for circulation among all of your Churches within a few days. It is one of the most notable addresses given in our generation by a great statesman on the absolute necessity of the Church being the forerunner of progress and civilization in all parts of the world.

I wonder if we realize how important is the place that God has given our nation along all lines of progress? I do not believe it is too much to say that America has been given the first place commercially, politically, and religiously in world progress in our generation.

We recognize that this is true commercially—that our trade with the world is greater than any other nation. We ought to realize that it is so politically: no other nation has the influence to-day in the councils of the nations that our own has. No one could have brought about the treaty of peace between Japan and Russia, among all the leaders of the nations, but our own courageous President Roosevelt. [Applause.] China remembers very well that a few years ago, through the foresight and vigor of our great statesman, John Hay, that nation was saved from dismemberment, and she is not likely ever to forget that blessing. Even in India, under the British flag, where it was my privilege to work as a layman for ten years among the students of Calcutta, the American missionary has an influence that the English missionary, even, doesn't have; not that the English missionary isn't as capable and courageous and consecrated, but because many of the natives have the idea that he is in some way the representative of the government under whose flag he dwells. And the American missionary is free from any suspicion of that kind. You all know, who are familiar with the history of Japan, that our American missionary force has been prominent and most effective both in diplomatic negotiations and in introducing Western civilization to that empire. So that, all around the world to-day, we ought to realize the fact—for it is a fact, without any boasting—that we have the place of primary opportunity and influence and responsibility not only along commercial and political lines but along definitely spiritual lines. And it would seem that we should realize that we have those obligations in order that we may rise up and worthily discharge them.

I have no particular zeal for the Laymen's Missionary Movement nor for any other human organization that is destined to pass away when its usefulness has been fulfilled. I believe the only organization in the world that is going to abide forever is the Church of Christ. [Applause.] All these other human organizations are merely temporary helps to enable the Church to fulfill the great purpose of our Lord; and I do not believe that any of these would be necessary if the Church were in the united condition that our Lord prayed she might be. I believe it is only because of our unfortunate separation into various bodies that we have to have some platform on which we can come together; and in view of the world opportunity with which we are confronted, I believe that the Laymen's Missionary Movement presents such a platform, on which men of all Churches can study the religious situation of the world, and then can act coöperatively in meeting that situation; for we have come to the point on the foreign mission field where we are quite satisfied to trust each other as denominations to preach a saving gospel.

No one of our denominations is large enough and strong enough to consider the possibility of covering with its own representatives the entire non-Christian world. And so our foreign missionaries, face to face with heathenism, have come to feel that the conditions that divide Methodists from Baptists and Baptists from Presbyterians are insignificant in the presence of the great spiritual destitution of these nations; and they are entirely satisfied to turn over a whole State or Province to any denomination that can enter into and evangelize it. So it has come to pass that the Foreign Missionary Boards of North America have been meeting together year after year for the last fifteen years, planning their work on the coöperative and comprehensive basis, and not on the competitive basis. May the day come when, in our own country also, we may stop our competition in order that every man may have a field as large as he can occupy, and in order that every spare man and every spare dollar may be put into a field where nobody is now at work! [Applause.]

I have been up and down this country for a number of years, traveling from coast to coast and from the Lakes to the Gulf, and I give it to you as my solemn conviction that of the 136,000 ordained ministers of the Protestant Churches in this country at the present moment we could easily spare anywhere from twenty to thirty thousand of them, who are now working in small fields, where there are more Churches than are really required to supply the religious needs of the community. And those people, with their support, if we were working on a truly coöperative basis, could work wonders by occupying great fields where no one representing any denomination is now at work. [Applause.] We cannot, of course, in any mechanical or arbitrary way force such union, but our missionaries have got to the point where they are willing and able truly to coöperate. And that is only the prophecy of the good time coming, when we here shall also get into this splendid relationship here at home.

Now, what is the outstanding fact that faces the Church of Christ to-night as a whole? Your denomination has been deliberating here for three days about its share of the non-Christian world. I hope to be able to set your part of the field into its relationship with the whole field in order that you may realize your opportunity in the comprehensive scheme to evangelize the whole world.

The chart here behind me indicates the entire amount spent by the Protestant Christian Church throughout the world on this missionary enterprise last year—$22,460,000. Of that amount, about $9,500,000 came from the United States and Canada, about nine and one-third millions from Great Britain, and about three and a half millions from the other countries of the world. I think you will be struck with two facts on that chart: First, that Great Britain gave about as much as we did, although she has only half our population and less than half our wealth. That means that Great Britain is doing twice as much in proportion to her wealth as we are doing for the evangelization of the non-Christian world. It would be well to realize, along with that, another thing: that Great Britain and the United States together are now doing eighty-four per cent of all the foreign mission work done in the world. That gives very great significance to the fact that this Laymen's Missionary Movement has already spread to Great Britain. At the invitation of the Missionary Societies in England last year six laymen went over there to speak on the advantages and desirability of the men of the English-speaking world uniting in one coöperative, comprehensive movement for the evangelization of the unevangelized world.

We supposed that, on account of the conservatism of England and Scotland, they would want to think it over for six months or a year before taking action; but they were so wonderfully prepared, providentially, for this same movement that within thirty days there was a national organization of the Laymen's Missionary Movement in England and another in Scotland. Each of them raised on the spot, as you are doing here now, money to support a Secretary and to meet other necessary expenses. And during the last month the Secretary of the Scottish Laymen's Missionary Movement has been traveling up and down the United States and Canada, in cities where great forward movements have been undertaken, in order that he might study the secrets of this Movement and apply our methods to the cities of Scotland and England. It is an inspiring thing to me that, overleaping all political barriers, the Christian men of the English-speaking world are now actually united in one great missionary movement. [Applause.]

How far does this $22,000,000 go in supporting an adequate missionary force in the non-Christian world? Your Church and all the Protestant Churches of Christendom are now supporting thirteen thousand men and unmarried women missionaries. There are about five thousand wives of missionaries on the field; but we leave them out of the calculation for the moment, not because they are not splendid missionaries, but because ordinarily in calculating the missionary force necessary for the field either a man or an unmarried woman is assigned to a district. The consensus of judgment of different missionary bodies in the various countries is to this effect: If we are going to evangelize the whole world in this generation, we ought to have about one missionary, either a man or an unmarried woman, among every twenty-five thousand of the people to be reached. Thirteen thousand missionaries, each with a field of twenty-five thousand, can look after 325,000,000 people; but that leaves 675,000,000 others absolutely unprovided for.

I want you to realize, first of all, how great an undertaking it is for thirteen thousand missionaries to evangelize three hundred and twenty-five millions. Bear in mind that we have in this country 136,000 ordained ministers, in addition to twenty millions of Church members like you and me. And among this force of foreign missionaries there are only six thousand ordained missionaries. We are expecting that force not only to evangelize a population equal to the United States, but equal to all North America, plus South America, plus Great Britain, plus Germany, plus France, and about twenty millions of others thrown in for good measure! That is the kind of gigantic undertaking our present missionary force is facing. And when they sent back to the home Church the request for enough missionaries to put only one among every twenty-five thousand, thereby assuming the responsibility themselves of evangelizing 325,000,000 of non-Christians, I believe it was the greatest single act of faith on the part of a great body of Christians which has ever been known in human history. [Applause.] And yet, when they have accomplished that magnificent result, do we realize that there will be 675,000,000 still unprovided for? That is the reason of this convention to-day. That is the reason of the Laymen's Missionary Movement and of all the forward movements in all the Churches— for a larger sacrifice of life and of treasure, in order that the whole world may be evangelized in our generation.

What is the proportion of the entire field that ought to be undertaken by the North American Churches? I am going to ask you to kindly give your opinion about this before I proceed. Let me remind you, first of all, of two facts before I ask you to answer the question: That the United States and Canada are giving forty-two per cent of all the Protestant foreign missionary money in the world, yet we are only doing half as well *per capita* as Great Britain. From these two countries the bulk of the force must come. Now, in view of those facts, what proportion of the non-Christian world would be reasonable for our Churches in North America to evangelize? I wish I could have fifteen or twenty answers from you, just what you feel about it. What do you think the percentage of the field is that we ought to cover from this country? Please give me your best impression.

A member: "Sixty per cent."

A member: "One-half."

A member: "All of it."

Mr. White: "We want to let Great Britain have part of it."

A member: "450,000,000."

Mr. White: "That is a little less than fifty per cent."

A member: "Two-thirds."

A member: "Eighty-four per cent."

Mr. White: "That is twice what we are doing now."

A member: "Seventy-five per cent."

Mr. White: "Well, now, one man suggested a little less than fifty per cent. I think I will let you vote on the question. How many would be in favor of North America undertaking at least fifty per cent of the work? Those favoring this please hold up your hands. [Audience here raise their hands.] That is very good. Thank you. How many think we ought not to take that much? I do not see any hands."

On the basis of our doing fifty per cent of the whole work, we would have five hundred millions of the non-Christian world to reach. Our home field contains fifty millions of people who are now outside the membership of all our Churches. But in the foreign mission fields there are 500,000,000 of people whom we must evangelize from America, if they are ever evangelized at all. I wonder how many have been thinking of this foreign missionary problem in that proportion. Nobody in this audience doubts for one minute that the Christian Church in this country is entirely capable of evangelizing America in this generation. The only question is whether we are going to make possible the evangelization of the rest of the world. And I want you to realize, inasmuch as we have already agreed that 500,000,000 is the lowest number we ought to reach from this country—I want you to realize what that means. That means that every man of us has ten times as many people to reach in the foreign fields as at home. That means that every congregation here has a field ten times as big outside of America as at home. That means that your denomination, and every other denomination in America, has ten times as many people to reach away from America as here. We ought to think of that as we think of the prayers we are to offer and the life we are to invest and the money which we are to put into the evangelizing of the non-Christian world. These are the three avenues of power by which the world is to be saved—prayer, life, and wealth. I do not know how many of us are praying for the whole kingdom, but no one could really pray the prayer which we offered unitedly awhile ago without praying for the whole wide world: "Thy kingdom come, thy will be done on earth as it is in heaven." Our Lord was not talking about North

America or the United States or the State of Tennessee; he was talking about the whole world. The other question is the life we are going to put in and the treasure. How much life would be needed if we put one among every twenty-five thousand in the world of non-Christians? That would only be twenty thousand missionaries from North America.

I was reminded very vividly, as some of the Chattanooga Committee took me out through Chickamauga Park, over this historic battle ground, of a far greater sacrifice that was made by our States and our homes a generation ago. From the State of Illinois, one soldier out of every seven of the entire population went to the front; from the State of Kansas, one out of every six; from the State of South Carolina, one out of every five; from the State of Louisiana, one out of every four; from the State of North Carolina, 20,000 more soldiers went to the front than they had voters in the State. [Applause.] That is the kind of sacrifice that a nation will make when it is desperately in earnest. And do you mean to tell me that if the Church of Christ became in earnest about evangelizing the world it would not give one of its sons or daughters out of every 1,000 of its membership in order that the message of the Prince of Peace may be heralded around the world?

I was very much struck with the inscription on the Georgia monument this afternoon: "To the lasting memory of all her sons who fought on this field—those who fought and lived, and those who fought and died; those who gave much, and those who gave all—Georgia erects this monument." [Applause.] That's the kind of spirit with which we must confront this great world problem—those who are willing to give much and those who are willing to give all. [Applause.] The Senator who was with us this afternoon said: "There is not any recognition there of those who only gave a little." And in the last great rounding up that is coming yonder in the future there will be recognition that you and I will desire—only for those who have given much or who have given all. And I believe our reward and happiness, in the presence of our King, will be largely in proportion as we have given to his service and glory.

Now, it is very easy for you to make calculations from these figures. If there are 500,000,000 of people who must be reached from America, and 20,000,000 members of the Protestant Christian Church, about how many would that be for each one of us to reach? That would be about twenty-five, wouldn't it? You have 1,700,000 members, or a little more, in your denomination, Bishop Wilson was telling me. If you multiply 25 by 1,700,000, about how much do you get? About 42,500,000. Your Mission Board estimates your field abroad at forty millions. This is not too much for your denomination, if you take merely your *per capita* share of this responsibility. I wish you would realize that other denominations also are undertaking their share. The Southern Presbyterian Church believe they are responsible for twenty-five million of those people, and they are trying to send out missionaries enough to evangelize that many. The Northern Presbyterians believe they are responsible for one hundred million, and are trying to send out missionaries enough to reach that many. They have had one convention, with over 1,000 men present, in Omaha; and another in Philadelphia, with 1,600 men present; and these conventions of men, largely laymen, voted it to be their consensus of opinion that the Presbyterian Church ought at the earliest possible moment to multiply its force of missionaries from 800 to 4,000, and its funds from an aggregate of $1,200,000 to $6,000,000 a year, or an average of $5 per member for the whole denomination. Already many of their congregations have risen to that standard and gladly provided $5 per member.

So, when you are asking your denomination for an average of $2 *per capita,* it is only giving you the opportunity to measure up to your obligation in this world campaign, for I am sure that you will not be satisfied until it has become universal. The Congregationalists of North America say they are responsible for seventy-five millions of these people, and they are making their plans on that scale. The Northern Baptists say they are responsible for eighty millions. So, between one denomination and another, the whole field is being divided up. Unless you reach your field, it will not be reached at all. I want you to see how economical and conservative it is that your committee should ask you for only three million dollars a year in order to evangelize forty million people. First of all, we will take this fact: There are nearly eighty millions of people in the United States. Forty millions is half of that whole number. Do you realize that the Methodist Church in these Southern States has half as many people to evangelize yonder in the Orient as the whole population of the United States? Now, they ask for three million dollars a year to do that, and you voted to undertake to raise three million. How much do we spend among a similar number of people each year in America for religious purposes? Well, we spend very nearly three hundred millions of dollars for religious purposes in the United States every year, if not quite that amount. That would be $150,000,000 spent on forty millions of people, wouldn't it? And you are asking for $3,000,000 to spend among a similar number. That ought to be reasonable and conservative. If you spend $3,000,000 a year for the next twenty-five years, how much will that total be? Three million times twenty-five will be seventy-five million. That is less than $2 on each one of the forty millions, isn't it?

I believe we can evangelize the whole world at an average cost of not more than $2 for each person to be reached. That is all your Board has asked for; that is all you yourselves have voted to raise; and it is important that you get that raised as speedily as possible, if you are going to evangelize these forty millions of people in this generation. For do you realize that they are dying at the rate of more than one million a year out of your own field? Almost as many dying every year as you have members in your entire denomination in this country. How many of them are you reaching every year now on the basis of $2 being enough to reach one individual? You are spending, I believe, about $750,000 on foreign missions a year. That would reach approximately 375,000 people. But if you reach 1,500,000 a year, in order to cover the field in twenty-five years you will have to raise far in excess of that. More than a million each year are dying who have not yet been reached by any of your representatives, and I hope that you will toil and pray and sacrifice so that at the earliest possible moment you will swing out into these fields a force that will be able to evangelize them; and I believe that your Church doing this will lead other Churches to similarly occupy their fields, until all over Christendom we shall have a rising up, one denomination after another, to say: "We believe the time has come when we should seriously undertake to obey our Lord." And I have the greatest confidence that you are going to undertake to do this, because during the last few months there has been such a marvelous uprising of men in the United States and Canada to undertake to do similar things.

I have been for twenty years thinking about this missionary problem more than any other. During that time I have been for ten years face to face with conditions yonder in India; but I will declare to you that I have had more encouragement during the last six months to believe that the world will actually be evangelized in this generation than in all the other nineteen years put together. [Applause.] During the last six months, under the auspices of the Laymen's Missionary Movement, united campaigns have been held in twenty-two cities of the United States and Canada. Let me indicate to you briefly what those cities have done. Six cities on the Pacific Coast from which I have just returned (Spokane, Seattle, Portland, Greater Oakland, Los Angeles, and San Diego, in which there is a total of 112,000 Protestant Church members) gave last year $116,000 to foreign missions. They decided this year to try to raise $470,000 from the same constituency. [Applause.] That is a little more than four times as much as they have been giving. Nine cities in the South and the West (and you will be interested in the names of those cities)—Topeka, St. Joseph, St. Louis, Nashville, Knoxville, Atlanta, Charlotte, Norfolk, and Richmond—those nine cities gave last year to foreign missions an aggregate of $181,000. Representative gatherings of their business men discussed this matter, and decided what they ought to do. They have decided to undertake to raise, not $181,000, but $705,000 annually for this object. [Applause.] That means that in these fifteen cities—and not one of all the cities visited has failed to take active, aggressive action in the matter—that means that these cities have undertaken to quadruple their missionary output. Surely this is the most hopeful action in behalf of missions which has been taken in modern times. This Missionary Movement is sweeping through Canada in the same way, reaching from Toronto to Halifax. They gave there last year in seven cities to missions an aggregate of $345,000. They have now undertaken to raise $877,000 per year. This means that the Church is rising this year, as in no preceding year in all its history, to see that the message of Christianity is heralded around the world.

It is a great thing to be living in these days. More has happened in the last ten years than in the previous one hundred and more. More is going to happen in the next twenty-five years than has happened in the last twenty-five hundred. I would rather live now, for the next twenty-five years, than all the nine hundred and sixty-nine years that Methuselah lived; for a great deal more is going to happen. It seems better to live now than at any other time during all history. The one great question that confronts you and me and all Christians living in our time is the evangelization of the world during our generation, making this gospel absolutely universal. I am sure we can do it. Why, it only means, on the financial side, about one street car fare a week on the average from the Christians of this country. When the Protestant Christians of North America give an average of one street car fare a week, that will be $50,000,000 a year for foreign missions. I believe it can be done. I believe there are many indications that the Church is going to do it.. [Applause.] And I believe that God wants you and me personally to have a larger share in bringing about this evangelization than we can begin to realize and comprehend to-night. There are individual men now living who by their influence, direct and indirect, are going to be the means of carrying the gospel to a million or more individuals. What a glorious opportunity it is to live with such possibilities! That man had the right conception of life who said: "I would rather save a million men than save a million dollars." [Applause.]

I have a friend in Montreal who supported me for ten years in Calcutta, paying all my salary. He supports seven or eight missionaries in other parts of the world. He might have been a millionaire or a multimillionaire by this time if he had thought the best thing to do with money was to hoard it, but he thought the best thing to do with it was to unloose it through Christian personality out in the dark parts of the earth. And that man, to my certain knowledge, by that kind of disposition of his wealth, has been able to carry the gospel to tens of thousands of people who otherwise never would have heard it. My friend Dr. Goucher, of the Methodist Church of Baltimore, has during the last twenty years invested about $100,000 in India. With what result? There are in that district fifty thousand members of the Methodist Church who twenty years ago were idolaters. In that particular instance every two dollars invested led to some heathen soul accepting Jesus Christ as his Saviour and identifying himself with the Christian Church. And it will not be very long until that fifty thousand Christian people have become one hundred thousand. In a few years more they will become five hundred thousand, and I do not know how great the company may be that will meet and greet our Lord when he comes if they go on, under his blessing, multiplying as they are now doing. There is no other investment of life or money in all the world that can be made that will tell more powerfully for time and eternity than investing in personality along spiritual lines out in those great, dark places of the earth. And there is a place for just as many of you men and women as can afford to do it—to put one hundred, five hundred, one thousand, or ten·thousand dollars a year into this enterprise of redeeming the world.

I was riding along with a Baptist minister in a train sometime ago. In our conversation he said: "The most generous person in my congregation is an old colored woman. She can neither read nor write, she was born a slave, and does not have a penny which she does not earn over the washtub; yet she gives $50 a year for foreign missions. I went to her and told her that she was giving too much; that she could not afford so much. She replied something like this: 'You certainly would not take away from me the very greatest pleasure of my life. Why, very often,' she said to me, 'when I am at work over the washtub, and the sweat is falling down off my brow into the soapsuds before me, these sweat drops remind me of the jewels I am laying up in the presence of Jesus.'" That old black woman was carrying the gospel to about twenty-five of her sisters and brothers at the ends of the world every year by her humble sacrifice and love.

On the west coast of Africa a missionary station was established. Among the converts was a young girl about sixteen years old. The natives were taught to give their best gifts on Christmas to the Saviour, whose birthday was being celebrated. Their very poverty kept them from giving anything of great value; but if anybody could give a penny or two, that was counted a great gift. Most of them were not able to do that. They would bring a handful of vegetables from their gardens, or something of that kind. But on this occasion this girl in the procession, when she got in front of the preacher, took out a silver coin worth eighty-five cents and handed that to the minister as her gift to Christ. It was so large an amount for a girl in her position to give that he felt some hesitation in taking it. He thought that she had probably stolen it; but, lest it might create confusion, he accepted it for the moment, and then called her aside at the close of the service to ask her where she got it. She explained to him in her simple way that, in her desire to give something to Christ in some way worthy of his love and sacrifice for her, she had gone to a neighboring planter and voluntarily bound herself out to him as a slave for the rest of her life for this eighty-five cents, and had brought the whole financial equivalent of her life of pledged service and laid it down in a single gift at the feet of her Lord!

I am glad to have a gospel to preach that is capable of doing that for a savage, and I feel like asking my own heart to-night whether there is anything so glorious, so divine that we can do with our lives as to bind them in voluntary, perpetual slavery to Jesus Christ for lost humanity's sake, and to say to him: "If God will show me anything that I can do for the redemption of the world that I have not yet undertaken, by his grace I will undertake it at once." For "I cannot, I dare not, go up to judgment till I have done the utmost God enables me to do to promote his glory throughout the whole, wide world."

My fellow-Christians, I believe all of us would be fully satisfied with that kind of a life purpose a thousand years from to-night. [Applause.]

VI.

THE ONE GREAT MISSION OF THE CHURCH.

God is moving, through his Church, upon all the nations of the earth; he is stirring things out East; he is waking them up; he is letting them know that there are things besides their old civilization; he is letting them understand that there are some things higher than their superstitions and idolatries; he is giving them to feel that there are forces and agencies that do not belong to this world, to which they must give heed or perish. They begin to hear the muttering voice that comes back to them from the world, from the nations, and from the kingdoms of even this earth: "They that will not serve thee shall utterly perish." They are turning to the missionaries; they are turning to the civilized agencies and courting the commercial forces; they are turning to all the outside world to find out what these things mean; and they have not begun to learn yet. They are just waking up. But by and by, when their eyes are opened, when they see the form of the Son of Man in the furnace into which they have been cast, and feel the touch of his hand, then they will learn that he is indeed not only Lord of all, but the Saviour of all. And the Church will come to them as his messenger, indeed, with his power, presenting his life, and holding them forth before the world and making it to know that he, and he alone, can save them. They will learn that there is no other name given under heaven whereby they can be saved except the name of Jesus of Nazareth. That is what the Church will give them; and they will learn that from the Church, but *you* have to learn it first.

(72)

VI.

THE ONE GREAT MISSION OF THE CHURCH.

BISHOP A. W. WILSON, BALTIMORE, MD.

Mr. President: First of all, I want you to understand that when you are talking about the Church you are talking about that which I consider the greatest thing in earth—the greatest thing in heaven, I will say. I am not going to give it the second place to any organization or association that may be devised or conceived of among men; it stands absolutely first in its character and in its power. I know that it is a very customary thing among the leaders of thought in the various departments of secular life to sneer at the Church; and when we want to bring the principle of virtue that belongs to the Church into practical operation in the departments of secular life, they will talk about it in their patronizing way, "We are not leading a Sunday school," or something of that sort. Well, that is just what you should expect. Such wisdom belongs to the Church, and not to the princes of riches in this old country; and you may rest assured that these princes will not know it until they are finally overcome by it, as they are going to be.

The Church has its qualities and power, because, first, it has the essential, fundamental, indispensable truth, the truth that belongs to all, and that is going to abide when all the mere formal statements in other departments of life shall have been forgotten. "Whether there be knowledge, it shall vanish away;" but this knowledge shall not vanish away. It is not in the abstract merely; it is the living truth; it is a concrete form, and has been represented to the world in a personal form. You cannot kill it; you cannot hide it; you cannot put it away in the vaults of your laboratory and let it lie there to be forgotten or unearthed by scholars in the ages to come. It is a thing of such

(73)

vitality that it holds its place in your household to-day, in your counting office, and in your bank; and wherever you may find yourself, in social or in political life, this truth of the Church confronts you and demands acknowledgment, recognition, subjection; and if you do not yield to it, once your disobedience has been established, there is going to be a reckoning.

There is one thing that reminds me that the Church of God alone is the pillar and ground of the truth. That is why I hold it first. I hold it first because it represents to the world the highest ideal of character and of love. I do not care what you may say about the men who have led armies and been foremost in scientific pursuits in different ages of the world, in study—aye, even in character and social life—you may give them all the courage to direct and all the honor they may have bestowed upon them; but after all, I affirm, none of them have ever approached within seeing distance of the ideal that is furnished by the Church of God for human attainment.

We do not stand upon the moral level of the secular life with any of its qualities, its polish, its education, its gain in any direction; we do not stand there and say: "We are going to measure up to this and bring man up to it." But we get above that level, and say: "The only ideal is that which comes down from God out of heaven; and unless there be a God, you will not know what man is or can be." [Applause.]

We want to sit in the heavenly places. We claim a right to associate not only with humanity under secular conditions, but with the best and highest forms of creation in any and all worlds. [Applause.] We affirm that it is the right and prerogative of the Church to raise men that shall be able to confront God himself, through God, and walk in fellowship with his Son; so that his Son may be the firstborn among many brethren. But we do not stop short of that. No other organization or association on earth, no agency that man ever dreamed of, has ever accomplished such results as those. They have all had their level, and their ideals have produced local or national fame.

If you want to make a statesman, you take a course in the political school. Aren't they splendid schools for the education of manhood? If you want to give a man power among men and great intellect, you put him through your scientific courses, and give him instruction in philosophy; and he comes out simply to tell you that you do not know anything, that you should learn the feats in the gymnasium, that you should learn the different theories that the university teaches—if you don't know these things, you don't know anything. But we say the man that knows God and Jesus Christ knows everything that is worth knowing in this universe. [Applause.] He is bound to come to know, in the ages to come if he does not during this present life, everything that is to be known. I wish Bishop Hendrix would use his facile pen on that sort of studies to work up that first chapter of Colossians. I marvel that we have not made more of it. It contains the supreme philosophy of this and all worlds. And it is going to set aside all pretensions of science—aye, and all speculative philosophy down through the process of creation, down into the historic experiences of our humanity, until it touches the very bottom phases of life and death; then it will lift the whole up to the level of God, and raise everything with itself up to God. [Applause.]

That is our philosophy, and that is the school we are learning in; and when the intellect gets out of the secular teachings into that sort of truth and works along those lines, it is going to be settled where the higher courses in learning can never bring you. That is what we want, and that is what the Church represents. And I want you to remember another thing about it: the Church stands upon an immovable foundation. The side issues may be discussed; but set them aside for future consideration. There are a great many things that, in their present status, we see through clouds; we do not know what to do with them; but the great solid foundation, the thing that can never be moved, is that on which the Church builds, and that upon which she alone stakes her existence and her whole character. We do not stake it upon any speculative information, whether in theology or philosophy; we do not stake it upon any political view; we stake it simply and only upon the averment and presentation of Jesus Christ himself. "Upon this rock will I build my Church, and the gates of hell shall not prevail against it."

The Church has a power that no other organization, association, or agency of this world can claim or dares to claim. To prove you this, I need only quote the words of St. Paul concerning the strength and power that Jesus had given to his disciples, "All things are yours," when the Church was laboring under the feet of imperial brutality, when it was groveling in the earth, when it was spending its life to keep itself from utter destruction, when it was absolutely made up of the meanest specimens, according to this world's judgment, of our humanity that could be found, the slaves of the world, the poor, and the outcasts.

In all the world, with all its reforms and all its historic movements and all its speculations about the future life, you alone have the power that death shall never conquer, that will stand against any assault that may be made against it in this world and the worlds to come, for the eternal life itself is yours. You can make it triumph over all the forms of adversity that may be brought to bear against you. Life, death, things present, and things to come! Sweep the universe and gather into your thought all the resources of God everywhere—"they are yours." The Church has it to command. "They are yours."

Go to your highest legislative halls, and ask them, when they make their plans for the control of great interests and the direction of great movements—ask them what are their resources. They will begin to count them out in great form, and tell you: "We have the majesty of the law; we have the power of the government; we have the hand of taxation upon the wealth of the country." Yes, and what do they do? We have been at it for centuries, and had all of these things, and more than I can name, and they are trying to get more; and as they gather them, one after the other, they don't avail in the great need of the government and of society.

There is as much poverty to-day in our great country as there ever was in the world's history. There is as profound degradation of character. There is as supreme lawlessness. There is as much of all evil among men as there ever was in the world, except just where the Church has laid its hand upon men and said, in the Master's name: "Be thou clean." Only there has there been redemption.

Governments never redeem anybody. Legislation has never saved anybody. Wealth has not saved anybody. Heaven help us, it has done a vast deal on the other side. Wealth does not help to redeem men. The one power that the Church has under control, that God has put into your hands—the power of the Spirit of God, that cleans and saves every man that truly believes in Jesus Christ—that is the saving power, and that is the supreme power in this world. [Applause.]

I never go into a little prayer meeting, where two or three are gathered together, without a feeling of reverence. Usually they are poor people. There may be but two or three, but He is with them. They have that privilege, and can stand there in His presence and call forth the mighty powers of His government that control His interests and that pertain to them in life. And when a whole Church comes together, with hundreds of men and women present who recognize but the one Lord of all, I bare my head reverently and acknowledge that I am in the presence of the greatest power that earth or heaven can show.

One of the things that we have been troubled with in the years past is that our own people, while they owe everything to the Church of God, have yet depreciated their Church. They are snarling among themselves because of some little imperfection and because of some dislike of the measures that do not meet their wants or offend the taste of the secular class. That is too often the cause of the Church being disfigured and spotted here and there. But, in spite of all those little outbreaks of mere petty passion or local prejudices or personal opinion, I do not hesitate to say that the Church of God is the representative of him before the world, and all the petty passions and outbreaks are but pustules on the surface.

I want you to hold to that. Don't be thinking about your little community, with its surface outbreaks; don't be thinking about your poor little habitation. The church that was built fifty years ago may be nearly worn out, and you can't afford to build another; but the Church in the wilderness is as good as the Church in Solomon's temple. Don't fret or worry about those things. Just think that, if there are but a half dozen of us here that believe in the Son of God, we have the Church of God here; and that is the mightiest power in this community or in the country or in the world. [Applause.] Only think about that, and work on that line, and you will come to realize what it is to be in the Church of God. I thank God that I have a place in his Church, and you are never going to drive me out. [Applause.] If I haven't a little place here, I will go out in some little rural place, among a simple folk, and in their way worship God and the Father of our Lord Jesus Christ, and cast my lot with them. But the Church has got to hold on to me, because I am going to hold on to it. [Applause.]

Now, if I am right about the Church, what is its condition? Does it live simply to enjoy these prerogatives for itself? You say: "I am going to make myself great, and to get up into the highest heavens, where I can look down upon all the rest of the race in my superiority." I think not. I don't think that is the idea. We sometimes talk with men who act as though they were the whole of the business themselves, and as if they thought He had gathered all the resources of the earth and concentrated them on one person, putting that man above all the rest of the race. O no; that is a very different thing. It is a good thing to convert one and bring him up into the presence of God; but it is not his to go there alone; he must stretch his arms out and gather the crowd in and pull them up with him. [Applause.] That is what conversion means. If it means anything, it means unselfishness. If it saves one, it will save all who believe from the everlasting fires.

That is the idea. This great Church of God, with all its resources, with its command of all the powers of heaven and earth, was intended to do the greatest thing ever done in heaven or earth. Do not forget that. I haven't any faith in anything but the Church, as God's agent, for bringing about the great results that we seek. Other agencies, under the Lordship of Jesus Christ, may contribute to help the Church; but the Church is to do the work after all.

Most of the people of our country, and the English too, talk as though they thought that the gospel had its beginning right here, and was suited only to our peculiar views and institutions, and was not adapted to these lower races out in the East. It was begun out there. Peter and Paul and men of that sort were men that would be counted inferiors if they were among us to-day; and you would not give much heed to them, because they belonged to those superficial and half-trained races of the East. That is wonderful. Though apostles, they looked like barbarians. But they will tell you about a civilization of which you never dreamed. Now, that gospel comes to you, and lets you know that it was not meant for you in the first instance. Nobody ever said to you, or can say to you, that God first sent his Son Jesus Christ to bless you. He did not. He sent him to somebody else first. And out of that center, out from that Eastern country, he sent his messengers through all the world; and their message got hold of you Western people and lifted you out of gross idolatry and made you what you are.

We have been looking at things from this side, and we have not seen really what a Church is intended for. When we talk about improving this work, you begin to think about a few preachers going out to do the thing, like a Samson shouldering the whole work upon themselves. "Let them go out and do the work. That is right. But we have work to do at home." Yes, you have work to do at home; that is true. But your work to-day at home as laymen is to get the money to send the men out there to build up God's kingdom in all the East and everywhere else. [Applause.]

He that is rich unto himself and is not rich toward God is the poorest man on the face of the earth—so poor that our Lord did not hesitate to say of him: "Thou fool!" [Applause.] That is what you laymen have to learn. The Church of Christ can be carried on to its fullest extent only when the whole body of it works together. We have about six thousand preachers, I think, in our Church in this country; and there are twice as many more in the other Churches. What are they lacking? It is money. We haven't enough to minister to the people at home. If the laymen are not going to do the work, it never will be done. If the preachers are the workers, what are the laymen? Are they to simply sit about and let the preachers go into the active work and fix up the places and fill their mouths with all the earthly goods while they do nothing? Is that God's way? O no.

You talk about the preachers as leaders sometimes in a kind of patronizing tone; but you never accept them as leaders; you don't intend to do it. You say: "Well, you can do in your line and in your way the things that you want to do; but you cannot control us. We are going to do what we think right. We are making our own money, and will spend it in our own way, and live according to our own notion of things." If that is what the Church means, it is the worst failure that ever had its beginning on earth.

I am going to say this: God never commenced or instituted a proceeding or movement that was or can be a failure. But the fact is we have a mission that is so great that it will require all the vitality, all the manhood, all the energy, all the intellect, all the heart and enthusiasm, all the wealth, and all the culture among the laity as well as the preachers.

We are getting scarce of preachers. I was going to say I was glad of it, so the people would have to do something for themselves. Well, we cannot have enough preachers, I suppose: partly because you are too stingy to pay them, and partly because God intends that the laity shall learn that the work of the Church of God is in their hands, and not simply in the hands of the preachers.

Many years ago, when I was Missionary Secretary, I was pleading for the cause of foreign missions in one of the towns out here in Eastern Kentucky. One man of means, who happened to be in the church at the time, came to me afterwards, and said: "I have no use for foreign missions. We have up this creek here settlements where there are hundreds of people who have no more Christian teaching than the heathen in the Far East." "Well," said I, "it is the supreme disgrace of your Church here that it is so. You have a body of five or six hundred who profess to live in Jesus Christ; and yet you allow these people to die at your very doors, and never offer them the bread of life. The curse of God will be on you for it."

I acknowledge with profoundest sorrow that the words spoken in the address of the Mayor last night were literally true: that we have a lot of young men and women in the fastnesses of the mountains and in our rural districts that have never heard the word of God. It is true also that we cannot afford to let them go. I want to raise them to the level of all our Christians; and that can be done with a little labor at home, so that they can expend themselves in giving the gospel to all the world. [Applause.] They are the sort to do it. I tell you, that sort of a man will make the best sort of missionary. He is a strong man physically; and when he gets among the heathen, he is not subject as readily to attacks of the diseases which are so prevalent there, and he goes out with the qualities and requirements to teach the word of God. Take the first ministers of the gospel. God trained them from among the fishermen and lower strata of life, so that when they came to their task they were at their best physically and intellectually. They went out with the gospel penetrating the innermost chambers of their beings, permeating, saturating, and controlling them in every fiber; and when they went out, furnished and trained by the Saviour, the best Teacher the world ever saw, these fishermen, with no training in the rabbinical schools, turned the world upside down.

We have come to the point where you laymen will have to take hold of this thing and work it out. I have got to the point where I want to see the laymen take hold of every interest in the Church and push the foreign missions to a successful place, more successful than they are at present, and not let the missionaries do all the work. [Applause.] I want to see them not only manage the money matters, but also assist in other interests of the Church. We want praying men; we want men who are in constant communion with God; we want men who take their ideals of life not from the countingrooms of the banks and merchants nor from the legislative halls or political systems; but we want men who take their ideals from their fellowship with the Son of God. [Applause.] These are the men who can do the world's work, and none other. We cannot afford to let the thing fall into the hands of at least semi-secular men, who would do the work now and then, five minutes a week, for that is all they do. Some of them come to prayer meeting; but the most of them do not. They do not know how to pray. They will come to church Sunday morning, if they feel well enough; Sunday night they cannot come, for they say: "Once a day is about as much as we can stand." We cannot expect much from that sort of men. We have to get men with the enthusiasm of the Son of God. The laity of the Church must be baptized into Christ. They must have the spirit of Christ in them, and that every day and hour, praying for it, working for it, living for it, and dying for it. [Applause.]

We want the laymen of the Church to get in that condition; then the Church will have the power to reach all the nations, and we will lift the nations up and give the world the spectacle of nations conquered without the blare of trumpets, without the explosion of gunpowder, without the show of battle ships, without any of the horrors of war. We will give them the spectacle of nations conquered by the voice of the Prince of Peace; we will give them the spectacle of the greatest results in earth or heaven, wrought by the means of a pure, spiritual life and the power of Jesus Christ—power such as God uses, and nobody but God and those whom God wants and delegates to do his work. That is what we want to see.

6

Now, the one great interest of the Church encompasses all the interests of life. I do not believe in any business in which Jesus Christ is not a partner; I do not believe in any legislation where he does not sit in the speaker's chair; I do not believe in any government where he does not occupy the executive seat; for he is Lord of all. And he is not going to defend anybody, whether he sits on the kingly throne or whether he rules in the presidential chair, unless that ruler upholds his kingdom. He is going to hold his own as King of kings and Lord of lords over all nations and everywhere.

He is moving, through his Church, upon all the nations of the earth; he is stirring things out East; he is waking them up; he is letting them know that there are things besides their old civilization; he is letting them understand that there are some things higher than their superstitions and idolatries; he is giving them to feel that there are forces and agencies that do not belong to this world, to which they must give heed or perish. They begin to hear the muttering voice that comes back to them from the world, from the nations, and from the kingdoms of even this earth: "They that will not serve thee shall utterly perish." They are turning to the missionaries; they are turning to the civilized agencies and courting the commercial forces; they are turning to all the outside world to find out what these things mean; and they have not begun to learn yet. They are just waking up. But by and by, when their eyes are opened, when they see the form of the Son of Man in the furnace into which they have been cast and feel the touch of his hand, then they will learn that he is indeed not only Lord of all, but the Saviour of all. And the Church will come to them as his messenger, indeed, with his power, presenting his life, and holding them forth before the world and making them to know that he, and he alone, can save them. They will learn that there is no other name given under heaven whereby they can be saved except the name of Jesus of Nazareth. That is what the Church will give them; and they will learn that from the Church, but *you* have to learn it first.

Now, when you have done this yourselves, and consecrated the whole business, consecrated your plans, your families, your wealth, your legislation, everything; when you have put his seal on the whole—then, I say, the Church will have accomplished the work

God wants done in this world, and there will be such a clamor as never was heard.

Do you know what you will have done then? You will have done away with all wars and conflicts; you will have swept out the stain and disgrace that is in our cities by reason of the vices that are controlling so many civilized communities; you will have brought a reign of harmony and purity and peace—a magnificent thing—between the kingdom of God and the world. In our American strongholds, in which we take such great delight, we shall know that no injustice can find place. A man will recognize his fellow as his brother. They shall stand upon the same level, because they recognize one and the same Lord. Then the battle ships will disappear, armies will disband, wars will cease, and desolate places will be built up, and the old habitations that have been in ruins for centuries past will become beautiful cities.

When the Church of God shall have done all that, then the world shall proclaim deliverance everywhere. He is going to do it through his Church. And it will not stop there; for in the ages to come the song of the redeemed shall be heard yonder in the heaven. And it shall be known by the Church what are the exceeding riches of his grace. Not only that, but the principalities and powers of the heavenly places will turn their faces toward the Church in its perfected state, in the exercise of all its marvelous power, and see the manifold wisdom of God. The whole of his mighty work shall be carried on through his own people, and we shall know then what a power the Church has been and what a marvelous commission it has had to accomplish in the earth.

You and I have it to do. We have to do it at any cost. We can afford it. If it takes one hundred and fifty or two hundred thousand dollars in Soochow, China; if it requires one hundred thousand for Korea; if it requires five million for Japan; if it requires enormous sums undreamed of to-day to carry on this work through the heathen nations of the world and to help men up to this higher fellowship with the eternal world—if it takes it all, in God's name, in Christ's name, let us give it. [Applause.]

The Christ needs it. It is all his. "Freely ye have received, freely give." And when you have done that, your last sacrifice and song shall be to Him who loved us and washed us from our sins in his own blood, to whom be glory and dominion now and forever. Amen.

II.

THE OBLIGATION.

VII. THE DUTY OF THE STRONGER TO' THE WEAKER RACES.

VIII. THE SUPREME OBLIGATION OF THE HOUR.

IX. THE CHALLENGE OF THE CITY.

X. THE CALL TO GO FORWARD.

INTRODUCTION BY BISHOP E. R. HENDRIX.

King Edward VII., the most perfect gentleman in Europe, the great diplomat, never did a more gracious thing than the sending as his representative to this country of this great gray head that all men know. [Applause.] We hail him to-night on behalf of our people as the personal friend of William E. Gladstone [Applause], in whose Cabinet he sat an honored counselor. We hail him as a man who, like Gladstone, when an Oxford student at graduation, had the "Double First," the highest distinction possible in an English university, bestowed upon him. [Applause.] We hail him to-night as a professor in the University of Oxford, with a period of twenty-three years as a member of the British Parliament, and with yet a longer period, and who has won, by common consent of his countrymen and of the members of Parliament, the title of the most accomplished member of the British Parliament. [Applause.] The man of letters in public life is what our honored guest stands for before the world. While a professor in the University of Oxford he made a practical study of our own great country. By repeated visits and the weighing and sifting of his material he has given to the world the very best work on the American government in that immortal work: "The American Commonwealth." [Applause.] We hail him to-night as the great humanitarian—the one who stood for "home rule" in Ireland, the one who believed that the Boer War was unnecessary [Applause], the one whose eloquent voice was heard with Mr. Gladstone's in denouncing the Bulgarian atrocities. [Applause.] This is he, Privy Councilor, member of the Cabinet, man of letters, whom the King of Great Britain sends to our country as his personal representative. He does not come to us as a diplomat; he does not seek to bring closer relations between Great Britain and America. These nations are far above diplomacy: they are held in bonds of kinship. He comes not with a diplomat's arts to win our confidence; he had that before he came. He speaks straightforward those great truths which we believe in common, and which are so sacred to our hearts. We hail him to-night as the representative of three sovereigns. The year that Queen Victoria was crowned, in 1838, God gave her, as one of her coronation gifts that should help to perpetuate the glory of her reign, James Bryce. [Applause.] And so during that long reign he lived and wrought, ever ripening in knowledge and influence. As his great chief, unhappily retired now from the Premiership, said of him: "He has traveled everywhere; he has even been to the top of Ararat; he has read everything; he knows everybody; and he is the one who reflects such honor upon his noble Queen—the queenliest of women, the womanliest of queens." He lived to see her great reign close without a reproach, to see her imbedded in the hearts of her people, helping to establish the English dynasty and exerting an influence which will be felt through countless centuries to come. He serves also her honored son, who came with bowed head to that throne made doubly sacred by his mother's occupancy of it. He comes as the servant and representative of the king under whom he has served, in his Cabinet and as an honored member of the British Parliament, standing, like the king himself does, for peace, representing what is best in English traditions and thought. But, thank God, to-night, Mr. Bryce, you come to us the representative of another Sovereign, the King of kings and the Lord of lords. [Applause.] You represent our Protestant religion; you represent our holy Christianity. An imperialist, we welcome you because we are imperialists, believing in the extension of a kingdom that shall cover all the earth until the kingdoms of this earth shall become the kingdoms of our Lord and of his Christ. [Applause] On behalf of this representative body of laymen, it gives me the greatest pleasure to welcome you and to introduce you as the speaker of the evening. [Great applause.] [In honor of the speaker the whole audience rose to their feet.]

VII.

THE DUTY OF THE STRONGER TO THE WEAKER RACES.

HON. JAMES BRYCE, AMBASSADOR FROM GREAT BRITAIN.

I FEEL emboldened to address you on the topic before me because there is nothing which has brought the hearts of Americans and Englishmen nearer together than the work they have tried to do on similar lines for the kingdom of God in foreign lands. We have been in this modern world the two great missionary countries. We have not only felt it to be one of our highest privileges and duties as Christians to support the gospel in all countries, but we have also done it on the same lines, in the same faith, following the same principles, always trusting to the truth and not to force. And I am glad to tell you that wherever I have traveled (and if I had not traveled in many countries, where I have seen many missions, I should not attempt to address you to-night) I have found the American and English missionaries working side by side, in the closest relations, always helping each other.

Now, such a meeting as this to-night is the most conclusive proof of the interest which you of the South take in the cause of Christian missions, and it indicates that the laymen are doing it; that you are not leaving it to the clergy alone to tell you what your duty is, but have met to confer with one another as to how it may best be performed. Realizing this, it is not necessary for me to dwell upon the good that is being done by missions nor upon the duty we have to support them. This Convention alone is a sufficient proof of that. And the vigorous religious life which is pulsing through all the veins of the South finds inspiration not only in wanting to help your own people, but in wanting to help those beyond.

That is what ought to be felt by every Christian who thinks for a moment what his Christianity means, who thinks what he

(87)

would be if the light of the gospel had not shone upon him. He must feel that the very highest not only of his duties, but of his privileges, is to endeavor to give that light to others upon whom it has not yet fallen. It is the light that lighteth every man that cometh into the world. There is no greater privilege you or I can have than to help that light to shine in the dark places of the earth. And every man who feels not only what he owes to himself, but what his whole country owes to Christianity, will see that his country is foremost in the work of missions. Think of what you in America and we in England would be if we had not been Christian peoples for fourteen hundred years. All that time, although we have not profited as we should have done by its teachings, Christianity has been saving us from many at least of the evils in which our pagan forefathers lay sunk, and has been leading us onward and upward until many faults and vices of the Old World have been put behind us, until many moral truths and ideals essential for life have been revealed to us which the heathen world has never known.

If you should take our Christianity away from us, you would take away all that makes our true national greatness. Therefore, though we do not ourselves go out and preach the gospel to every creature, still we must feel, as Christians, that there is no duty nearer to us, or speaking with a more imperative voice, than the duty of trying to spread the truth of the gospel.

It was through Christ that there was first revealed the essential unity of all mankind and that all men were born brothers. If we believe that, we have a duty to those without as well as to those within. And I think it is pleasant to know that by degrees we have come more and more to feel that our duty in supporting those who diffuse gospel truths is far higher than any that we owe to the particular denomination to which we may belong. Each of us is connected with some particular religious body; sometimes because we think it is more closely conformable to the teachings of Scripture, and sometimes, perhaps, because of our associations in early life. But I hope we have reached the time when we feel that the essential truths of Christianity by which we live are higher and deeper than any differences that divide Christian denominations. When we feel that, we want to give the heathen not what belongs to any one special denomination or another, but the truths, especially those contained in the words of our Lord himself, which are the very foundations of our Christian faith. With this realization of the essentials of Christianity and of the duty of all Christians to work together will come also a new and higher conception of the work of Christian missions.

Time was when the success of a mission was measured by the number of congregations which the missionary was able to form in some heathen land to which he was sent and the number of converts which in each year he was able to add to the fold. That was natural. It was well that little centers should be built up; it was well that the converts be made; but too much stress was laid upon that as if it had been the whole work. We have come now to a larger and broader view. The preaching of Christianity is part of a great movement by which we are trying to reach not only the soul of the individual whom we may desire to convert, but also the whole people. We want to raise the people as a whole, to lift them out of the mire of the ignorance and vice and the low conceptions of Deity and humanity in which they have been lying, and to set them upon a higher plane with nobler ideals. That new view of missions is the Christlike one and open to all, although we may be divided as to the form in which essential truths had best be given.

Something of the same kind has happened at home. You who carry on the evangelistic work in the cities know that whenever you establish a home mission in the crowded slums of a great city you try not merely to preach to the people, not merely to learn the languages of new immigrants from Europe and to give them Christian ideas, but also to raise their life in every phase, to teach them cleanliness and the care of health, to give them better views of social duty, to cultivate a taste for reading, to gather them together in little social meetings—in one way or another to raise their conception of what life should be. When you do that, you make them all the fitter to receive the gospel. And I believe that those who have conducted evangelistic work of this kind have found that the work advanced far more rapidly in this fashion.

So is it also when we preach the gospel among the heathen. We lift them altogether, and desire not only to make Christians of them, but also to free them from the base, low life they have led and from their unworthy conceptions of the divinity of which they have sometimes had glimmerings. Thus missions must now be regarded as parts of a great world movement—the influence now exercised by the civilized upon the uncivilized or savage peoples.

There is in our time more than ever there was before a contact of the civilized and the uncivilized all over the earth. The world has grown smaller; steam and electricity have brought its parts together; and as the civilized races have spread out over its surface, there is no place where their influence is not felt; and with the exception of two ancient empires in the East, pretty nearly every part of the world has been brought under the control of some of the white civilized races, and even those empires are now in close contact with white races. Now, that is a new phenomenon. And under these circumstances missions are inevitable, because the civilized and the uncivilized are being brought together; and if Christianity is not brought to bear upon those uncivilized races with which we are now coming in contact, their last state may be worse than their first. I shall presently come back to that point. Meantime let me as a traveler— a traveler who has seen missionaries at work in a good many parts of the world—bear testimony to the splendid work which is being done in our own time as well as in times past by Christian missionaries. There have not been any nobler examples of devotion to duty, of self-sacrifice, of the renunciation of the ordinary pleasures and joys of the world for the sake of a higher calling than those which our missionaries have given during the last eighty years. I want to pay especial tribute to the work which is being done by the many missionaries of this country. I have seen them particularly in two places: first in India, where their work is admirable, and where some of your missionaries are the wisest men, who know as much about India and are as much worthy to be listened to on that subject as any men I have met. And I want also to pay a tribute to what they have done in the Turkish East, where they are placed among Mohammedans and certain non-Protestant churches. Those Eastern Christian peoples have suffered a great deal, and they have, I fear, a great deal yet to suffer. I need not tell you what is the unhappy life of many Christians in that country. Some thirteen years ago tens of thousands were murdered; many of them were women, who might have saved their lives if they had spoken three words to renounce Christianity; yet, like the martyrs of the apostolic **age,** they refused to sacrifice their Christian faith, and went willingly to death for the sake of the Lord they loved. Among these peoples it has been the duty of your Christian missionaries to labor. And the best work that has ever been done among them has been by your American missionaries. Whenever I wanted really to know what was happening, whenever I wanted to enable my friends to find some means of relieving the famine-stricken and unhappy people, whenever I have desired to find out what could be done politically to alleviate the sufferings of these oppressed and martyred races, I have always found that the best thing to do was to turn to the American missionaries. And I have often heard from members of these ancient Churches the warmest acknowledgment of the great services which your missionaries have rendered them.

Now, when one thinks of the splendid work which missionaries have done, when one thinks also of how long they have been at work, and when one thinks of the advantages which the missionaries of the great civilized nations ought to have, are you not sometimes surprised that Christianity has not overspread the whole world? Why is it that more progress has not been made? Think of the beginnings of Christianity, when Paul and the other apostles went out to make those first missionary tours, recorded in the Acts of the Apostles. They went to a few in number, through a pagan world, a world which was dominated by ancient and powerful religions, where all the authorities and secular powers were on the side of the old religions, and where before long those powers, the emperors and their governors, put forth their whole strength to resist and extinguish Christianity; and a series of cruel persecutions took place, extending over nearly three centuries, by which it was attempted to root out the new religion from the earth. Those persecutions failed. Christianity spread itself over the empire against all the power the empire could put forth, and made its way in the teeth of persecutions until at last it grew so strong that the emperor was obliged to recognize it; and from that time forth it became the dominant religion. It did that work in three centuries.

Since that time nineteen hundred years have passed, and Christianity has had all the material forces of the world on its side, nearly all the power, all the learning, and all the civilization, except during a short period when Mohammedanism was at its

height. Why, then, has it not succeeded in converting the whole
earth? And why does not the name "Christian" belong to the
entire globe, as it belonged to the later Roman Empire in an-
tiquity?

That is, indeed, a question worth asking. It is a question I am
sure you have often asked yourselves. It is far better for us to
reflect on what we have not accomplished, and try to discover
why it is that we have failed, than it is to exult in what we have
accomplished. It may be that we shall discover some of the
causes which have weakened us and prevented us from obtaining,
with material advantages on our side, what the apostles and their
successors obtained with all the forces and powers against them.
I am going to give one reason; it is not the *only* reason, but it
is a reason which has often been brought forcibly home to me
when I have been traveling and watching the limited success
which has come to missions in some foreign countries where you
cannot blame the missionaries because their zeal and devotion
are evident.

The preaching of the gospel is only one of many things which
have been taken to the uncivilized during the last four centuries
through their contact with the civilized races, and some of those
other things have largely neutralized it. That contact began
with the discovery of America by Christopher Columbus. What
was the first thing that happened when the Spaniards and the
Portuguese began to settle in the American islands and continents? One of their objects was to convert the heathen. They
took out a great many friars with them, and set them to preaching, and the cross was carried up and down the islands, and the
friars preached; and the natives, whether or not they understood
and believed, were at any rate baptized and compelled to say that
they were Christians. We cannot blame the Spaniards for want
of zeal, whatever else we may blame them for. They thought
they were saving souls, whether by persuasion or force; and I
suppose they would have thought it wrong not to use carnal
weapons in that warfare. But the Spaniards did something more
than this. Though the friars came to preach, the adventurers
coming along with them came with a great thirst and greed for
gold. That was what they sought in the New World. Finding
gold ornaments among the people, they asked where they came
from; they hunted for the gold mines, and put the natives to

work in them. They set them also to till the soil, and those poor, weak, simple-minded natives, accustomed to raise just enough food to support themselves, and dancing in the sun in the careless way of the savage, were driven to work under the stern eye, and perhaps the scourge, of a Spanish owner and taskmaster until in the islands of Hispaniola (now Hayti and Cuba) the whole population died out under the severities of the Spanish rule within thirty or forty years after the discovery of the islands. The same thing happened in most of the other Spanish islands. Wherever the Spaniard went he seized the land of the people, reduced them to slavery, and forced them to work in the mines for him.

That was probably the most harsh and terrible form which the contact of a civilized race with an uncivilized ever took. It ended with the extermination of the natives. And yet something of that kind, though not so bad, has been going on ever since. Wherever the strong races who, like the Spaniards, had horses and firearms, races with the appliances of civilization at their command, have come into contact with weaker races, that sort of thing has happened. Everywhere the native has gone to the wall. Sometimes, where the native race was weak, it has been extinguished; it either dies out under hard treatment, as did the natives of the Antilles, or under the diseases which the white man brings with him or through use of the liquor which he has brought them. In one way or another the native races, if not extinguished, have at any rate become demoralized. They lose what have been their native customs and whatever strength these customs had, and find out that it is far easier to acquire the vices of the white man than to imitate his virtues.

I do not want to overstate the case. I do not deny that some of this was inevitable. The contact of a superior civilized race with a barbarous race must always bring certain evils to the weaker. But the evils need not have been so great if the civilized men who went among the natives had only behaved like Christians. Unfortunately, that was just what they did not do. There were always a few good men among them who tried to protect the natives, men even among the first Spanish conquerors (certainly some of the Spanish clergy, who did all they could) ; but the forces of rapine and avarice and the sort of contempt which the strong man feels for the weak have brought little but suffering to these weaker men. The land of the native was very often taken without giving him anything for it, and he was driven away if not killed. The trader who went among the natives cheated them, and did what was even worse: he sold them vile liquor that ruined them body and soul. And I am sorry to say that that is going on in some places still. It would have been a good thing for the natives if the art of distillation had never been discovered.

And yet it was only the other day that we awakened to a sense of the tremendous evils we have wrought among native peoples by the sale of drink. It does harm enough among white people, but it does far more among a savage or semicivilized race. They are not used to it or seasoned to it as in a certain way, it is to be feared, a number of our population have become. It demoralizes them; it works like poison upon them; it destroys them.

Now, these things have had a great effect upon the work of Christianity. How was it possible for the natives not to look at the practice of the Christian as well as his preaching? The missionary represented a religion of justice, of peace, and of love. But with the missionary came the man who tried to take away the land of the native or sold him worthless goods or intoxicated him with his liquor. How was it possible for the natives, when they saw these men who called themselves "Christians" just as did the missionaries, not to feel that there was a great variance between the practice and the doctrines of this religion? The saying is attributed to some African prince that the process going on in his country was: "First missionary, then trader, then army." The missionary came first, and well it would have been if he had been left to do his work alone. But before the missionary had succeeded in Christianizing the people the trader came to undo the missionary's work. And even where the white man did not rob or injure the natives there is something in his attitude when he finds himself among an uncivilized people that is not kindly, that is not Christian. He acts toward them as if they were persons to whom he can do whatever he likes.

If any of you have ever traveled in a foreign country among a savage people, you will know what I mean when I say that it takes almost the temper of a saint to keep you from treating with arrogance or scorn a people who are very much weaker than yourself and who frequently provoke you by an astonishing want of understanding. Nothing but a sense of human duty and Christian duty will prevent a man from acting harshly or unfairly when he is placed in such conditions. ·

Now, this attitude of the civilized stronger race has been one of the great obstacles to the advance of Christianity. In Africa, for instance, and in India, if the conduct of Christians had been on a level with their teachings, large parts at least of those countries would to-day be Christian countries.

There were times when the governments themselves behaved very badly. It has been only in the last forty or fifty years that Christian governments have awakened to their duties. Governments have latterly tried, and I think they are honestly trying, to protect the natives. This is not yet the case in all parts of the world. There are lamentable exceptions. But it is the case wherever either the United States or Great Britain holds sway. I am perfectly certain that your government and my government are doing their best wherever their flags fly to protect the native in every way they can. And I can say from having traveled in India that it has been the sole and whole-hearted object of the English government to administer absolutely equal justice in India between the European and the native and to give the native as good a government as the circumstances of the country will permit.

But even where the government is good, it is possible for the private adventurer to do a great deal of harm. He it is who discredits Christianity. While the missionary is preaching the private adventurer is going about cheating the native and selling liquor to him, trying to get his lands from him, treating him always with scorn and contempt. That is what stands in the way of the progress of our religion; and that is why Christianity spreads more rapidly while adversity and persecution give it the opportunity to show the distinctively Christian virtues of faith, constancy, humility, and love than when all the power of this earth is on its side. The Christian religion advanced faster against the hostility of Roman emperors like Nero, Decius, and Diocletian than it has advanced with all the strength of civilization behind it, because the temptations to abuse strength are great and have been yielded to. It is not that any power has gone out of the gospel; it is not that Christian nations at home are any less zealous; but it is that other men have gone on undoing the Christian missionary's work all the time he has been preaching.

If that be true, what is our duty as Christian men and women? That is the point I want to bring before you to-night. I only venture to do so because, having seen something of the contact of civilized and uncivilized races, and having watched the difficulties that hamper the missionary, I am anxious that all of you should know what the traveler feels to be the duty of every nation which calls itself Christian in all those countries where it can exert its influence. That duty certainly is not to ask the government to use force. We want no more action like that of the Spaniards who carried the whip and the sword while the friars carried the crucifix. We believe the blessing of God will not rest upon any such method.

We even desire that the governments shall not give any political advantage to the missionaries. The more that missions are severed from political power, the better. But we do desire that you should strengthen the hands of the civilized governments which desire that Christianity shall bring justice and peace with it, and that the native shall be protected.

Now, you can do that. You can strengthen the hands of these governments; you can encourage your own government to lay down and carry out rules for the protection of the native, which I am sure the United States government does desire to carry out honestly and in the right spirit.

We in Britain want to do the same; and we are always appealing to our government and assuring them that they will have and do now have the spirit of the British public behind them in endeavoring to protect the native. And I trust that if there are still parts of the world in which the natives are not being protected the public opinion of America and of England will speak out and say that it demands that the natives everywhere have care and protection.

Our duties do not end with subscribing to the missionary societies. It is our duty to watch wherever over the world the advance of Christianity is being hindered by bad practices of nominally Christian men. Therefore, let us restrain the adventurer and the trader if he wants to wrong the natives by force or fraud, and absolutely prohibit the sale of liquor to the natives. And let us also support the government in endeavoring to have the natives considerately treated. They ought to be regarded as children; they ought to have the measure of indulgence which is given to children; and under the conditions in which their life has been passed, they ought not to be expected to rise at once to the level of civilized man.

The position is now becoming critical. You are often told—and you are told with truth—that this is a critical time for civilized countries. It is a time when there are all sorts of new movements, all sorts of new ideas, when many ancient landmarks have been removed, or at least when some people are trying to remove them; it is a time, particularly in your country, when you are receiving great new masses of population; and in Europe it is a time when all sorts of new political movements are beginning to agitate the old countries. But the critical feature of the time is not so remarkable in civilized countries as it is in the racial situation of the world at large, because, so far as we can see, the new forces visible in Europe and America, which are affecting your political and social life, may continue working for the century or more before there will have been any permanent far-reaching change.

But as regards the relation of the races of mankind in the world, if you will look at the changes which have taken place within the last fifty years, you will see that by the time another fifty years has passed the whole globe will have been overspread by and come under the control of the civilized peoples. If you will except the two great empires of China and Japan, Old World empires which have suddenly come to the front again in our time by entering the circle of the civilization which they had so long excluded, you will find that all the rest of the earth's surface is now under the control of a few white races; and before long all the native organizations will have disappeared. The native tribes will have been broken up, native kingdoms will have vanished, native customs will have gone; everywhere the white man will have established his influence and destroyed the old native ways of life. Things which have lasted from the Stone Age until now are at last coming to a perpetual end, and will be no more. They will vanish from the face of the earth. This is a phenomenon which has never happened before and can never happen again.

Why is the position so critical? Because, when all these savage and semicivilized peoples have lost their ancient organizations, their ancient customs, and their ancient beliefs, they will along with these things lose also their ancient morality, such as it was, which had its sanctions in their ancient customs and beliefs. If you destroy these, their morality falls to the ground and is gone, and they are left with nothing, adrift, rudderless upon a wide and shoreless sea. You may say that their customs were often bad, their morality often immorality. That is true. Much of it ought to disappear. But at the same time some of these old customs had a certain beneficial control over their conduct; they molded their lives, and in many cases they were a foundation for a kind of morality which prescribes behavior tending to virtue, such as good faith (at least with one another), hospitality, and compassion toward the helpless. There are savage peoples who have these virtues, and you will find they rested on beliefs which are now perishing.

That is why the present moment is such a precious and critical one. If these peoples are losing the old customs and beliefs which have ruled them thus far, the time has come to give them something new and better. This is the moment; this is the accepted time; this is the day when God, speaking to us who have overspread the world, us who have taken these people under our control, commands us to feel the moral responsibility that lies upon us and the Christian responsibility that lies upon us to think for and care for these weaker brethren. If they are under our influence, they are in our keeping, and we shall be responsible to God for them. We have disturbed their ancient ways of life for our own interests, because we went among them some few doubtless with a desire to do good, but the great majority from a desire to make money and to exploit the world's resources for the purposes of commerce. We are taking the agricultural wealth from the soil, the forests from the hills, and the minerals out of the rocks for our own benefit.

Are we to do this and yet not be responsible in God's sight if we fail to exert all our efforts to give these people by our own conduct a just view of the Christianity we desire to impart to them? They are, through the will of God, in our keeping. And it is even more our duty than it ever was before to treat them with justice and tenderness while we seek to lead them into the true Light.

GROUP OF CONFERENCE LAY LEADERS.

Begin at top, and read from left to right

R. H. WESTER, DR. S. C. TATUM, J. S. STEEL, L. H. IRELAND, JNO. P. PLETYJOHN, F. B. THOMAS,
DR. J. W. VAUGHAN, F. M. DANIEL, T. J. WATKINS JUDGE A. E. BARNETT.

VIII.

THE SUPREME OBLIGATION OF THE HOUR.

The most mysterious thing in the world almost is the influence the heavenly bodies have upon the tides of the ocean, as twice every day they are lifted heavenward to be swept back far into the heart of the continent. Nobody can explain it all. Nor has anybody been able to explain that mysterious sense of obligation that sways men. How do men come by it? The animals do not have it; they cannot think profoundly; they have but instincts, and think only things. Man thinks thoughts, invisible thoughts. That shows his alliance by nature to God. And the more profoundly he thinks, the more loftily he thinks, the nearer to God he is. Man belongs to the invisible worlds.

And when there comes into a man's life a power that summons him to do the best in him, that stirs motives that he never knew of before, that raises his energies until there has come a new breath into his humanity, that tells of God moving upon man—this same power is going to give man life and to give him life eternal. It is God. He has registered himself in the gift of his Son, who came among men teaching a salvation that gives men a measureless depth, breadth, and height in the love of God, who thus registers his own infinite nature and makes it manifest in man.

(100)

VIII.

THE SUPREME OBLIGATION OF THE HOUR.

BISHOP E. R. HENDRIX, KANSAS CITY, MO.

My Dear Brethren: Will you pray while I speak? This is the most solemn hour in your life or in mine. This is "high tide on the coast of Lincolnshire;" and the tides of the Spirit, like the tides of the ocean, register themselves in terms of the shore.

You never saw high tide in midocean; no man has ever seen it there. We know there is high tide as we study the land. We know these accumulated waters have been lifted up to the bosom of God and sent back to bless the earth; and as they speed onward toward the land the putrid shore is cleansed; as they speed shoreward the belated merchantman that could not get over the bar is lifted, and the ocean hurls itself in mighty tidal rivers far into the heart of the continent. Then we know there has been high tide at sea.

So it is with the tides of the Spirit. God manifests himself in such a time as this; and this is the proof of the invisible, when it is registered in terms of the visible. The proof of the existence of the Holy Spirit is seen when he moves upon human spirits. This was what Pentecost meant. It was God, the Spirit, registering himself in terms of consecrated manhood; when young men saw visions, when old men dreamed dreams, when the Church was born again to a new life, to a holy zeal, to a larger consecration, to a wider mission. That was the way in which the tides of the Spirit registered themselves. The apostles displayed it of old, when men were speaking in many tongues, when there was the glory of holy zeal upon their brow and in their speech, and the Spirit of God was poured out among men.

And so it is in our day; so it is, thank God, to-night. God is registering himself in our methods, in our work, in our organiza-

(101)

tion, thank God, and from this time forward, I trust, in our whole lives.

O what a motto to take from this great gathering, "Missionary Work Is a *Man's* Work!" Don't leave it longer to the children and the women. [Applause.] Let's recognize God's claim upon our manhood. Take home with you that other great motto: "I would rather save a million souls than a million dollars." [Applause.] And go home to take God into partnership with you. Lay up your treasure in heaven; transmute your gold into immortal spirits saved by the blood of Christ. O let there be a great company from the heathen world to welcome you into everlasting habitations! Ours is the conquering Lord. And when I look out on the conquering march of the strong Son of God, I find that he has never touched a life that would listen to him that he did not master. He mastered Matthew, with his passion for gold; and on that day he left his bank and became an apostle of the Lord Jesus Christ. He mastered Peter, with his passion for the sea, the strongest passion almost known to men; and on that day he left his nets and went gladly to follow Jesus, and became a fisher of men.

Jesus weak? "Look at the men he has mastered!" Why, it is he who has made the great nations of the world. The leading nations of the world to-day are Christian nations. The great navies of the world to-day belong to Christian peoples. The wealth of the world to-day is in Christian hands. There is no heathen nation in the world to-day that can go to war without the consent of these Christian nations that hold the purse of the world.

The intellect of the world to-day bows before Jesus. The heart of the world to-day, bleeding to the core, responds to the call of Jesus. I thank God the capital of the world is being held under his scarred hand. O Son of God, lift us all up to thee, and then hurl us out like the tides to bless every shore under heaven! [Applause.]

Jesus not only mastered the great minds of the world; he made them. It was he that summoned them to their best thinking; it was he that deepened their motives of life; it was he that called out their best energies. "My sheep hear my voice." Obedience to him, response to his call, is knowledge of his abundant life. But the measure of a man's responsiveness is the measure of his greatness. Responsiveness is but man's responding to God, recognizing God's claim, seeking to meet the obligations that God puts before us and on us.

The most mysterious thing in the world almost is the influence the heavenly bodies have upon the tides of the ocean, as twice every day they are lifted heavenward to be swept back far into the heart of the continent. Nobody can explain it all. Nor has anybody been able to explain that mysterious sense of obligation that sways men. How do men come by it? The animals do not have it; they cannot think profoundly; they have but instincts, and think only things. Man thinks thoughts, invisible thoughts. That shows his alliance by nature to God. And the more profoundly he thinks, the more loftily he thinks, the nearer to God he is. Man belongs to the invisible worlds.

And when there comes into a man's life a power that summons him to do the best in him, that stirs motives that he never knew of before, that raises his energies until there has come a new breath into his humanity, that tells of God moving upon man— this same power is going to give man life and to give him life eternal. It is God. He has registered himself in the gift of his Son, who came among men teaching a salvation that gives men a measureless depth, breadth, and height in the love of God, who thus registers his own infinite nature and makes it manifest in man.

Now, we well know that a man without the sense of responsibility is not fit to be a witness or a juror in a court of justice. He would be dismissed from the witness stand or jury box if he declared himself without any sense of obligation. It would indicate at once that he had not attained his manhood, that he was arrested in his development. A man who has no sense of obligations to his fellow-man, of the relations to God out of which obligations are born, is unfit for citizenship. The higher the obligations, the more perfect the citizen and the more profoundly devoted to the nation. On the higher relationship and the conscious obligations imposed treaties are formed and contracts are made. All laws of business are based upon this sense of obligation.

Why do you shy at contracts with heathen nations? Because no conscience has been awakened, and no such thing as full responsibility has been developed. There seems to be something incomplete in any man, in any nation, that ignores its contract, that is not bound by this sense of obligation. But in a man conscious of this obligation, bound by his word, bound by his obligation to God, there is something to build on. Thus contracts are made, business relations entered into, great treaties formed that have bound the nations together. My brethren, the most powerful influence at work to-day on the human race is the sense of obligation. It calls man to his best, to his highest, to his noblest; and who has ever thus awakened it but Christ? And it is Christ, then, who has developed this in man, who has sent men from the humbler tasks to the larger tasks, from mere pursuit of wealth to the pursuit of souls, making them desire a million souls rather than a million dollars.

So the most wonderful power of to-day is the sense of obligation; and the nation whose judiciary ranks highest, whose treaties are held most sacred, under whose flag human life is most secure and property the safest, is the nation that meets its obligations squarely as they come up. That is what Christ does with the individual. He takes the man from the lower strata, taking him from a life of lust and degraded conditions to a noble and pure and consecrated manhood. My brethren, with this knowledge or sense of responsibility, I see him calling you and me to greater lives, to larger things, to more commanding efforts, to better investment of our lives for God and man. My brethren, I am heartily tired of thinking of the gospel in terms of a postage stamp, as we are now doing. Once there was a poor man just recovering from fever. The physicians said that he could take only two or three spoonfuls of soup each meal, and said: "You must do everything else in the same proportion." After a while the patient said to his nurse: "I wish you would bring me a postage stamp; I want to read a little." [Laughter.] He thought that his ability to read should be measured also in proportion to his ability to eat and his ability to drink. My brethren, do you know that that is just what we have been doing as a Church? We have been reading a postage stamp. That is about all our strength has permitted us to read. We can read only what is on a postage stamp, "The United States of America, Two Cents," when we plan to give our gospel to the heathen world. That is more than you are giving now for each one of these forty millions of people that are set apart as your legitimate field. You are giving at the rate of one and one-half cents a year for each—not even the price of a postage stamp. My brethren, it becomes our great Church to think in terms of millions, not in terms of a postage stamp. [Applause.]

We gave last year, for all purposes, $10,895,000, with our nearly 1,750,000 members. We are beginning to think now in terms of millions of dollars. In one year (1907) we increased the value of our Church property $5,000,000; we added for preaching and teaching for the home Church $5,000,000; while we are giving, including what you do for Church extension, less than $1,000,000 for the spread of the gospel among the needy at home and abroad. This was given this last year. Thus we spent more than $10,000,-000 on ourselves; and when you come down to what you have given to the great outlying fields, you are thinking in terms of the postage stamp, my brethren, rather than in terms of the living Christ and of the great commission of our Lord. Away with these little ideas of our obligations and of our work! They are unworthy of the Christ that bought us, and of the love that redeemed us. Christ has come to make us care, my brethren; he wants to master us until we recognize his supremacy in our lives; and the measure of Christ's supremacy over us and the measure of our consecration to his service is the measure of our greatness.

Take a man like Peter. What would Peter have amounted to if Christ had not awakened the sense of obligation? What Church would bear his name to-day had it not been for Christ awakening this obligation in him? But in that hour when Christ took command of Peter's ship, he took command of Peter; and when Jesus said, "Cast your net on the other side," Peter used a term that is not used anywhere else in the gospel but by him. He said: "We have toiled all night, and taken nothing; but, Captain, Captain, if thou command, I'll let down my net on the other side." Men said: "There's a new Commander on Peter's boat to-day." And there was. That is a word, "Epistata" or "Commander," that is used nowhere except by Luke and where Peter used it; and later he repeats it. It is in that critical hour of the storm when Peter came to him and said: "Captain, Captain, carest thou for me to perish?" Christ had taken possession of Peter's boat and Peter's nets and Peter's life; and there was growth from that hour. Then there was responsiveness; then there was conviction; then there was greatness of motive.

Brethren, laymen, may I say this word to you to-day? Let the Lord be henceforth the Captain of your life. Take him on board

the ship. Let him enter your countingroom, and every day recognize him as the Lord of your business; and under that influence
you will know the sense of obligation in its blessed inward reach,
as blessed also in its outward effects, until your lives will grow
great under his hand. For Christ immortalizes every man who
puts himself and his possessions completely in his control. How
he immortalized that widow that day when, as I heard an ex-
President of the United States say, "he took the widow's mite
and set it in his crown!" The crown jewel of my Lord was a
widow's gift, because it was her all. And when we put our all in
Christ's hands, we are, like Peter, in partnership with him. He
has absolute control over our lives. That is what made him the
leader in the group of the apostles, the heroic figure that our Lord
honored and trusted in the ministry of the world.

Now, my brethren, I make this appeal to you to-night as the
supreme obligation of the hour. We must think larger thoughts.
Save us, save us, O our Christ, from these little views! Call us
to thine own side and give us convictions; bring the best that is in
us to thy service, and make us thine, thine indeed. Let us be
swayed by purer, deeper, higher motives. Use us, O Lord!

Lord Beaconsfield used to say: "Let me know the passions of
men, and I'll tell you the history of the men. Let me know
the passions of a nation, and I'll tell you the history of the nation."
I put it in better form than that: Let me know the motives of men,
not their passions, and I'll tell you then what the men are and
what they will become. Let me know the commanding motive of
a nation, then you can cast its horoscope. When the Son of God
came into the world, he came absolutely to change the whole nature of man's life by teaching his motives until the foundations of
man became of greater depth than were ever found in man before.
No human soul has ever been swayed with such devotion as Christ
has awakened in men to do their best and be their best. Some one
asked Jenny Lind what was the secret of her successful life, how
it was that she reached such multiplied thousands—sometimes
twenty thousand at a time—with that wonderful voice. This was
her response: "I always sing for the ear of God." O, do you wonder that she reached the ear of man? My brethren, when there
are motives that sway us until the consuming passion of our lives
is to sing for the ear of God, to preach for the ear of God, to live
for the service of God, then we put forth the best that is in us, and

live wholly for God. O, my brethren, what we want is the supreme effort; what we want is the motive that lifts. The measure of any man is his lifting power. The ordinary man lives; the great man lifts. How much are you lifting, and what power is that back of you making you lift? The supreme obligation of the hour is to think greater thoughts, to be swayed by profounder motives, to consecrate all our lives to nobler deeds.

My brethren, the heroic age of our religion is just about to dawn. We had a little test of it in the first century. There has been no intervening century so closely resembling that first century as this twentieth century, when the Church has a fresh commission from our Lord to give the gospel to the whole world. There is something to live for again. It is a *great* task that always raises up men; and a *great* work will not lack volunteers. When Stanley made his last adventurous trip into the heart of Africa, he wanted a few companions. He called for volunteers, and twelve hundred men volunteered to accompany him. There was something about the difficulties and perils of that march through the dark forests that seemed to appeal to them, and twelve hundred men stood ready to go. When that great voyage of discovery was proposed to the South Pole and the ship needed to be manned, permission was given to appeal to the members of the different ships of the British government for volunteers. A small crew only were needed, and nearly the whole channel fleet said: "Send me! Send me!"

It is this that is going to stir the Church to its very core; for we see by our acceptance 40,000,000 of people in the foreign field challenging us, with 8,000,000 people belonging to us in the home field, nearly 2,000,000 more of which are so related to us that they must look to us for the gospel; so that not less than 50,000,000 of people are recognized as *our* immediate field. When the Church begins to say, "Yes, we'll give the $2 a member per year to secure the $3,000,000 for this purpose," then we'll begin to do something that will show that we recognize the sense of obligation and the supreme obligation of this hour. O then what a glorious Church you will be, "fairer than the moon, brighter than the sun, terrible as an army with banners!" O blessed Redeemer, may this time soon be! O, my brethren, what our Lord wants now is consecrated lives. "Present your bodies as a *living* sacrifice." When good Bishop Wilmer lay on his deathbed, one of his daughters asked him if there was any special place where he would like to be buried. He said: "My child, I have never seen the place where I would like to be buried." Thank God, I haven't either. If I had my way, I should like to tarry until my Lord shall come, if I can only have a part in this great conquest for the kingdom of my Lord. O let us not be in a hurry to go!

Men, men, I appeal to you, don't look with discouraged hearts on this oncoming war nor slink from the field of conflict. It is all right to look on it from the glorious heights of heaven; but ask to have a part in it. Get your convictions from the heart of God. That is where this missionary problem is, that is where to find it, and that is where all of us can find it. And then in the heart of God you will find the great motive of love and the secret of the consecrated life for the winning of this world. This is the supreme obligation. It is the same, my brethren, that it has been since my Lord, with those last words on his lips, put that blessed obligation on the Church. They were his last words. O let us not disappoint him! May it be our daily thought and our daily prayer to obey that supreme command!

The other night when our Ambassador-guest from across the seas was here, and in introducing him I made mention of the fact that God gave him to the good Queen in the year of her coronation, I thought of what transpired on the day of her coronation. She was only a slip of a girl, with some seventeen or eighteen years behind her; and her people thought the ordeal would be most trying when she was crowned that day. The great "Hallelujah Chorus" was to be the signal for all to arise. But they said: "Your Majesty may just remain seated while this chorus is rendered." And so, in obedience to this injunction, she remained seated. There were standing the dukes and lords and marquises and counts—the noblest men of the realm, the greatest minds, the purest lives were all represented there. But as the great gathering began to sing, "Hallelujah! hallelujah! hallelujah!" they saw the timid, shrinking Victoria arise from her throne, and with streaming eyes she too sang, "Hallelujah! hallelujah! hallelujah!" And they knew that God had given them a queen after his own heart as well as a queen in name. [Applause.] So that beautiful life, ripening with the years, finally found its expression in a beautiful characteristic incident. Her chaplain one day preached a sermon upon the coming of Christ, and when he should come to claim his own, when the kings of this world should become the acknowledged followers of our Lord. Those near the royal box saw the Queen's lips quivering and her eyes fill with tears. When the service was ended, she signified to her chaplain that she would like to see him alone. He came into her royal presence, and saw that she was profoundly moved; and finally he said, "May I ask why your Majesty is so moved to-day?" and she said, "O that I might be alive when the dear Lord shall come!" And when he asked, "May I ask why your Majesty so wishes to be alive when the Lord shall come?" she replied with choking voice, "That I might lay this crown at his feet." May we too, with the good Queen Victoria, help to crown him Lord of all! [Members: "Amen!"]

O men, lay everything at his blessed feet, and crown him Lord of all! Give your sons and your daughters to this work; those of you that can give your own lives to this service; and let us address ourselves to this great work until he comes and finds us watching in that day! [Applause.]

IX.

THE CHALLENGE OF THE CITY.

Not long before Mr. Bryce was sent to Washington a company of Americans called upon him as they were about to sail for their home. He said to them: "Go back to that splendid world across the sea, but don't you make a failure of it. You can't go on twenty-five years longer as you have been going on in your great cities without putting us liberals in Europe back for five hundred years." That means, my friends, that we cannot go on for twenty-five years more as we have been going on without putting civilization back for five hundred years. In recent times various States have not dared to intrust their larger cities with autonomy. Certain powers of self-government have been taken away from them and lodged in the Legislatures of the States, lest the rich be despoiled through the suffrage of the poor. But, my friends, the day is surely coming when the city will no longer go down on its knees before the State Legislature and beg permission to do this or that. The cities will take into their hands their own affairs; and not only so, but when they have come to full self-consciousness they will take into their hands the affairs of the State and of the nation also. Rare, indeed, is the great city which is not dominated by the saloon; and this is often true of small cities as well. Madison, Wis., is the seat of a great university, a small city characterized by exceptional intelligence, precisely where you would expect to find ideal citizenship, and yet I heard an ex-Mayor of that city say: "The city of Madison is governed by its one hundred saloon keepers. It is they who decide who shall be nominated and who shall be elected in both the Democratic and Republican parties."

(112)

THE CHALLENGE OF THE CITY.

DR. JOSIAH STRONG, NEW YORK CITY.

Mr. Chairman, Ladies and Gentlemen: A religious meeting was once opened with prayer by a colored brother. He prayed appropriately for the speaker, that he might have inspiration, liberty, power, and just as he was about bringing his petition to a close it occurred to him that there was to be a second speaker. So he proceeded to pray for the second speaker, and in so doing quite exhausted his vocabulary. Just as he was again bringing his petition to a close it suddenly occurred to him that there was to be a third speaker. He hesitated a moment, then said: "O Lord, have mercy on the third speaker!"

I think, when it comes to the fourth speaker, Mr. Chairman, the petition ought to be: "O Lord, have mercy on the audience!" [Laughter.]

We are now to consider the problem of the city. I have an acquaintance who said he would rather be his own grandson than his own grandfather, which is a very concrete way of saying that the world's future is to be better than its past, and which I believe with all my heart. But I would rather be myself than my remotest descendant, because, my brethren, we are living in what I believe will prove to be the supreme transitional period of the ages; and the great transitional periods of the past have been the periods of supreme opportunity—the mighty hinges of history, on which have turned the destinies of States, of nations, of civilization. Broadly speaking, the civilizations of the past have been rural and agricultural; the civilizations of the future are to be urban and industrial.

There have been great cities in the past, and of course there are to be great agricultural interests in the future. But there is

8   (113)

taking place a shifting of influence and of power and of population, the consequence of which we have only begun to conceive. The problem of the city is the problem of civilization. The city paganized means civilization paganized. The city Christianized means the world Christianized.

We are loath to recognize the fact that the marvelous and disproportionate growth of the city during the past forty or fifty years is to continue. You are more or less familiar with the facts. At the beginning of the nineteenth century three per cent of our population lived in cities. At the beginning of the twentieth century thirty-three per cent; then one in thirty-three of our small population, now one in three of our large population. Then there were only six cities in the United States of 8,000 inhabitants or more. At the beginning of the twentieth century there were 517 such cities. Men who have not yet learned the causes of this disproportionate growth of the city have generally concluded that it was due to the peculiar conditions of our new civilization. But there has been a similar redistribution of population in Europe, and even in Africa and Asia. Wherever the new civilization has gone, there the city has sprung into marvelous life.

In order to appreciate the problem of the city we must recognize the fact that its disproportionate growth is not temporary. This redistribution of population, this flowing of a mighty tide from country to city, is to continue. It is due to several causes, which are permanent. One is the application of machinery to agriculture. A commission of the government, appointed some years ago to inquire into the effects of such application, reported that four men with machinery could then do the work formerly done by fourteen. What becomes of the othen ten? They are forced out of agriculture. Another cause is the application of machinery to manufactures in the city, which attracts these men from the farms. A third cause is the building of the railway, which makes the transportation of population from country to city very easy; and furthermore, it makes possible the transportation of food so as to feed any number of men gathered at one point. There has been many a famine in the cities in the past when grain was rotting on the ground only a few leagues away.

Cities have always been as large as they could well be, for man is a gregarious animal. It has been difficult to provide water and food and fuel for dense populations. But these limitations are now removed, and it has become possible to feed 10,000,000, 20,000,000, or 30,000,000 people gathered at one point; hence this inherent tendency in human nature toward segregation is free to-day to assert itself. But, as I say, men are very loath to recognize this fact. They have discovered that this redistribution of population complicates both the problems of the country and of the city, and hence raise the cry: "Back to the soil! Back to the soil!"

Good friends, we might as well try to reverse the motion of the earth on its axis and turn it back into the age of homespun. We might as well try to hang up the Tennessee River on a clothesline to dry. We are fighting against the stars in their courses. No man who has any appreciation of economic laws doubts for a moment that this disproportionate growth of the city is destined to continue.

For the last sixty years and more—ever since the United States government took census reports on this particular point—the percentage of men engaged in agriculture has been decreasing, and the percentage of men engaged in the mechanical and fine arts has been increasing. These arts are pursued in the city; hence the disproportionate growth of the city.

There was a time when as many families could win a living from the soil as could find land, and each was practically independent of all the world. But that was in the age of homespun, when the farmer and his wife knew in a rough way ten or a dozen trades between them, so that they could produce the necessaries of life for themselves. They had few, if any, luxuries. That day has forever passed in this country. The farmer of to-day can produce by hand, say, one-tenth as many things as his grandfather could, but he wants about ten times as many. He must, therefore, produce food for the market, that he may exchange his products, or the money received for them, for the products of our factories. That is to say, agriculture has become a part of organized industry, and is therefore as dependent on the market for its prosperity as is pig iron or any other product.

Who would attempt to provide for all the idle people in our cities by setting them to making pig iron? It would simply glut the market. And it is just as easy to glut the market with food products as with iron or cotton.

There is a well-known economic law called Engel's Law, according to which it has been absolutely demonstrated that, as civilization rises, as income increases, the proportion expended for food decreases. Here is a man who has an income of $1,000. He presumably has all the food he needs. His income gradually rises, we will suppose, to $100,000 a year. He doesn't eat one hundred times as much as he did before; he doesn't eat any more. He doesn't spend one hundred times as much on his table; he cannot. He may spend a little more, perhaps twice as much. But he can easily spend one hundred times as much on houses and grounds, on equipage and furniture, on art and books, on statuary and gems. His wife, if her bank account is good enough and her taste is bad enough, can wear $1,000,000 worth of diamonds. [Applause.] There is no limit to expenditure in that direction except purse and taste, and these are not fixed limits. They are artificial limits, and they are rapidly changing. There is a natural limit to the amount of food a man can eat, and therefore a natural limit to the amount of food the world can consume. When the world has been adequately fed, the population which gains its livelihood by producing the world's food can increase only as the world's population increases.

On the other hand, the population which gains its livelihood by the mechanical and fine arts can increase as rapidly as the world's population increases, multiplied by the world's increase of wealth, which is increasing at an enormous rate. Evidently, therefore, those who gain a livelihood by the mechanical and fine arts will necessarily increase more rapidly than those who gain their livelihood by producing the world's food; and as such people live in the cities for the most part, the cities must necessarily continue their disproportionate growth.

The wealth of the city already dominates the land. In the middle of the last century more than one-half of the wealth of the United States was in the rural districts. Before the close of that century more than three-fourths of that wealth was in the cities. While the wealth of the rural districts increased fourfold, that of the cities increased sixteenfold. And the influence of wealth is like the pressure of the atmosphere: it is felt in every direction.

Again, the press, generally speaking, gives direction to public opinion, and public opinion in the United States determines our national policies, home and foreign, and the press is to be found in the city.

Already the city dominates the land by the influence of its wealth and by the influence of the press, and in due time the city will have that power which in a democracy belongs to the majority. At the present rate of the city's growth, in one generation's time there will be 20,000,000 more people in the cities than there will be outside the cities in the United States. Do we apprehend what that signifies?

The distinguished guest of this Conference, an admirer of our institutions and our most friendly critic, the distinguished Ambassador from the Court of St. James to Washington, said, a few years ago: "The one conspicuous failure of American institutions is the government of her great cities." And we know it is true.

It is a comparatively easy matter to govern a small city. It is increasingly difficult to govern that city as it grows larger. And our larger cities, like New York, Philadelphia, Chicago, have become a stench in the nostrils of the civilized world.

Not long before Mr. Bryce was sent to Washington a company of Americans called upon him as they were about to sail for their home. He said to them: "Go back to that splendid world across the sea, but don't you make a failure of it. You can't go on twenty-five years longer as you have been going on in your great cities without putting us liberals in Europe back for five hundred years." That means, my friends, that we cannot go on for twenty-five years more as we have been going on without putting civilization back for five hundred years.

In recent times various States have not dared to intrust their larger cities with autonomy. Certain powers of self-government have been taken away from them and lodged in the Legislatures of the States, lest the rich be despoiled through the suffrage of the poor. But, my friends, the day is surely coming when the city will no longer go down on its knees before the State Legislature and beg permission to do this or that. The cities will take into their hands their own affairs; and not only so, but when they have come to full self-consciousness they will take into their hands the affairs of the State and of the nation also.

Rare, indeed, is the great city which is not dominated by the saloon; and this is often true of small cities as well. Madison, Wis., is the seat of a great university, a small city characterized by exceptional intelligence, precisely where you would expect to find ideal citizenship, and yet I heard an ex-Mayor of that city say: "The city of Madison is governed by its one hundred saloon keepers. It is they who decide who shall be nominated and who shall be elected in both the Democratic and Republican parties."

My friends, our great cities are, for the most part, dominated by the saloon and the gambling hell. What if the city is controlled by its worst elements when the city dominates the nation? We are on probation; we have about one generation in which to make the city capable of self-government; and I know of no way to make the city self-governing except to make the citizen self-governing. I thank God we can begin with the child to-day. Our day of grace has not yet passed; but, my fellow-citizens, we have not one day to lose.

That we may better appreciate the problem, let us dwell for a moment on its complexity. The population of the typical city is thoroughly heterogeneous. A czar may rule successfully over one hundred races, perhaps; but a democracy must be more or less homogeneous in order to be successful. There is no great city in the United States that has not fifty or more nationalities living in it. There are sixty-six different languages spoken in New York to-day—if the number hasn't increased since we investigated the matter, which is likely. I must not be understood to cast reflections on our foreign population. As our Irish friends might say: "Many of our best American citizens were not born in their native land." [Laughter.] Most of us were Americans by accident; they are Americans by choice. And when they become educated in American institutions, their patriotism puts ours to shame.

I remember reading a letter of a young man who came to this country young enough to get the advantage of our public school system. He then took a course in Columbia University, where he graduated. After graduation, he wrote: "Now, at the age of twenty-one, I am a free American citizen, with only one great desire in life, and that is to do something for my fellow-men, so that when I die I may leave the world a bit the better." - Now that young man was a Russian Jew. [Applause.] And I want to say to you that that Russian is a better American, and that Jew a better Christian, than many a descendant of the Pilgrim fathers who is to-day living a selfish life.

Foreign immigration furnishes magnificent raw material out of which to create American citizens; and if the immigrants do not become such, it will be our fault rather than theirs. That is part of our problem and part of our responsibility; but we must recognize that this vast body of foreigners coming to us greatly complicates the problem of the city. The proportion of illiterates among these foreigners is nearly three times as large as among the native whites. The proportion of paupers among them is very much larger. The foreign by birth or parentage in the United States constitute about one-third of the whole population, but furnish nearly as many paupers as the native whites and blacks put together.

Crime is greatly increased by immigration. In a given population there are two and one-half times as many criminals among those who are foreign by birth or parentage as among the native American stock. And I want to say to you, my friends, that in eighteen of our largest cities the population which is foreign, by birth or parentage, is two and one-half times as large as the native white population, which means that if we do not Americanize this foreign population it will inevitably foreignize us, and in so doing foreignize our civilization.

Not only is the population of our great cities heterogeneous, but the great problems of the new civilization huddle together in the city; there is the supreme problem of wealth in its relation to poverty; there Dives and Lazarus face each other; there wealth is piled many stories high, and there is the wretchedness of the slum.

The problems of vice and crime are aggravated in the city. Philadelphia and Pittsburg are not exceptionally bad cities, and yet to a given population in the State of Pennsylvania there are seven and one-half times as much crime in Philadelphia and nearly nine times as much crime in Pittsburg as in the same population in the rural districts.

We, then, establish certain tendencies. One is the tendency of the city to grow more rapidly than the whole population. Another is the tendency of the city to come more and more under the control of the worst elements of its population as it grows larger. Another is the tendency of pauperism and vice and crime to increase in the city, and this is more especially true of the slum.

Perhaps you will remember that a few months ago there was a town blown up by the explosion of a powder factory. Neither saltpeter nor sulphur nor charcoal, taken separately, is explosive, but united they make gunpowder. Neither ignorance nor crime is revolutionary so long as they are entirely comfortable; nor is poverty revolutionary so long as it is controlled by intelligence and conscience. *But poverty, ignorance, and crime combined make social dynamite,* of which the city slum is the magazine, awaiting only a casual spark to burst into terrific destruction.

We have seen what are the principal tendencies in the city which cause alarm. I need not argue to this audience that the great conservative institutions of society on which we must rely to meet these dangerous tendencies are the Church and the home. Are they growing proportionately fast in the city? Are they increasing as the population of the city is increasing?

As to Churches, we find from one-fourth to one-tenth as many Protestant Churches in our cities to a given population as in the whole country. And the proportion is decreasing. There are only about half as many Churches to the population now as there were fifty years ago in the cities. In other words, here is a tendency on the part of the Church to grow weaker as the city and its dangerous elements grow stronger.

How is it with the home? The census shows that on the farms, out in the country, about two-thirds of all the farmers own their homes. As we come to the cities of 100,000 inhabitants, that proportion rapidly decreases. When you reach cities the size of Boston, 18 per cent own their homes. As the cities become larger, real estate becomes more valuable and fewer men can own homes. When you come to Manhattan, less than 6 per cent own their own homes.

Property makes a man conservative; but if a man has nothing to lose by an uprising or revoluton, he is much more apt to be revolutionary. The larger the city, the more likely it is to be dominated by the worst elements of society, the smaller is the strength of the Church and the proportion of homes, and hence the city becomes the hotbed of anarchism and of socialism.

My friends, the supreme problems of civilization are in the city; and it is in the city that they must be solved. I have not time to take up to-day what I believe to be the method of solution. I believe that problem has been solved; I believe that nothing remains to-day but to convince Christian men and women of the effectiveness of the methods which have been tested now for twenty years and to induce them to apply this solution to the problem of the city.

I desire to use the remainder of my time to show you that the problem of the city is not simply a profound national problem, but is the supreme world problem.

We have heard much, but not too much, of the awakening of China. Hundreds of miles of railway have been built, and thousands of miles are projected; steamboats ply on the rivers; thousands of miles of telegraph wires have been strung; factories have gone up, which are being kept busy day and night. The industrial revolution is well under way in China.

The new civilization of the Western world was created by the industrial revolution; and wherever human muscles toil, there the industrial revolution is bound to go, because machinery is bound to go. It is destined to invade every country in the world. And we can anticipate what the effects of that revolution will be in Japan and China and India, because we know what its effects have been in every country in Europe and in every State in the Union.

Let us glance briefly at a few of the results of the industrial revolution. One is this disproportionate growth of the city, which is caused by the redistribution of population, the emptying of villages into cities. That movement was most marked in this country from 1880 to 1890, and during that period more than

10,000 townships in the United States lost population, notwithstanding the general growth. In the State of Illinois 792 townships lost population, while Chicago sprang from 500,000 to more than 1,000,000. That was not exceptional. In every State of the Union and in every Territory of the United States that same movement from country to city took place. In every State and Territory there was an increase of population, save only Nevada; but, notwithstanding that increase of population, there were more than 10,000 villages that lost population—villages being emptied into the cities. Six hundred and forty-one townships in New York lost population, and nearly a thousand in Pennsylvania. The same process is going on here in the South. You will find, if you will look up the facts, that hundreds of townships have lost population, while the cities have grown 40, 50, 80, 500, or 1,000 per cent in ten or twenty years.

There is one other result of the industrial revolution to which I wish to call your attention, and that is the geographical scattering of the family. Boys and girls in the agricultural age, the age of homespun, stayed at home; the home was the factory. The industries have now been carried from the home to the city, and the boys and girls have followed. When farmers' sons are agriculturists, they are anchored to the soil; when they become mechanics, they are scattered over all the land by the vicissitudes of the labor market.

Now, mark you, my friends, in Asia there live one-half of the human family, and in China and India alone 700,000,000. It is significant that most of these millions live in villages. The Blue Book of India tells us that there are upward of 500,000 villages in India. And Arthur Smith, one of the best authorities on China, tells us that there are not less than 500,000 villages in China.

Every civilization has passed through the village stage. Asiatic civilization was arrested at that stage. There are very few great cities in China, notwithstanding the great population—not so many millionaire cities as there are here in the United States. Another characteristic of Asiatic peoples is the patriarchal family, on which are based the religions of Japan, China, and India.

The industrial revolution has been in progress for some years in Japan, and the results which have attended it in Europe and America have already appeared there, and precisely the same results are beginning to appear in China. What does this mean? It means that many thousands of villages in Asia are to be emptied into the cities yet to be built in China and India; and it means the geographical scattering, and therefore the destruction, of the patriarchal family.

The social systems of Asia are based on the village as the religious systems of Asia are based on the patriarchal family. The industrial revolution is destined to turn and overturn and overturn until these foundations of Asiatic institutions are ground to powder. That is the meaning of the industrial revolution; that is the meaning of "something doing" throughout Asia and throughout the world, of which we heard last evening.

The supreme marvel of the nineteenth century was the awakening of Japan. The supreme wonder of the twentieth century, I believe, will be the awakening of China and India.

Think of China—gray with years when Rome was founded, more ancient than ancient Abraham—traveling by the lightning express, riding on electric cars, sending telegrams, talking over the telephone, reading Confucius by the incandescent electric lamp! What incongruities! What juxtaposition of East and West! What confusion of the centuries! Can we ever again be surprised? Yes, there is one more wonder. That remarkable woman, the Dowager Empress, was the representative of conservative China, and, as such, imprisoned the young emperor, who is the representative of young and progressive China; and let me say that in so doing she illustrated David Harum's interpretation of the golden rule: she did what the young emperor was intending to do to her, and she did it "fust." This same representative of conservatism hitherto sent a commission to our country and to Europe to study constitutional government, with the promise that she would give constitutional government to the 400,000,000 of China.

Good friends, China is already awake! Japan is already awake! India, with her 300,000,000, is already awake! In God's name, isn't it time for America to be awake? [Applause.]

There are to be thousands of cities built in Asia during the

twentieth century; and it is the first time in the history of the
world that it has been possible to develop a new civilization in
the light of science. The city is to dominate not only this nation, but China, India, all Asia, and all the world.

The government of the city is to be the political problem of
all lands; the evangelization of the city is to be the religious
problem of all lands; so that the city is the problem of home
missions and foreign missions alike. The tremendous social
problems of the city are attracting the attention of the wisest
in America and Europe; and Asia is soon coming face to face
with them.

As the result of twenty years' study, I wish to say that I believe, to the very center of my being, that these problems can be
solved, and solved only by the application of the principles of
Christ's teaching. [Applause.]

Look ye, then, ye men of this Missionary Movement, see what
the Missionary Movement means! It has not only its spiritual
aspects, but also its social aspects, its industrial aspects, its physical aspects of every sort; and let us remember that moral and
spiritual progress depend not only on spiritual causes, but also on
physical conditions.

The problem of missions is as broad as the problem of civilization; the problem of missions is as broad as the world; and its
very essence is the problem of the city.

I can take only a very few minutes more, and let me devote
that time to this point: God has laid a responsibility upon this
generation such as he never laid upon any other, because he has
given to us such an opportunity as he never gave to any other.
He has placed in the hands of this generation such resources to
meet that problem as were never placed in the hands of any
other, for our God is a reasonable God.

One of the most striking characteristics of this new civilization is the enormous increase of wealth. One speaker last evening referred to the fact that our wealth is more than $100,000,-
000,000. In 1850 the wealth of the United States was $7,000,-
000,000; in 1904 the wealth of the United States was $107,000,-
000,000. That has been the increase within the memory, within
the business career, of some of you men. It is as if the people
of the United States had been given the touch of Midas, which

transmutes everything into gold. There is nothing like it in the history of other nations, because other nations are not using machinery as we are, and no other nation has carried the division of labor as far as we.

Not only is wealth increasing at an enormous rate, but the rate of increase is increasing. The average increase of our savings over and above all expenditure and all waste durng the ten years from 1890 to 1900 was $6,400,000 for every day in the year. The average increase of wealth over and above all expenditure during the first four years of this century, the latest for which the treasury has issued any statistics, was $13,000,000 a day— more than twice as great as it was during the last decade of the last century.

Let us suppose that the rate of increase from 1900 to 1904 does not continue, but that it falls back one-half, as a result of the existing conditions. What will the wealth of the United States be in that fateful year of 1940, when the city will domi- nate the nation? According to the supposition, our wealth in 1940 will be equal to all the wealth of the United States in 1900, plus all the wealth of France in 1900, plus all the wealth of the empire of Germany, plus all the wealth of Russia, plus all the wealth of Great Britain, plus all the wealth of New Zealand, plus all the wealth of Australia, plus all the wealth of India, plus all the wealth of all the colonies of Great Britain throughout the world. My friends, such wealth is not only stupendous, it is absolutely appalling! Such wealth will put a strain on the moral character of this nation such as no nation on earth has ever endured. Spain was at the acme of her power when the gold and silver of the New World were poured into her lap. She could not endure the strain, and she fell to the lowest place among the nations. Brother men, nothing will save this nation from the curse of wealth but the consecration of wealth. [Ap- plause.]

Luxury has always been degrading, and wealth has always been dangerous. Every nation, every age has needed the stim- ulus of poverty to develop its resources. We must struggle if we would be strong. What are our young men to do without this stimulus, unless indeed they learn to consecrate their wealth and, practicing daily self-denial, regard themselves be-

fore God as his stewards? We need for Asia's sake to consecrate our wealth; we need for our own sake to consecrate our
wealth.

Years ago our fathers looked out on this broad continent and
gained inspiration for consecration from the fact that they were
engaged in the statesmanlike work of creating a nation. Men
of to-day, we gain inspiration for this needed consecration from
the fact that we are engaged in the Godlike work of shaping a
world! [Applause.] No such opportunity ever came to any
other generation, and therefore no such responsibility was ever
laid upon any other generation.

And, let me say, my friends, the supreme opportunity—and
therefore the supreme responsibility—is laid upon America. I
haven't time to show you—but I could show you—that, in God's
providence, America is a great political, social, religious, and
economic laboratory, where are being worked out the supreme
problems of the new civilization for all the world.

It is true the industrial revolution is older in England than in
the United States; but we have carried the division of labor farther than England, and therefore we have gained more experience. And England, France, and Germany are sending their
commissions to the United States to learn from us.

We call this continent the "New World;" we call Asia the
"Old World." But, good friends, America has become the old
world in experience with these new problems; and Asia is to-day
the new world, just entering upon this new era. And it is for
us, as for no other nation, to give her the illumination of the
gospel applied to the solution of these problems in our own national life. How can our citizens go to China and tell them that
Christianity will solve their problems, unless we apply those principles to our own problems? [Applause.]

There can be no national secrets to-day. Japan and China
know of the degradation of our cities; they know of our com-
mercialism; they know of our greed and graft. If we do not
conquer ourselves with the gospel, we can never carry a conquering gospel into all the world.

Brethren, if I have given to you the impression that there is
any occasion for panic or discouragement, I have belied myself.
I believe the world is growing better every day. [Applause.]

I do not believe that the Creator of this world will ever cease to be its Governor. I do not believe that He who gave his Son for the redemption of the world will ever forget to love it. [Applause.] I have confidence in God. I have confidence in God's word; and it seems to me that we have an expressed promise in this Word touching the redemption of the city. [Applause.] At the beginning of this divine-human Book our first glimpse of man is in a garden; it is a paradise of perfect beauty, of perfect simplicity, of perfect innocence. It is a paradise of virtue unfallen, because of virtue untried. We turn to the close of this Book and we catch another glimpse of man in a perfected estate. We see in that vision not the beauty of innocence, but the beauty of holiness. We see not the uncertain, the unstable peace of virtue untried, but the established peace of virtue victorious.

In that first picture we see individualistic man; in that second picture we see social man. In the first we see unfallen man, sustaining right relations to his Creator; in the second we see redeemed man sustaining right relations to his God *and* to his fellows. [Applause.]

The story of this marvelous human drama begins in the country; it is consummated in the city. The crown and consummation of our civilization, the full coming of the kingdom of God on earth, is typified not by a garden but by a city—a Holy City, into which shall enter nothing unclean, nothing that maketh a lie.

Paradise lost was a garden; Paradise regained, my brethren, will be a city. And it is your privilege and mine to be co-laborers with God unto the coming of his kingdom in the city and in the whole earth. [Great applause.]

X.

THE CALL TO GO FORWARD.

9

Your civilization is stagnating and putrefying with material prosperity. The moral miasmas which arise from your accumulated and unused wealth threaten the well-being of all classes. The pestilence of greed pervades all places, sometimes penetrating to the pulpit even. It corrupts your politics and defiles your social life; it divides families with feuds and sets communities at variance with each other; it moves capital to oppress labor and labor to defraud capital. What at last is your question of capital and labor but a contest of greed? Were the wages of labor or the returns of capital ever so great among any people? What then are they quarreling about? What is the meaning of their strife over money except it be that each is mad because both cannot get all of it? I confess that I cannot get interested on behalf of either contestant. It is a quarrelsome greed that animates both parties. If it were a contest of eagles, vying with each other as to which could fly nearest the sun and hide himself deepest in the rays of that radiant orb, I could watch the contest with eager interest. But over a contest of vultures, as to which shall get the largest share of the carrion which they have jointly discovered, my enthusiasm refuses to rise. We have struggled for wealth, and when we have won it, we have held on to it with such adoring tenacity that covetousness has tainted all our ideals. We make money not only the measure of material values, but the standard of human life itself. We are beginning to feel that to be without money is to be without character, and that we can do without character if we can only have money. Our competitions are ignoble rivalries, and our social system is rapidly becoming a race course for the display of vulgarities. We are the bondslaves of the bond market and most truly the "serfs of the soil."

(130)

X.

THE CALL TO GO FORWARD.

BISHOP W. A. CANDLER, ATLANTA, GA.

You may conceive of three things we could do with reference to this matter of foreign mission work: We could go backward, we could stand still, or we could advance. Practically, however, there are but two, for standing still and going backward are about the same thing.

We must advance, and for reasons that will occur to you without much suggestion from me. Consider what would be the effect upon ourselves at this period of the world's history, confronted by all the spiritual wants and national needs that have been set before us this evening, if we either stood still or went backward.

What would be the effect upon ourselves? We will begin with the very least effect: It would not be good even for our earthly interests, not to speak of our higher concerns; it would not profit us financially; for as the nations are Christianized and begin dealing with the other nations in the earth they become more and more prosperous themselves, and therefore more and more profitable to their associate nations. We might say of them to-day that as long as they are unchristianized they are unprofitable members of the family of nations. It may interest certain members of this convention to be informed that if by education, evangelization, civilization, or what not you could get all the Chinese gentlemen to put on one more shirt a year it would raise the price of cotton not less than a cent a pound. [Laughter.] But that is a very low consideration. Missions pay, but they cannot be sustained by mercenary motives.

A higher consideration is what effect the abandonment of the work of foreign missions or retrogression in the work would have upon our own confidence in our own Christianity. Any religion

(131)

that is willing to divide the world with any other faith is, by the very fact of its willingness to make such a division of the earth, proved to be insincere as to its own conviction of its truthfulness.

When the king of Israel had brought before him two women contending for the same child, each pretending to be its mother, he settled the issue shrewdly when he proposed to divide the child between them—to cut it in two. The spurious mother agreed, being willing to destroy the child in order to win a point; but the genuine mother resisted the proposition most strenuously, for the child was more to her than victory over an opponent. In like manner, if the Christians of the world are willing to divide the race, giving some nations to paganism and some to Christianity, they thereby proclaim both the spuriousness of their faith and their lack of love for men. But Christ will have no partition of the planet. He claims all souls. Wherefore our religion is necessarily, in a sense, nobly intolerant. It is intolerant of all pagan faiths as truth is intolerant of falsehood or as love is intolerant of lust. Knowing that it has come from God, it refuses all compromise, and insists that there is not room enough in the world for both it and any other competing faith. [Applause.] There is not standing room on the planet for the religion of Jesus Christ and any opposing force whatsoever. [Applause.]

There are some in our day who affect great generosity toward pagan religions. They call their flabby folly "mental hospitality," I believe, and talk of God's having come to certain nations through Buddhism, to others through Mohammedanism, and to others through Brahmanism. This is the veriest nonsense. God has not left himself without witness in any nation; by the voice of both Providence and the Spirit he has called all men everywhere to repentance. But all these pagan faiths and idolatrous superstitions have made men deaf to the voice of God and heedless to the divine commands. God has no more approached men through them than the broken-hearted, grief-stricken father of the parable approached his prodigal son through the hardened citizen of the far country to whom his wayward child had joined himself. These enslaving superstitions send God's children to the hardships of the most degrading courses of life, and neither God nor any good man can look upon them with any degree of toleration. It is not possible to arrange between them and Christianity any sort of *modus vivendi.* It is war to the death between Christianity and every high thing that exalteth itself against God and his Christ.

I remember that about the years 1886-1888 this sort of pseudo-liberality was quite prevalent in some quarters of our country. Certain missionaries of the American Board were giving that Board considerable trouble by sundry speculations through which they assumed to be the special champions of God's love toward heathen men and his liberality toward heathen faiths. Some of those men were in Japan, where they were a specially noisy nuisance to all sincere servants of Christ. But where are they now? What has become of them? They are no longer in Japan. They have failed as missionaries and returned home or gone to ruin. When I was in Japan, two years ago, I heard nothing of them. But I found a venerable man still there with whom those vanished apostles of liberalism were not very sympathetic in their day; Dr. Davis was there, and he is there to-night. I saw him when I was in Japan. He was worn with years and wasted with toil, but full of hope and zeal, as loving to the Japanese as he is loyal to Christ. I can never forget his great sermon to a large congregation composed of missionaries of all the evangelical Churches, in the course of which he cried out with thrilling eloquence: "Doubt your doubts and believe your beliefs, and give Christ to Japan." Dear, brave, orthodox Dr. Davis is there yet; but the apostles of compromise have left the field. Perhaps they are still philosophizing in and around Boston.

Men who run after sterile speculations, men who make fine-spun and foolish distinctions between the divinity and the deity of our Lord Jesus Christ, who appear anxious to show themselves more broad-minded than divine wisdom and more tender than God's love, and who think that Christ may be useful, although not indispensable, to the heathen world, will not remain on the foreign field even if they go there. They may go out impelled by curiosity to see strange things or by a spirit of youthful adventure; but they will never endure for long the hardships of missionary life. They hurry home whenever the pinch of battle comes on. [Laughter.] For one, I do not blame them. He is a foolish man indeed who will separate himself from kindred and friends and native land to carry a colorless, bleached gospel to a pagan people. Since such a man believes that the heathen world can get along without Christ, he demonstrates that it can get on very well without himself. In fact, the liberalist is not needed in any land. He is not needed at home or abroad, on either side of the world, in the Far East or in the Near West.

Suppose we desired to redeem a dark and degraded ward of one of our great cities and engaged one of these apostles of liberalism, with his hair-splitting speculations, for what we call slum work. Imagine him mounting a "goods-box platform," surrounded by a company of forlorn and forsaken men, adjusting his eyeglasses, and, beginning in the lisping accents of a dainty and artificial elocution, to say: "Gentlemen, you know the most learned men of our remarkable age have discovered there were at least two Isaiahs. And you know the book of Job is only an ancient Oriental drama, and Ruth is a Hebrew idyl." What would his audience do? Well, some one of the crowd would probably say: "O, come along, boys, there is no use listening to that stuff. Let's go and get a drink." [Laughter.] Preachers and performances of that type are worse than useless in the slums of the home field, as they are purposeless and paralytic in the presence of the heathen.

Now, I have a practical proposition to submit. In the heathen world we find the greatest moral destitution, and the type of Christianity which I have been describing is absolutely palsied and ineffective there. The slums of our great cities are the points of direct need and most dangerous strain in the home field, and this emasculated gospel is worthless for redeeming the slums. It can do nothing, therefore, on either side of the world at the points where men most need help. Can that be a gospel at all which fails where a gospel is most sorely needed? Now, here is a scientific test for the gospel of liberalism. [Laughter.] That test is what you might call the "inductive process;" and when tried by induction, liberalism is found wanting. [Applause.]

But if you do not speedily carry the true gospel of Christ to all the world, you will inevitably persuade yourselves to accept the lazy liberalism which is content to believe that any religion is a message to men from God. You cannot long hold with strength the truth of Christianity unless you hold it as the one faith which all the nations must have, and undertake to do all that in you lies to give it to them. [From the audience, "Amen! Amen!"]

The fact is, it is inhuman for a man to have any truth which others need and selfishly withhold it from them. For instance, a few years ago a man discovered the anti-toxin which overcomes diphtheria; but he reserved to himself a royalty on its use, and he has been censured by all good men everywhere. His selfishness has killed the glory of his discovery. The world uses his remedy, but despises his spirit. His remedy has gone round the world without a missionary society to send it. Men of nobler mind than the discoverer have given it to mankind. True men will not hold any truth in selfishness.

If I knew all the arithmetic that is known—but I do not [Laughter]—if I were the only man in the world who knew arithmetic, I would be bound to give the knowledge of it to all the rest as far as my ability would go. If I were the only man in the earth who was acquainted with the theory and application of electricity, I would be bound to impart the secret to all others. How much more are we bound to give to all men the knowledge of Him who is the "Light of the World," the "Sun of Righteousness, with healing in His wings!"

But having considered somewhat the effect upon ourselves of going backward or standing still in the work, let us now consider what would be the effect of such retrogression or stationariness on the unchristianized nations. Even if their faiths could be justly regarded as comrades of Christianity and partial revelations from God, they cannot maintain their old systems much longer. Pagan faiths are doomed; and if Christianity fails to occupy pagan lands, the nations who dwell in them must soon become faithless people, "without hope and without God in the world." You have heard what our friend, Mr. Ellis, has told us of the perishing cults of the Orient. Mohammedanism is also paralyzed and prostrated; it is strong to persecute, but feeble to redeem. Pull away its political supports, and it will fall prostrate upon its face, never to rise again. Its chief supporter is aptly called the "Sick Man of the East."

And all forms of religion, except evangelical Christianity, are "sicklied over," not with the "pale cast of thought," but with the palor of perishing superstitions. Stricken with blindness in the blazing light of modern times, they walk like blind men are led, held up by the hands of political guardians and conducted by the manipulations of priestly guides.

Take Romanism, for example. It is a degenerate form of Christianity, although in many respects more pagan than Christian. It is doomed, although its final judgment may be postponed for a season and its fall may be delayed. A few days ago one of its archbishops in our own country was reported in the press dispatches as predicting and lamenting the early disestablishment of the Roman Church in Italy. In Austria there is a great movement away from Romanism. In old Spain, the most loyal of the papal nations, a religious reformation is setting up. In Portugal, belated and benighted though it be, the light of a new religious era is appearing like the dawn. All the world knows of the revolution going on in France. Latin America, from Mexico to Terra del Fuego, is penetrated through and through with evangelical influences; while Romanism is semi-moribund, its most marked evidences of vitality being mostly such as come from the stimulation applied by a progressive Protestantism. In Cuba, for example, our missionaries have driven the Romish priests to preaching as they had never done before Protestantism entered the island. When I first visited Cuba, in the winter of 1898-99, I found few seats in the churches. There was provision made for kneeling before images and prostrating the body before high altars, but little or no provision for sitting down and hearing a sermon. It is not so now. In all the churches there are seats—somewhat variegated, like Jacob's cattle, but seats nevertheless. In one cathedral I counted, when attending services, twelve different kinds of chairs and benches. The Catholic fathers had evidently gathered sitting devices in a hurry; and in that place before a small congregation, sitting on the assorted seats, a priest was doing his best to preach a sermon. He was evidently not used to such work, and most of his talk was an incoherent rant against "los Protestantes;" but he was doing, I doubt not, the best he could. At any rate, I was willing to find him guilty of an assault with intent to preach. [Laughter.] Henceforth Romanism must preach in Cuba or go out of business; and it may be that it will have to go out of business by trying to preach.

The Protestantized Romanism you see in our country is bad enough, but it is infinitely better than that which one meets in what are called "Roman Catholic countries." The case of Romanism here is a good deal like that of Cleopatra's Needle. As long as it stood in Egypt it remained almost unchanged for centuries; but when it was brought into the atmosphere of England and set up on the banks of the Thames, it began to crumble. If it had not been treated speedily with a coating of paraffin, it would have disintegrated utterly. So Romanism in the United States has had laid on its outer surface a paste of Protestantism to keep it from going to pieces. In the lands where it has had its own way, and stood up in its character, naked and undisguised, the people are turning away from it.

So also the superstitions of Asia are discredited and doomed. They continue to exist, and millions of people still adhere to them formally. Social usages, domestic customs, political forms, and commercial interests combine to give them a semblance of strength; but they are decayed at the center, and their fall at last is as inevitable as the operation of the law of gravitation. Buddhism in Japan, for instance, is doomed. It is said that under its shelter are housed eight million gods in Japan, and I suppose the figure is not too large. But there are more gods in Japan than there are Japanese men and women who sincerely worship them. Perhaps some of you have seen what a Georgia farmer calls a "new ground." It is a tract of ground only partially cleared of the trees. Perhaps half of the larger trees are "cut around" in order to kill them, although they are left standing. Those trees do not fall down the first year after they are girdled with the gashes of the death-dealing ax; some of them may put forth for one season a few leaves. But it is not safe to walk under them when the March winds of the second year are blowing over the "new ground." Dead limbs and decaying trunks are then falling all about. In a few years they are all gone, and in a decade even the stumps have disappeared and the old roots in the ground have rotted. Well, that is the condition of Buddhism in Japan to-day. It is "cut around" and its leaves are withering. When I was in the old capital of Japan, Kioto, the property of the greatest Buddhist temple there, perhaps the greatest in the world, had been levied on for debt, and the official corresponding to the sheriff of our country had advertised it for sale. The sale began on the day we left the city. The authorities of the temple had borrowed money to keep it up, and they had pledged city property for the payment of the debt. Their revenues had so fallen off in the meantime that the bankers to whom they were indebted had obtained judgment against them in the courts, and were proceeding to collect the debt by sheriff's sale. Yet that is one of the newest and richest temples of Buddhism in the world. When it was erected, not so very long ago, its huge columns were lifted into their positions by cables made from the hair of the women of Japan. I saw the cables in the temple. When a woman will part with her hair, native or artificial, to build a temple, she is certainly devoted to the religion for which it stands. [Laughter.] A temple to which the women of Japan, a generation ago, gave the hair off their heads cannot now command money enough to keep it out of the hands of the sheriff. Buddhism and Shintoism both are losing their grip on the Japanese people. It is hard for them to retain the respect of people whose increasing enlightenment daily discredits all superstition. The Japanese people are learning on all lines of knowledge. Just think of their progress in medical science alone! When the armies of Japan went into Manchuria to meet the forces of Russia, scientists were sent before them who analyzed all the water on the way, and placarded every pool and well and stream, warning the troops against all the water which was not fit to drink. By consequence, sickness in their camps was marvelously diminished. The superstitions of Buddhism cannot long survive alongside scientific methods of that sort. Whether Japan becomes Christian or not, it cannot remain Buddhist. It may become atheistic and agnostic; that is a real peril. Indeed, such has come to pass in a measure already. Western learning has been acquired by the Japanese faster than Christianity has been given to them, and by consequence many of them are to-day faithless and despairing. When I was there, in 1906, there was prevalent in the land, especially among the student class, an epidemic of suicide. Science had quenched the light of their old faiths without giving them the light of Christianity, and they had come to feel in such a faithless condition that life was not worth living. As my Brother Ellis has told you, sending your Western learning to Japan will not meet the needs of that brilliant but restless nation. The source of Japan's distress and danger to-day is the possession of learning without the knowledge of God.

And what shall we say of the situation in China? All over that awakening land there is a universal hunger for the "Western learning." Many things have conspired to bring on this yearning for the "new learning." China's war with Japan contributed to this result, as did also the Russo-Japanese war. Movements of international commerce and communication have had much to do with it. Christian missionaries have done most of all to create this condition. By all these influences the Chinese have been awakened to the fact that Confucianism and the system of learning arising from it cannot meet China's wants any longer. Hence the old system of education has been discarded. The examinations of the civil service now include the subjects of the "new learning," and thousands of students who have been studying for years the old Confucian classics with a view to promotion have been called upon to throw all their work away and start over again. And they have done so without the slightest protest or disturbance. No fact could be more convincing that China is awakening and has determined to acquire the arts and sciences of the Western nations. Hence the Chinese are calling for Christianity, not directly, to be sure, but indirectly by their demand for the "new learning;" for, as Dr. Anderson told you this morning, their thoughtful men know full well that they cannot acquire the learning of Christendom without absorbing the religion of Christendom. Herein is a constraining call to go forward. Can we stand still or go backward with such an immeasurable opportunity before us? Can we with bread enough in our Father's house to spare refuse to feed this hungry nation, the most populous in the world, but starving for want of spiritual food?

What of Korea? There is the most pathetic case of all. The Koreans are very poor, and they are industrially hopeless. Some centuries back their industries were prostrated and their artisans were carried into captivity by Hideyoshi, who is called the "Napoleon of Japan," and who was as cruel a monster as the Napoleon of France. In fact, Napoleons anywhere are horrible creatures. Well, this "Napoleon of Japan" carried away Korea's industrial arts by taking captive their artists and artisans, and he thus prostrated their industrial system. Since his day corruption among Korean officials has made the prostration still more profound. Korea is, therefore, inexpressibly poor and industrially hopeless. The very motives for industries have been taken away by oppression and corruption.

The Korean nation is also religionless. Centuries ago Buddhism was the religion of Korea; but the Buddhist priests, who are the Romanists of the Orient, intermeddled so mischievously with politics that their religion was outlawed. The old dynasty with which they had been in league was dethroned, the capital was moved from Songdo to Seoul, and it was decreed that no Buddhist priest should put foot in Seoul forever. No priest has been there in all these later centuries until since the Japanese occupation. Buddhism, being thus discredited at court, fell into decay everywhere else in the land, and so Korea was left without any religion. But renouncing all religion cannot destroy the religious principle in the human breast, and so the religionless Koreans turned to a grotesque spiritism and devil worship. The spirit world broods over them, and drops fear upon all their lives and pours grief into all their souls. I think the most bitter cry my ears ever heard was one which broke upon the night air near our mission compound one night in 1906 when I was there. I did not, of course, know the meaning of the words, but the cry was burdened with grief. I asked the missionary what it meant, and he replied: "Some one is dying down there." I then learned that when one is dying among the Koreans a member of the family will get upon the roof of the little mud house and cry after the spirit: "O, dear one, do not depart. Come back! Come back!" Here, then, was a sorrow-stricken man, calling in vain after the loved but departing spirit, and knowing nothing of Him who has brought life and immortality to light in the gospel.

Korea is politically hopeless also. The Koreans desire political independence first of all. If they cannot have that, they would prefer next the suzerainty of China because it is nominal and light. If that is denied them, they would like to have a protectorate by some Western power, Russia or the United States, because they fancy such a protectorate would be too far off to oppress them, and would bring them material gains. The last thing in the world they want is subjection to Japan, and that is what they have. They know what "benevolent assimilation" by the Japanese means; and they may well abhor it, however it may be disguised by fair words.

What does this poor, oppressed, and religionless people need? What do they ask at your hands? They do not need your philosophy; they have had the Chinese classics for centuries, and they have had thinkers among themselves since the days of King David's reign over United Israel. If that is all you have to give them, you need not go forward to help them.

The supreme, imperative need of Japan, China, and Korea— the crying want of all the nations of the Far East—is Christianity. These nations are not savages; they are heathen, but they are no more barbarians than were the men of ancient Greece and Rome. Cicero, the orator, was a heathen, but he was not a savage; he was a thinker and a man of letters. Herodotus, the historian, was a pagan, but not a barbarian. He was a cultivated man, who recorded for history nearly as many untrue things as Lord Macaulay. [Laughter.] Virgil was a heathen, as also was Homer before him; but even the sublime Milton did not disdain to make their epics the models of his own heroic verse.

So also these Orientals of whom I have been speaking are not savage, although they are pagans. And they are not bad warriors. Even the Chinese, who have been accounted a nation of cowards, can fight. They are not afraid to die. I must dissent with deference and hesitation from one thing said by Dr. Anderson this morning. He said the Chinese were not a warlike people. My reading has given me the impression that before the setting up of the Tartar dynasty they were very warlike, and in our day we may see what the scientists call a "reversion of type." It is said they ran away from the battle when they met the Japanese army in Korea. I do not blame them; and that affair does not prove them cowards. As I have been told, Li Hung Chang brought on that war, and got large gains out of it. In preparing for it Li Hung Chang, individual, traded with Li Hung Chang, official, selling him, among other things, some badly assorted arms and ammunition. The caliber of the guns and the size of the fixed ammunition were not the same; and when the time came to use them, they couldn't get the ammunition into the guns. You see, that wasn't good ammunition to fight with. Well, they ran. What would you have done? [Laughter.]

Let me tell you: You allow these people time to wake up—and they are going to wake up—then indeed you will have something to consider. China awake without Christ will be a "yellow peril" in truth. Certain gentlemen in Congress, who have been eating I don't know what, are having periodic nightmares about Japan coming over here and raising a row. Japan is not coming over here for a fight soon, if ever. She wants no war with the United States. It would not suit her. Let Japan engage in a war with us, and what would be the result? There would be three or four months, perhaps, during which we would not be very successful. But then China would wake up, and say, "I'm going to take Korea back;" and Russia would get even for her grudge; and then our forces would get in good shape, and there would be a setback to national ambition in the "Land of the Rising Sun" for several centuries. They know all that just as well as you do. [Applause.] Japan is not caring especially about matters in America.

Now, you have been in the harvest fields—that is, some of you have—and you have sometimes stirred up an old mother quail, and she would go off limping on one leg and one wing, and you would go after her. She would lead you thus far afield, and after she was sure you were far enough away, to your great surprise you discovered just as you were about to catch her that she was certainly convalescent as she flew away out of sight. Do you know what was the matter? Her young were in an opposite direction from that she led you.

Japan will seem to make much ado about a San Francisco school question; but her young are in Manchuria and Korea. If she can secure cotton lands in Korea and wheat lands in Manchuria, and colonies in both, she can lay the basis for commercial success; and then she can do anything, but not before. There is no immediate danger from Japan.

But you let China wake up and train millions of troops in the Flowery Kingdom and create a navy, but remain heathen at heart, and then no man can foresee what will follow. If China should fall into the habit of fighting, there is no saying what would happen.

We talk about the "Far East." There isn't any "Far East;" it is the "Nigh East" now. Bishop Pierce went overland from Georgia to San Francisco in 1859. He left Georgia in April and reached San Francisco about the middle of June. He rode in a stagecoach most of the way. He was a long time in getting to the end of his journey. He called on Capt. W. T. Sherman on his way, at Fort Davis, and the Captain entertained him hospitably. But Captain Sherman came through Georgia five or six years after that and the Bishop did not entertain him, so far as I know. [Laughter.] But with Captain Sherman's help and the aid of many others it took Bishop Pierce two months to make the trip. But I left Atlanta on July 18, 1906, and ate my breakfast in Yokohama, Japan, on August 8. On landing I sent my wife a cablegram, and came mighty near getting the answer before it started. [Laughter.] You see all lands are close together now.

Queen Victoria, in her time, fell down the stairs of Windsor

Castle and sprained her ankle. This mishap was known in New York several hours before it happened. If the cablegram had gone on around the world, her Majesty might have been fore-warned, so that the accident need not have occurred. [Laughter.] The ends of the earth are close together now.

Thomas Jefferson said, and afterwards Mr. Lincoln stated the idea more fully, that this country would have to be all free or all slave territory. The notion was combated for some time. Lee and Grant and Johnston and Sherman took up leading parts in the debate toward the close of the controversy. We found out, after that protracted and somewhat warm argument of four years, that the thing was true. [Laughter.] The conviction has deep-ened ever since until now nobody doubts it. [Applause.]

The ends of the earth are closer together now than Washington and New Orleans were when Thomas Jefferson was President. [Applause.] Take, for example, the battle of the Allies before the walls of Peking. We knew the results of the fights of each morning by reading the evening papers. But when Andrew Jack-son—I think in the State of Tennessee he is called familiarly and affectionately "Old Hickory"—when Andrew Jackson fought Gen-eral Pakenham at the battle of New Orleans, they fought some days after the war between England and the United States had closed. [Laughter.] Just think of men fighting battles when there was not any war going on! But Andrew was fond of that sort of thing. He was at New Orleans, so remote from Washing-ton, however, that the authorities at the national capital could not tell him to stop. And he never would stop until somebody told him to do so, and he did not always stop then. [Laughter.] In Jackson's time news traveled slowly. It is not so now.

Thus by rapid transit and speedy communication the possibility for Christianizing this world is thrust into our hands, and that great achievement will have to be accomplished by evangelical Christianity, and largely by the Christianity of the two great English-speaking nations. [Applause.]

The ends of the earth are close together, and all men now are neighbors. National isolation is impossible. All things found in one land run rapidly through all lands. Contagions of world-wide evil and movements of universal good are possibilities. The evangelization of the world is not beyond the power of the great English-speaking nations, and it seems as if this great and blessed work had been committed mainly to their hands. [Applause.] There are some evidences that they are conscious of the solemn responsibility. The Protestant Churches of the world contribute annually a little more than twenty-two million dollars to the cause of foreign missions; and of this sum, the Churches of the English-speaking nations give above eighteen million dollars. The Anglo-Saxon nations take the lead in this mighty movement for the redemption of the sinning and suffering.

If you good people who are not Methodists will not listen, or take it amiss if you hear me, I will say another thing in this connection. What I am about to say is true, however, whether you hear it or not. It is this: Methodism will have to do a very large part of this great work of evangelical Christianity in the Anglo-Saxon nations. Its doctrines and its polity give it special qualifications for the work of foreign missions. It believes in the possibility of saving the whole world, and not a mere fraction called the "elect." It sends out preachers without waiting for them to receive calls. The motto of its ministry is: "The World Is My Parish." Methodism is thus pledged to and prepared for planetary preaching. It must ever heed the "call to go forward" to the "regions beyond."

Moreover, we can offer no excuse for failing to go forward. We cannot say that we have not men enough. More men offer for the foreign field than we send out. Our mission boards lack money, but not men; and our people have in their possession all the money required for this great enterprise. Alas! they have it, and they hold it! Some men think less of their lives than others do of their gold. A holy man will give up his son or a consecrated mother will yield her firstborn for the work of foreign missions, while their neighbors professing equal faith will withhold most stubbornly their dollars from the cause.

I recall a case in point. When I visited Cuba the first time, just after the Spanish-American War, conditions were very hard and unhealthy there. Yellow fever laid its victims in the streets, and starving people met you on all sides. After looking into the situation, I returned to seek a man for the mission in Havana. My mind turned to an admirable young man who had been a student in Emory College when I was President of that institution. He was a member of the South Georgia Conference, as also was his honored father; and as the session of that Conference was at hand, I went down to the place of its meeting to see him. An elder brother of the young man had died on the mission field, and was buried at Durango, Mexico. I naturally feared the affectionate father would be unwilling to give another son to a mission then so dangerous to life; and I went hesitatingly, wondering how I would be able to overcome his objections. But when I met him, he said: "We gave Robert to Mexico; and when I read your appeal for Cuba, I said to my wife that you would want George for Cuba." And then he added with deep emotion: "We are glad to give him also to the work." The grand old man and his devoted wife rejoiced in giving two sons to the foreign field. But when I appealed to a rich man for money to send George MacDonell to Cuba, he gave me grudgingly the pitiful sum of twenty-five dollars. Alas! alas! that money is so dear and "flesh and blood so cheap!"

Money is all we now need to evangelize the world. Thousands of men are waiting to be sent out. All the doors of all the nations are open to receive them. Only the money is wanting which the work requires, and the members of the Churches have that if they would only part with it for the promotion of God's cause among men. We can give no excuse for not going forward except the niggardliness which withholds the means, and we certainly cannot plead our sin in defense of our delay to go forward.

It is of no use to say we cannot go forward because of the "financial panic." The panic is rightly named; it is a panic, and in it there is nothing but panic—unreasonable fright sprung from insane selfishness. I have seen financial crises before this time which had economic reasons to justify and explain them. But there is no reason for this panic. Not a statistical fact nor an economic principle justifies it. It is simple, senseless fright. A man asked me the other day when I thought it would end. I replied: "In the name of sense, how can I know?" You see a dog running at breakneck speed down the street with a tin can tied to his tail. Some silly boy started him going, but all the philosophers in the earth could not tell when he will stop. The whole movement depends upon the strength of the string and the tail. [Laughter.] The poor creature's mind has nothing to do with it. He ceased to reason when he began to run. After once entertaining the thought of running, there was no room left in his brain for any other idea. Auto-suggestion to change the current of his

10

reflection and bring him to a standstill is out of the question. And that is the case with you business men. When you get over your unreasoning scare, the panic will pass. [Applause.]

We have hid out in "old stockings" and safety vaults money enough for all the great work God wants us to do. We cannot truthfully say that we have not the resources required for a forward movement. Last year the government statistics, compiled from the tax returns of the American people, showed considerably more than one hundred billion dollars' worth of property in the United States. That showing was made from the books of the tax assessor; and if we swore to that official we had that much, we had it. [Great laughter.]

Your civilization is stagnating and putrefying with material prosperity. The moral miasmas which arise from your accumulated and unused wealth threaten the well-being of all classes. The pestilence of greed pervades all places, sometimes penetrating to the pulpit even. It corrupts your politics and defiles your social life; it divides families with feuds and sets communities at variance with each other; it moves capital to oppress labor and labor to defraud capital. What at last is your question of capital and labor but a contest of greed? Were the wages of labor or the returns of capital ever so great among any people? What then are they quarreling about? What is the meaning of their strife over money except it be that each is mad because both cannot get all of it? I confess that I cannot get interested on behalf of either contestant. It is a quarrelsome greed that animates both parties. If it were a contest of eagles, vying with each other as to which could fly nearest the sun and hide himself deepest in the rays of that radiant orb, I could watch the contest with eager interest. But over a contest of vultures as to which shall get the largest share of the carrion which they have jointly discovered my enthusiasm refuses to rise. [Applause.]

We have struggled for wealth; and when we have won it, we have held on to it with such adoring tenacity that covetousness has tainted all our ideals. We make money not only the measure of material values, but the standard of human life itself. We are beginning to feel that to be without money is to be without character, and that we can do without character if we can only have money. Our competitions are ignoble rivalries, and our social system is rapidly becoming a race course for the display of vulgarities. We are the bond slaves of the bond market and most truly the "serfs of the soil."

But if a generous portion of our vast resources were turned loose for the salvation of the world, we would be raised by the things which now drag us down. Our contests then would be not the barbaric rivalries of greed, but the holy competitions of beneficent zeal; we should then vie with each other as to who should have most of the glory of carrying civilization and Christianity into all the heathen lands. [Applause.] At last there is but one enterprise great enough to draw off the dangerous resources of Christendom and keep them at a safe level, and that enterprise is the great work of bringing the whole world to Christ. [Applause.]

Indulge me in one other reflection concerning how it would affect us if we stood still or went backward in the work of missions. To stand still or to go backward we must break with the Captain of our salvation. We must go forward or we will cease to follow him, for he is at the front. There are those who talk of "going back to Christ;" but he is not behind us. He is related to us as he was to Joshua when that leader of Israel saw him on the walls of Jericho. He gave Joshua to understand that he was there as the "Captain of the Lord's host," to take command in person on the field and lead the campaign for the conquest of Canaan. In like manner he now goes before the hosts of Christendom for the conquest of the world. He is not resting in the rear, but going on before. If we follow him, we go forth to certain victory, to a triumph which will bring peace to all lands and salvation to all peoples; if we refuse to follow him, we shall turn backward to a moral desolation of world-wide despair more terrible than the wilderness that was behind Joshua and Israel. We cannot turn back; we will not turn back; we will hear and heed the "call to go forward."

Already we see the dawning of the day that shall end in world-wide victory. The golden beams of its promise are stealing over all the earth. The high noon of the day of the Lord draws near, when, triumphant over all his foes, he shall be proclaimed by angels and men "King of kings and Lord of lords." [Great applause.]

III.

THE OPPORTUNITY.

——

XI. THE SUPREME OPPORTUNITY OF THE HOUR.

XII. CHINA: THE GIBRALTAR OF MISSIONS.

XIII. KOREA: A GREAT RELIGIOUS AWAKENING.

XIV. THE CHRISTIAN CONQUEST OF JAPAN.

XV. BRAZIL: A BUGLE CALL TO VICTORY.

XVI. CUBA: ON THE FIRING LINE.

XVII. MEDICAL WORK IN THE ORIENT.

While in India I had gone to see the Taj Mahal, at Agra. The Taj is a great mausoleum of white marble, built in memory of his wife by Shah Jehan. It is the finest piece of architecture in the world. I have seen most of the world's great sights—and most of them disappoint you—but the Taj Mahal satisfies completely. It is a feast for the soul that loves beauty. Whether you see it shimmering in the glistening noonday sun of India or bathed in the opalescent glow of eventide, the Taj is a dream of beauty. I walked about in its courts; I went through its corridors, where the light infiltrates through its alabaster screens; and then I went into that great pillared dome, where, inlaid with mother-of-pearl and colored stones, is inscribed the whole Koran. While I listened the guides evoked from the dome the echo which lives there and which speaks for fifteen seconds. I tested it by my watch, and found it so. Then, to my good fortune, the guides and the tourists all left; and, with my wife and two friends, I was alone in the marble rotunda. And I had an inspiration. I stepped over to one of the pillars and, raising my voice to the center of that great dome, as clearly and distinctly as I could I enunciated the Arabic name of God. For twenty seconds by this watch that name rose and swelled and circled and recircled and echoed and reëchoed and reverberated and volumed, until the whole vast dome was filled with the name of God. I come back to you to say that to-day, to whosoever has ears to hear, the world is echoing round with the name that is above every name.

(150)

XI

THE SUPREME OPPORTUNITY OF THE HOUR.

MR. WILLIAM T. ELLIS, PHILADELPHIA, PA.

Mr. President, Ladies and Gentlemen: I have come to you to-night not to make a speech (I cannot make a speech), but to tell you in simple words what I have seen.

I have seen, paradoxically, Southern Methodist crowds made up of yellow men. I recall, one evening in Kobe, I had gone to your night school, where a great company of Japanese pay a tuition fee to be taught English and the rudimentary branches of education; and the school was so successful that there wasn't room for them in the building. I saw the unusual procedure of a company of men outside of each window, standing on the veranda, with their heads stuck through the window; thus, in their eagerness, getting the education into their heads, if not into their bodies. You had not staff enough to teach them; so the teachers had called to their aid a young English clerk. When I came to the English class room, this emergency teacher was drilling them in English phrases, and the first phrase he was making them repeat after him was: "I have got a dog." They learned that model English sentence, and then he drilled them in another sentence: "There are many dogs in Hengland."

I could tell you about the son of the Southern Methodist missionary (I have made all kinds of criticism of missionaries, so let me tell this right at the fountain head of things), a bright American boy, about ten years old, who is the son of one of your men in Japan. I was in his city on a feast day, and it is the custom of the priests to put out in the streets the great temple drums, and trust the small boys to make racket enough to attract the attention of the gods. And this devout little Methodist was sitting astride a Shinto drum, banging away to attract the attention of the Shinto deities!

I have been a teacher only once in my life, and that was over at Hiroshima. I went to teach an English class for your Mr. Meyers. I didn't know how to talk Japanese, but we talked in English with some difficulty. It was at the time of the San Francisco disturbances. I said to the young men: "I am afraid you will want to break my head because I am an American?" One of them responded very quickly in his lame English: "There is no such mind in our hearts."

More seriously, I want to say that in Japan, Korea, and China you have, to my knowledge, a company of men and women whose work, if you knew it, would fill you with a deep and overflowing pride. [Applause.]

There sits on this platform a man whom I greatly desired to meet, because, when I was in Japan, I was hearing of him, North and South: "This is the way Dr. Lambuth did it;" "This is what Dr. Lambuth said." His far-visioned, statesmanlike, sanctified character has made an impression upon Japan that will not soon fade. [Great applause.]

I should like to philosophize, if I were able, about the way mission work keeps men young. Over in Kobe you have a Dr. Newton—I wish you knew your men better! If you did, you might take time from praying for them (I suppose you pray for them; you keep talking about that) long enough to give three cheers for those men and women! [Applause.] Dr. Newton would be counted an old man in America; I suppose you would superannuate him. I went over the Kwansei Gakuin with him. I found him a magnificent teacher and administrator, full of zest for the Japanese and for his institution. We went to the class room at lunch hour, and we came across some boys eating their lunch. They were caught by the President, and were very much embarrassed. Well, President Newton tried very hard to be very sober and dignified while the boys were looking; but when he got outside the doors he was younger than the small boys himself. That's the spirit of the "old man" on the mission field.

But all the while I have been talking I've been thinking about a spot in Japan which means more to Mrs. Ellis and myself than any other spot in all Japan. Down at Hiroshima there is an institution known to Japan—it should be known to all the South-land—called "The Hiroshima Girls' School." [Applause.] Gentlemen, I'm ashamed of you that you do not more worthily applaud that name—"The Hiroshima Girls' School." [Great applause.]

I'm going to get confidential with you men. I have been discovering, in the last few days, that there are a great many big men at this Convention, but a bigger man than any of you is Miss Nannie B. Gaines, of Hiroshima. [Applause.]

They had a feast of their leading citizens in Hiroshima a little while ago, and they invited one foreigner. The one foreigner they invited, and the one woman, was your Miss Gaines. [Applause.]

There is a woman who has achieved in that land a loftiness of character, a breadth of vision, a power of administration which would make her a great woman, by all the standards that determine true greatness, anywhere in the wide world. [Applause.]

I have so often thought, since knowing Miss Gaines, of the fair belles of your Southland, who shine in your social circles, how much more worthy, how much more great, in all things womanly and gracious and queenly, is this woman who has elected to give her life to a people of an alien tongue and birth! [Applause.] I have heard young women talk of social triumphs; to me it seems a diviner triumph for a woman to be loved and honored and followed, to repeat her life and her character in the lives and characters of hundreds of young women who are going to put their shaping hands on the new nations.

And with Miss Gaines at Hiroshima are a company of young women like unto her. I was there after Miss Lanius returned from her furlough and when Miss Williams came for the first time. Well, when the Ambassador reached Chattanooga yesterday, he was met out on the hills by automobiles and many of your prominent men. Miss Williams and Miss Lanius were not met by automobiles; but there was a great company of the people at Hiroshima gathered at the train—a line of four or five hundred young women, who stood waiting to give an ardent welcome to these young women who came to work among them. Do you know anybody in America who has achieved a social triumph like that?

Take the sister of a gentleman who sits on the platform—take Miss Margaret Cook, the brilliant head of the kindergarten at Hiroshima. [Applause.] I cannot understand why you Southern men should ever let any of those ladies get to Japan as "Miss" Somebody. [Applause.] I'm sure it is of their own choosing. [Laughter.]

But I mustn't talk further about Hiroshima; I have to talk for a moment about Korea. Let me not take up any of your individual missionaries in Korea, but one of your natives there. Do you chance to know—you see, I'm trying to try to make you brag about your men on the foreign field! Sometimes there are men in the North who think a missionary is an evil to be tolerated when he comes home. I hope better things of you—but do you happen to know, you Southern men, that the greatest Korean in the world, a member of the late Emperor's Cabinet, refused to take the principal office in the present Cabinet that he might become a teacher in your school at Songdo? [Applause.]

Do you realize that the future of Korea, that wonderful nation, is to be determined not by Marquis Ito, not by the civil and military powers of Japan, but by that handful of missionaries, by that growing—pentecostally growing—company of Christians who are making a new Korea, with a new life, a new hope? [Applause.]

I talked with your Mr. Yun Chi Ho. I went there as a newspaper man, to find out all I could about the situation, and I had to see the leading natives as well as the leading Japanese and Americans. Now, it is a great thing to see a patriot, in any land. Mr. Yun said to me, with an intensity which I cannot reproduce: "Mr. Ellis, the only light in the black sky of Korea is the Christian Church." [Applause.]

Just one word about China. I leave to others the details concerning your work, which I would like to dwell upon did I not feel called upon to give you a somewhat larger view to-night, if I may. There is a city called Soochow; and, by the way, you may go to Soochow from Shanghai by a railroad train finer than any that have been entering Chattanooga, and you will cross eight hundred bridges in going through Soochow, if you like to bridge your difficulties. [Applause.] At Soochow you will get to talking about the city's leading citizens, and you will hear mentioned two or three foreign names. I need not point out to you the significance of the fact that when a man attains an identity as a leading native citizen he has become a power in his community. I heard there this story: During the Boxer days there arose a riot in Soochow. A foreigner's sedan chair was going along (you travel over that city in chairs), and the mob began to cry: "Kill the foreigner! Kill the foreigner!" They were doing that very thing over North China at that time. The mob grabbed hold of the chair and pulled out the man who was in it, and then the leader turned round and said, disgustedly: "It isn't any foreigner at all; it's only old Dr. Park." [Applause.]

There is another man—I invite you to watch him blush while I speak [indicating Dr. Anderson on the platform]. He is trying to hide behind men not quite so good-looking as he. [Laughter.] I found in traveling over China a great many institutions of wisdom and learning, and it became my painful duty to try to put each in its place: which is best, which is second best, and so forth. I found two claimants for first place among the modern institutions of learning in China. One of those two is the Soochow University of the Southern Methodist Church. [Applause.] And as the President of that college, Dr. Anderson is a great man. [Applause.]

I want to talk a little more generally, if I may, to-night, because you would think, if I should talk about individual missionaries, that I had been subsidized by your Board, or something of that sort. [Laughter.] Well, from what I have heard from some of the brethren, I don't think you would suspect that I had been subsidized. [Laughter.] I have the unenviable distinction of being the arch-critic of foreign missions. I have written and printed more criticisms of foreign missions during the past two years than any other man alive. I went out as a newspaper man to find out what was what in foreign missions. I don't advise my brethren of the quill [aside to the press representatives] to take the same assignment.

It means, for example, that during the year I circumnavigated the globe. I traveled more than 35,000 miles. I traveled in steamships, in launches, in house boats, in canoes, in junks, in sampans; I traveled in innumerable wheeled vehicles, carriages without number, in jinrikishas by the hundreds. (The jinrikisha, you know, even if they don't have it in Chattanooga, is an enlarged baby carriage, pulled by a man. The word "jinrikisha" means "man-pulled car"—the original "Pullman car.") [Laughter.] I traveled in jinrikishas, in automobiles, in ehkas, in tongas, in droskies, in bashes, in wheelbarrows, in sedan chairs. I traveled on elephants, on camels, on buffaloes, on donkeys, on horses, and afoot. [Laughter.] I was feasted in Japan and mobbed in China. [Laughter.] I slept on the floor in Japan, in a bake oven in Korea, and out under the stars in India. [Laughter.] I shivered on 203-Metre Hill and suffered under 150 degrees of temperature in India; I bit the dust in North China—and I was bitten by other things all over the Orient. [Laughter.] I talked with more than a thousand missionaries on their fields. I talked with statesmen and diplomats—excuse me—yes, I talked with statesmen *and* diplomats, with native officials, with foreign travelers, foreign merchants, foreign editors.

I endeavored to find out what is what in this old world of ours; and, as a scout of civilization, I come back to you to-night saying, in the words of Samuel Johnson—words of which we are trying to make slang in these days—that "there's something doing" in the world.

There is something doing in the world—something significant, something portentous, something ominous! There is a surge, a swell, a billowing, a ferment, a very tidal wave of human feeling all around the world to-day. Define it? I scarcely know how. You may call it a wave of democracy, a wave of socialism, a reassertion of the old, old rights of individual liberty; you may call it the spirit of the times; you may, more searchingly and more truly, call it the Spirit of the living God! [Applause.] I can only say to you that, wherever you go in this old earth, even the most superficial and casual observer will find that there's something doing.

You are something doing! Did you ever stop to think of the significance of the phenomenon of this great laymen's gathering? This is unprecedented in the history of the Southland. What means this arising of strong men? Do you think that God calls his forces together for the fun of gathering them together? Do you think it means nothing that you have come from the east and the west and the north and the south to sit down and take counsel concerning the things of the ends of the earth? No! No!

What is God doing here with these splendid forces and equipment? What he is doing here has intimately to do with what is doing over yonder. There is such a thing as a divine concatenation of events. God's bells all chime in tune. He is doing something here; he is doing the same thing at the ends of the earth. For I am one of those who believe that the Lord God Omnipotent reigneth. [Applause.]

Consider with me for a moment what is known to all of you, concerning our land of America. We have been having during the past three years a revival—a civic, social, ethical, commercial, political revival—and the mourners' benches are full. [Laughter.]

Has it ever occurred to you that what is doing in America to-day, which I need not dwell upon, is one with what is doing in Great Britain also? You heard from the distinguished Ambassador, whose presence honored you last night, and whose reception honored both him and you, that there is not only in Great Britain, although he dwelt upon that, but that there is throughout the Far East a strange, critical movement in human society to-day.

Well, over in Great Britain they call it liberalism, laborism, or socialism—they scarcely know what to call it, but they know this: to-day Great Britain is in a social and political crisis such as she has not known for a generation.

There is "something doing" in Great Britain; there is also "something doing" in France. You read, a few months ago, of the separation of Church and State? I do not think you considered it an isolated thing, because you read behind the mere news of the day, and perceived that the event was only a symptom of a deep-running tide in the national life of France. There is "something doing" to-day in France.

Even Spain, as she sits in the ashes of her departed fame and glory and present shame, finds coursing through her veins a new purpose, a new life. There is "something doing" in Spain. We have all heard echoing from the guns at Casablanca that there's "something doing" in Morocco. The tidings of the foul murder of the crown prince and king of Portugal told you and me that there's "something doing" in Portugal to-day.

We read the dispatches from the brunette republic to the south, and we know that there's "something doing" in Haiti at this time.

Did you observe the paragraph in the newspapers a few weeks ago to the effect that Italian troops had been posted in front of the Vatican? Why? Was the pope in danger? I do not know. They did not know. They simply knew this: that Italy to-day is being shaken from top to bottom by this new "something" that is "doing" in the whole wide world.

I received a summons about a month ago to go to Turkey as a newspaper correspondent, that I may be in at the death of the Sick Man of Europe, because his cup of iniquity is at last full. This message came by the underground route, that it is nearly all over with Turkey. There's "something doing" there! There also continues to be "something doing" in Macedonia. Russia, as she raises her bruised, bewildered, and befuddled head amid the sound of bursting bombs, the wild cries of the smitten and persecuted, and the dull roar of red revolution, knows that there's "something doing" in Russia to-day.

Go down to Egypt, where the West touches the East. I found that the week before I reached Cairo Lord Cromer had paraded through the streets of that ancient city every available man and gun of his British Majesty's forces, in order to suppress and impress the revolutionary Cairenes. Egypt, the land of the dead, is becoming a nation of a living crisis. As the young Egyptian sits in the sidewalk cafés of Cairo, with his red fez cap tilted rakishly to one side, and his patent leather shoes crossed and stuck up in the air, twirling a swagger stick in one hand and sipping the Egyptian coffee, which is two-thirds grounds and one-sixteenth dust, he is talking of revolution, rebellion: life for the land of the dead.

Go down the Red Sea until you come to India. I was there about the anniversary of the Mutiny of 1857. It is not a reflection upon the distinguished Americanized guest who has so lately honored this city to say that there is certainly something doing in India because the British are waking up to it. [Laughter.] I was there, I say, on the anniversary of the Mutiny; and

I found the timid among the British folk scared lest India again should run red with the blood of the white man. The last copy of *The Pioneer Mail* from India, which I have in my room at the hotel at this moment, is full of dispatches concerning the riots in Tinnevelli, in Southern India. Riots in Tahore on the north, riots in Calcutta on the east, riots in Bombay on the west —all India has been swept with the fear of sedition, revolution, and rebellion. I do not think there will be another mutiny, for two or three reasons: There is not a cannon in the hands of the natives, and there is not a native who has access to any arsenal in India. I do not believe another mutiny could succeed. But I do believe that India to-day is on the verge of a graver crisis than that which startled the world in 1857.

And I had better say now, lest time should fail me later, that the solution of India's troubles is not the solution that the young Indians offer. India says: "If the British will move out, India's day of glory will come in." The Swadeshi Movement has for its watchword: "India for the Indian." I am bound to say that, if the British should move out of India to-day, the situation to-morrow would be vastly worse than it was yesterday.

India's need, and the need of the nations, goes down, down, down to the deep, deep, deep springs of human nature. The only sufficient remedy lies in a force that will be applied to the fundamental springs of human nature, which are religious. [Applause.] India *wants* self-government; India *needs* Christ. [Applause.]

Joseph Cook, a short time before he died, said: "The nineteenth century has made the world one neighborhood; the twentieth century must make it one brotherhood." [Applause.] India's need, and the need of the world, is for the spirit of brotherhood, which it can only learn from that Best Brother of mankind, the Nazarene. [Applause.]

But Joseph Cook should have gone a little farther and said this: "The world is a neighborhood; the world should be a brotherhood. A neighborhood without brotherhood is not a thing to be coveted, but to be feared." When, in point of fact, the Orient was months removed from us, we did not care that the Orient was immoral, that it was rotten, that it was dirty, that it was untruthful, that it was all the cruelty and awfulness that heathendom means. Then those conditions did not bother us. But to-day we are next-door neighbors to it all. And I say to you, with all the intensity of my being, that, if we do not make the world neighborhood a brotherhood, God help our children! [Applause.] On the basis of sheer self-interest, we are bound to be interested in the whole wide world; and that is the genius of this Laymen's Missionary Movement: it is interested in the entire big world. [Applause.]

Go with me from India to the Philippines. Sailing along the beautiful islands of the Philippines, at last you come to Manila. You will experience the thrill which every wanderer in foreign lands knows when once more he comes beneath the folds of his own flag. [Applause.] But you will have the added thrill of rejoicing that America has done as she has done in the Philippines. You will see that when Mr. Dewey planted the American flag there he was merely the unwitting agent of the great God who has universal and far-reaching purposes to fulfill. And you will see that in the Philippines the American men have accomplished more in ten years than Great Britain and the East India Company have done in one hundred years in India. [Applause.] If I were talking on a single country, I should be happy to tell you how the gospel has gone hand in hand with our flag in making over these wonderful, wonderful Philippine Islands.

But go with me to China—and now I have need of all my courage and self-confidence, for what can I say to you about China? You sit here in Chattanooga, the gateway to the South, the center of the world (some Chattanoogans think!) [Applause]; and while I rejoice in our American progress and pride, this criticism is to be made of us: we do not seem to realize that

"There's a world outside the one you know."

The center of the world's news to-day, my fellow-workers of the press, is not London or Berlin or Paris or Washington; the center of the world's news to-day is China. Napoleon Bonaparte, who was a seer, said once: "There sleeps China. God help us if ever she awake! Let her sleep!" I come to you well aware that you cannot understand what I mean; and I say to you that this great empire of four hundred million people, about whose awakening you have been hearing for decades—*China to-day is awake!*

When China was asleep, five years ago, it was as though China were a great jellyfish: you put your thumb in pressure on one side of the jellyfish and the indentation remained as long as the thumb was there, and the rest of the jellyfish did not feel it. To-day China is a mass of living tissue. Touch it never so slightly on one side, and the thrill will be felt to the farthermost ends of the empire. Let Japan misbehave in Manchuria, and she is boycotted in Canton. Five years ago China was a heterogeneous congeries of unrelated individualisms; to-day she is a homogeneous entity: she is one nation, with one purpose. Talk with the eminent statesman in Peking, talk with the coolie along the roadside, and they all say the same thing: China is going the one way; China is about to learn the wisdom and the weapons of the West. There is one China to-day. She has two hundred newspapers, great institutions of learning; students throng the doors of your Soochow University, and there is not room for them, because you haven't been ready for the emergency.

But listen! Listen! I am not an alarmist, but by the same deep, passionate, patriotic determination that China is resolved to learn and possess all that the West can teach and give her— by that same spirit she has determined to throw out the Westerner! And she ought to do it. She is right, by all human consideration. If I had been in China in 1900, I would probably have been a Boxer. If I were there to-day, I would probably be an anti-foreign revolutionist. When I consider what I have seen with my own eyes, not even taking into account the history of the outrages perpetrated by the nations, I do not wonder that China hates us with a perfect hatred.

The greatest task before civilization to-day—I do not limit it to Christendom—the greatest task before civilization to-day is the task of putting a new mind into awakened China. And I do not know how she's going to get that new mind unless she gets "the mind that is in Christ Jesus." [Applause.]

I cannot come to you and say that China wants the gospel; I do not believe she does. I cannot say that the world wants the gospel. I did not find that the situation in the world to-day is represented by the Macedonian man crying: "Come over and help us." I found the Macedonian man only in Korea and the Philippines; I did not find him anywhere else. Heathendom does not want Christianity, because it is heathendom. The situation is perhaps represented by what I found in the famine field of China. I saw hundreds and thousands of starving men and women and children there, in the villages and in the famine camps, where they were living on the cold, bare ground, the fortunate ones being sheltered by a little bit of straw matting. One day I went out with a missionary to give medical aid to some of the Chinese in these terrible straits. What do you suppose was the complaint we heard oftenest? They came to us saying, these men and women who were starving (and you need not take their word for the fact that they are starving; you cannot take a heathen's word about anything; but the unmistakable pallor of starvation on their face could not be gainsaid): "Even when we get to the relief station, and secure a portion of rice, we haven't any appetite for it. Can you give us something for our appetite?" Starving! yet saying, "Give us something for our appetite!" They did not know that they had reached the last stage of starvation and were dying. Ladies and gentlemen, that is the heathen world: it has no appetite for the bread of life, but it needs it supremely. [Applause.]

It would not be just to you if I took more time to dwell on the fascinating land of Korea, when Bishop Candler is to follow me. I wish I had an hour for Korea; I would tell you, ladies, about the hats worn by the women of North Korea. They are bigger than the "Merry Widow" hats. [Laughter.] Most of the Orient, you know, is so wise that its women do not wear hats. I wish we were as wise as they. But up in North Korea, in Pyeng Yang, the women wear bushel baskets over their heads which come down over the shoulders. When a man is around, they drop the hats down over their faces, and so can see just at their feet, "one step at a time." When they go to church, the door is too small to let in the hats. I wish we had smaller doors in our churches. [Laughter.]

You do not catch my meaning. [Laughter.] I would not be so ungallant as to suggest what you think I have said; I might have to answer to Mrs. Ellis for unadvised remarks like that.

[Laughter.]   I mean this: The Korean Church has a smaller door, spiritually speaking, than any other Church in Christendom, for this reason: there are so many people thronging into the Church there that the missionaries purposely make it difficult to get into the Church. Let me tell you, if I may take a minute for a story, this little occurrence: I went out itinerating in Korea, and we came to the village where we were expected, and the missionary found twenty-five candidates for baptism waiting for us the next morning. I thought twenty-five candidates didn't amount to much, and early in the morning, before breakfast, I took my gun and went out to shoot a goose—and the goose is still there; but I shot at him. I shot at a million of them, more or less, and didn't get one. But I came back and found the missionary looking at his watch. He said: "We must get busy. Here are twenty-five men to be examined, and we have to go over to the other village to-day." After a hurried breakfast, we sat down in the little room, about eight feet long, six feet wide, and six feet high at the ridgepole. There sat the missionary on the floor; alongside him his helper; then the three leaders of the local Church; then the candidate; then the newspaper man. (There were also about a million others, such as do not move in good Chattanooga society.) [Laughter.] Then he began the examination. Why, do you know, in Korea they make some of the converts learn to read in order to be able to read the Bible, and so fit themselves to pass this examination? I said to the missionary (for I had him translate every question to me): "Why, Mr. Hall, that isn't right. It is not fair to ask those questions. I could not pass that examination. I wouldn't try to join your old Church; you wouldn't let me in." It is harder to get into the Church in Korea than it is to get into the kingdom of heaven.

The missionary that day turned down some of the leading men of the community. Which of you pastors would dare to do that? But he did it. Then along came an old woman, with very much my state of mind: she couldn't answer the questions. But she was different from me in this respect: she said what I'll never say: "I'm only a stupid old thing. I can't answer the questions, but," she went on to say, "I do love the Lord Jesus, and I want to belong to his Church." That old woman for nine years had been a believer and had lived a godly life, as the leaders testified. That missionary redeemed himself in my eyes by having the grace to let her in.

In Korea there are better Christians than—I won't say Chattanooga—in Philadelphia. [Laughter.] They read the Bible more, they pray more, they study more, they have more people at the Bible classes in one region in Korea than you have people at the Laymen's Missionary Convention in Chattanooga. I was going along the highway in that village which I have mentioned, and I saw a man coming along with two half-lengths of telegraph pole on his back. As he came up to me his face began to crack and break into smiles as he saw me. I knew what was coming. When he came up to me and stopped (for the villagers regarded me as a kind of missionary-in-law), he shifted his burden to one side and grabbed me by the arm. They don't shake hands in Korea; they just grab you anywhere and squeeze. He laid hands on me and bade me be at peace, and I bade him be at peace. And he told me how joyous it was to be a disciple of the Lord Jesus Christ. And this young coolie in Korea was gladder to see me than any man in all America, because I was a humble disciple of his Lord and Master, Jesus Christ. [Applause.]

I have said enough to indicate that there is "something doing" in Korea; there is also "something doing" in Japan. I could tell you that you are not going to solve Japan's problems merely by teaching it the Western ways. There are men who say that our civilization is good enough for them. Teach them to study as we study; teach them to eat as we eat; teach them our manners and customs; teach them to dress as we dress; and still they remain heathen, with their vital needs unmet. Japan's ethics and morality, which she teaches in the schools, need at their base a vital, religious power. There's "something doing" in Japan. There's "something doing" all around the world.

That "something" may perhaps be best expressed, as I close, by a story. While in India I had gone to see the Taj Mahal, at Agra. The Taj is a great mausoleum of white marble, built in memory of his wife by Shah Jehan. It is the finest piece of architecture in the world. I have seen most of the world's great sights—and most of them disappoint you—but the Taj Mahal satisfies completely. It is a feast for the soul that loves beauty. Whether you see it shimmering in the glistening noonday sun of India or bathed in the opalescent glow of eventide, the Taj is a dream of beauty. I walked about in its courts; I went through its corridors, where the light infiltrates through its alabaster screens; and then I went into that great pillared dome, where, inlaid with mother-of-pearl and colored stones, is inscribed the whole Koran. While I listened the guides evoked from the dome the echo which lives there and which speaks for fifteen seconds. I tested it by my watch, and found it so. Then, to my good fortune, the guides and the tourists all left; and, with my wife and two friends, I was alone in the marble rotunda. And I had an inspiration. I stepped over to one of the pillars and, raising my voice to the center of that great dome, as clearly and distinctly as I could I enunciated the Arabic name of God. For twenty seconds by this watch that name rose and swelled and circled and recircled and echoed and reëchoed and reverberated and volumed, until the whole vast dome was filled with the name of God.

I come back to you to say that to-day, to whosoever has ears to hear, the world is echoing round with the name that is above every name.

God's great legions, visible and invisible—the legions of him whose stately steppings among the nations make human history —are swinging into line. Shall we, too, "fall in?"

> "He hath sounded forth the trumpet that shall never call retreat;
> He is sifting out the hearts of men before his judgment seat.
> O be swift, my soul, to answer him; be jubilant, my feet!
> Our God is marching on!"

[Great applause.]

XII.

CHINA: THE GIBRALTAR OF MISSIONS.

As we look back over the conflicts of the nations and the days gone by, we can everywhere see His hand guiding; and out of every conflict He has brought the sons of men into a brighter day, into a higher life. And He is still guiding. Several things indicate this. For instance, for this great work of to-day God needs a larger force than ever before. Many of us have been thrilled at the sight of St. Paul crossing, almost single-handed, over from Troas to Philippi, passing from Asia to Europe, in the name of God, armed only by the spirit and the power of our Lord Jesus Christ, to conquer the Roman Empire that then dominated the world. But Paul was going against a power that had won its place by the sword, that was dominating the world through the sword; a power that held its place in the world just so long as the hand that wielded the sword was strong. That was a comparatively easy conquest. But the world is being marshaled to-day against a nation whose power is not the sword, and never has been; and God needs a larger force, a stronger battle line, and more courageous leaders. This is clearly indicated to-day. Why is it that just as we are brought face to face with this great people of the East we have our great Laymen's Missionary Movement here in America? Why are you here to-day? It is simply because the Church of God is facing a problem that it never faced before, and God is gathering his armies and assembling his servants that they may take the land in his name. He wants the strongest and the best it is possible to get.

(168)

XII.

CHINA: THE GIBRALTAR OF MISSIONS.

DR. D. L. ANDERSON, SOOCHOW, CHINA.

Mr. Chairman, Ladies and Gentlemen: In our consideration of China this morning we must think first of how near China is to us to-day. Improved methods of travel have brought China so close to America that the good and the bad can easily pass from one country to the other, and has thus made China our very near neighbor. Only a few years ago we looked upon China as at the "ends of the earth;" now there are no "ends of the earth," and we in America to-day are standing face to face with the four hundred millions of China.

Our own people on the Pacific Coast complain a great deal of the evil coming from China into America. I can testify that a very great deal of evil goes from America into China. Very much of our vice, our immorality, our lowest forms of debauchery goes over in nearly every steamer that crosses the Pacific; and keeping this in mind, we see that the China question is one that concerns all of our people. It is not simply an obligation of the Church to carry the gospel unto all men everywhere, but this is a question that concerns every man in America. We are face to face with these people. We must necessarily have intercourse with them. It is a matter of vital importance what their character will be, for that must affect us. And so as we stand before them to-day, with the gospel in our hands, it is necessary that we should carry it to them, not simply that China might be saved, but that we ourselves might be saved and our own land and her institutions be preserved. [Applause.]

The great problem of the East, which is the problem of our twentieth century, must necessarily be solved in China. The conflict of the nations which has, in a sense, been a conflict between

(169)

good and evil, and so has resulted in the betterment of mankind, has ever been moving westward seeking a wider field. In all this the hand of God can be clearly seen, and he has so ruled that out of every conflict men have come into a brighter day and to the realization of a higher life. To-day the people of the West, having for nineteen centuries been under the training of the gospel that has brought to them unlimited development along all lines, holding clearer ideas of God and of his creation, of our Lord Jesus Christ, the purpose of his coming and the nature of his kingdom, possessing also a wealth of achievement in intellectual lines such as the world has never known before, having a monetary wealth undreamed of in any past age and a vast military power that is a burden even to the marvelous wealth of this present century, are now standing once again face to face with the people of the East; and in the foremost line on the one side stands China, and in the foremost line on the other stands our own land, America. We can easily see that the advantage is with the West; and yet our advantages are no greater than are necessary for the great task we have to perform. That task is twofold: first, to propagate the truth of every sort that God has revealed to us for the benefit of the world, especially the gospel of our Lord Jesus Christ; then also to receive from the East, from China, the truths that have dominated there so long and have preserved her life until the present time; and we must so give and so take that both the East and the West may be only benefited, that both may be brought into the larger kingdom of our Lord Jesus Christ.

It will be utterly impossible this morning to discuss China's system; enough to say that in that system we find much of God's eternal truth, a very great deal of it. Historians tell us how the old nations of the past grew up, how they lived, how they died, and how, dying, left a rich legacy of truth to the succeeding ages. But China, whose history dates back to the earliest period, stands alive to-day, and is ready to hand out to the world those great truths that have preserved her, and that she has brought down from the dim ages of the past. I know we have a way of declaring that China is alive to-day simply because no one has gone there to destroy her; and some even say that China is already dead, simply a putrid corpse, lying out there simply because no one has gone to bury her. But look into her history; that tells another story. Barbarous peoples, such as those who went down from the North and destroyed the Roman Empire, have time and again come down from the North upon the Chinese Empire—only they did not break it up. Chinese civilization was strong enough in every instance to conquer her conquerors and to preserve herself. And so, instead of being dead, she is very much alive; not effete, not powerless, but persistent, strong, energetic as ever in her history.

We do not like to acknowledge it, probably, and yet in some things her civilization has been developed to a higher point than our own; and in some things her ideals are nearer to those of the Lord Jesus Christ than ours. Take, for instance, the fact that we somehow still hold to the old idea that might is right; and we believe that in some way the kingdom of our Lord Jesus Christ is to be advanced in this world through the sword. Indeed, many in the Church, as they look upon our magnificent fleet now going out to the East, imagine that these gunboats will be influential in establishing the kingdom of our Lord Jesus Christ and in glorifying his name. Many among us still imagine that this can be done by physical force. We forget that that is not our Lord's idea. We forget that, when Peter drew that first sword for the honor of the Lord, the reproof came instant and sharp: "Put it up; they that take the sword shall perish by the sword." A system established by the sword can perish by it. The Son of God was establishing a kingdom that should never be moved, and the sword had no place in that kingdom. It is hard for us to realize this, though we sometimes sing, as we did in our Easter services in all of our larger cities the other day, saying:

> "Thou art sublime!
> Far more awful in thy weakness,
> More than kingly in thy meekness,
> Thou Son of God."

Yet while the song is still upon our lips, we fail to realize its true meaning. We are still dominated by the thought of our feudal age.

Now, if you will take China, her ideas in this matter are nearer to those of the Son of God than ours. She has always abhorred physical force, and it has been her rule for ages past in dealing with men to appeal to their intellectual and moral faculties, not to mere physical force. Hating war, having a contempt even for her own military officials, without an army in the past such as we would call an army—there have been great congregations of men, but not soldiers—yet China stands to-day a great empire. Do you remember that He said: "Blessed are the meek: for they shall inherit the earth?" I think the most striking fulfillment of those words that we have on earth to-day is the Chinese people. They have attained to their present position, have occupied so large a portion of the territory of the earth, not by the sword, but simply by the strength and superiority of their civilization. China did not grow by the sword, and I am confident that China never will be destroyed by the sword. There is not power enough in the mere physical forces of the earth to destroy her. So China stands to-day, strong in her ancient civilization, antedating all that of all other nations of the earth; strong in the truth that she has held and is still holding; strong in her vast territories, with her varied climate, rich in agricultural and mineral products; strong in her immense population, persistent, laborious, economical—and unwarlike.

And yet, weak. I do not know of anything on this earth to-day so pathetic as the position of the Chinese people. They stand, as our Master said, "as sheep not having a shepherd." There is no Head. The great moral system that has kept them through the past, and is still keeping them, has no head; for He is the Head over all, but they have not yet found that out. And so they are going about as blind, seeking for some one to lead them into the light. For as we come in contact with China over yonder we see her more intelligent men, and especially her younger men, holding on to the past, realizing that their empire has held a position of power and influence through all these years; and yet realizing also that there is now something wrong in it, though not exactly able to understand what it is. They are wishing for and seeking for the light, and are holding out a hand to the West, trusting that they may be led out into a brighter day.

Now, it is just at this time that our God has brought us face to face with these people; and I think I can safely say that the Church of God has never had such a task before her as she has to-day. We look out upon the world, and it seems to me that God has reserved this land of China until this hour, until his people could be trained and nourished through nineteen long centuries of experience in his truth and his guidance in order that he might prepare them for this great work, this conquest of China. And if we will consider the matter a little, I think we can see that our God is still leading as he has led in all the past.

As we look back over the conflicts of the nations and the days gone by, we can everywhere see his hand guiding; and out of every conflict he has brought the sons of men into a brighter day, into a higher life; and he is still guiding. Several things indicate this. For instance, for this great work of to-day God needs a larger force than ever before. Many of us have been thrilled at the sight of St. Paul crossing, almost single-handed, over from Troas to Philippi, passing from Asia to Europe, in the name of God, armed only by the spirit and the power of our Lord Jesus Christ, to conquer the Roman Empire that then dominated the world. But Paul was going against a power that had won its place by the sword, that was dominating the world through the sword; a power that held its place in the world just so long as the hand that wielded the sword was strong. That was a comparatively easy conquest. But the world is being marshaled to-day against a nation whose power is not the sword, and never has been; and God needs a larger force, a stronger battle line, and more courageous leaders. This is clearly indicated to-day. Why is it that just as we are brought face to face with this great people of the East we have our great Laymen's Missionary Movement here in America? Why are you here to-day? It is simply because the Church of God is facing a problem that it never faced before, and God is gathering his armies and assembling his servants that they may take the land in his name. He wants the strongest and the best it is possible to get. [Applause.]

And we see that he is laying his hand upon our educational institutions also, for our great institutions of learning, like Yale, Harvard, Pennsylvania, Virginia, our own Vanderbilt, and I know not how many others, are even now engaged in the work of missions in China, and are sending out numbers of their choicest young men into the field. God has put his hand on the educational institutions of this land—the institutions that we reckon as those of power—and is using them over yonder.

Then take another point: It is just at this time that God has created among the Chinese themselves a great need, a need for something that can be supplied only from the West, a need for something that the missionary is in the most advantageous position to give, and that is our Western learning, our Western education.

And you will find that their desire to gain this, their insistent demand for it—for it is a demand from the whole people—has changed their attitude entirely toward the missionary. Not long ago in China I was not a man; I was simply a foreign devil. Ten or fifteen years ago no man of any respectability would have had aught to do with us. But now that is all changed; and every barrier that stood between China and the West has been removed, and the only barrier now to the progress of the gospel among these people is the same one you meet with here every day; it is simply the world, the flesh, and the devil. Everything else is gone; and we can come in contact with these people, every class of them, for every door is open.

Don't think that the Chinaman is sitting down with his mouth open ready to take in our gospel; he does not know anything about it. But you can come directly in contact with him, with the Chinaman of every class; you are at full liberty to approach him with the gospel of the Lord Jesus Christ, and he is willing to hear it patiently. It is his great desire for this Western education that is moving him to-day. And the result is that the youth of China to-day, the young men and young women, are being thrown into the hands of the Church, into the hands of the missionaries, in order that they may train them both for this life and the life that is to come.

Now, take our institution in Soochow. In our school there we have to-day something like 218 students of the best in the land; they represent the very best. Practically every one of our students is the son of some high official or of some one of the literary class or of some very prominent merchant; not that the poor are shut out (we make provision for them), but many of the better class that we could not even speak to a few years ago are now seeking us. They do not come to beg anything at your hands; it is not "charity work," as you would call it; but each one of these men comes with the money in his hand to pay for full tuition and all expenses, and he pays a higher tuition than was ever heard of in that land, and is glad to do it.

More than that, last year we turned off a large number of applicants who could not be received. We did not have room for them, no room in the buildings, nor a sufficient teaching force to instruct them. What happened last year happened the year before; it is to happen again this year. I verily believe that we could double our number of students in a very short time if we had a larger equipment. I am confident of this; and I feel sure that, if we can only be allowed to grow and develop, in a comparatively short time, something like ten years, we could have a thousand young men there, representing the very best of young China, put into our hands to train for China and for the world.

Do you understand what this means? It means that the Church of God in America to-day—and I say America advisedly, because nearly all the missionary schools in China are American—it means that the American Church has the opportunity to-day of training the young men who to-morrow will be the leaders in China. It is in your hands; God has thrust it there.

And they come begging. We have had men to wait in our proctor's office for two or three hours, with their children and with the money in their hands, begging that their sons might be received; and we would have to say "no," for we simply could not take them. So this work is being pressed upon us. The fact that the gospel of our Lord Jesus Christ is being taught in the school is no hindrance whatever to patronage; the fact that every boy in that school has to study the Bible for three solid hours a week (and it is real study) does not deter. A gentleman who lives near Soochow said: "If my boy wishes to become a Christian and join the Church, all right; there will be no objection from me." He added: "I am too old for that sort of thing; but I want my children to have it all." His idea was that if they got the "new learning" in its fullness they would have to take the Lord Jesus Christ along with it; that somehow he was at the very heart of it.

Only the other day, at our commencement, which came off in February, we had a very prominent Chinese official to make the annual address for us. Although he is not a Christian, he is a man of intelligence and ability, educated in England; and he made the statement, and insisted on it, that the missionary schools were doing decidedly the best educational work that was being done in China. He insisted that our students stick to us, that moral training was essential in educational work, and that religion was absolutely necessary to make men. [Applause.] When you take that into consideration, the very fact that the education which we are carrying into China is a Christian education only makes it, in a real sense, more acceptable to the Chinaman; not that he understands Christianity, but he understands the necessity of moral and religious training. Any religion is better than no religion. It is impossible to-day to revivify Confucianism. The only religion in China to-day that has a future is that of our Lord Jesus Christ.

We have government schools in Soochow, organized by the government; and it has been their system to give free tuition to all their students; not only free tuition, but free board; and to give, besides that, to every student some three or four dollars a month to pay his incidental expenses; and yet, while that was the case, the best of Soochow and the surrounding country, as far as we could receive them, would come to us and pay all their expenses. They preferred our system; it was the better.

I want to say that we have the opportunity to-day to do a wonderful work in China; but what is lacking? Money. We simply haven't got it. And Bishop Wilson and Dr. Lambuth insisted that I should come over to America just at this time to meet you brethren and get in touch with this Laymen's Movement, that we might get from you what we need to carry on this work. As I told you, we are hampered now. We have about two hundred students, and have been standing at that point about two years. We cannot go farther until we get more men and more money. I will be glad to talk with any of you or any committee. We need another school building in Soochow; we also need larger dormitories. Bishop Candler asked me awhile ago if our dormitories were finished. I answered: "Yes; and we need another one now." We need residences for our teachers. We also need a larger tract of land; we have now nine acres, but we greatly need a plat of about ten more that is lying just alongside of us. In other words, we need in Soochow to-day about seventy-five thousand dollars. That may look like a big sum; but it would be a pretty small thing if spread out over this audience.

Then, if you are going to have a first-class educational institution in China (and you are laying the foundation there, or can lay the foundation there, for one of the great institutions of that great empire, an institution that in the future will rank something like Yale or Harvard in America), we must have an endowment so that we can carry on this work. Now, we have in Shanghai a piece of land that the Board proposes to turn over to us for an endowment.

We have about two and three-fourths acres of land in Shanghai that was bought by Dr. Allen some twenty-five years ago. The

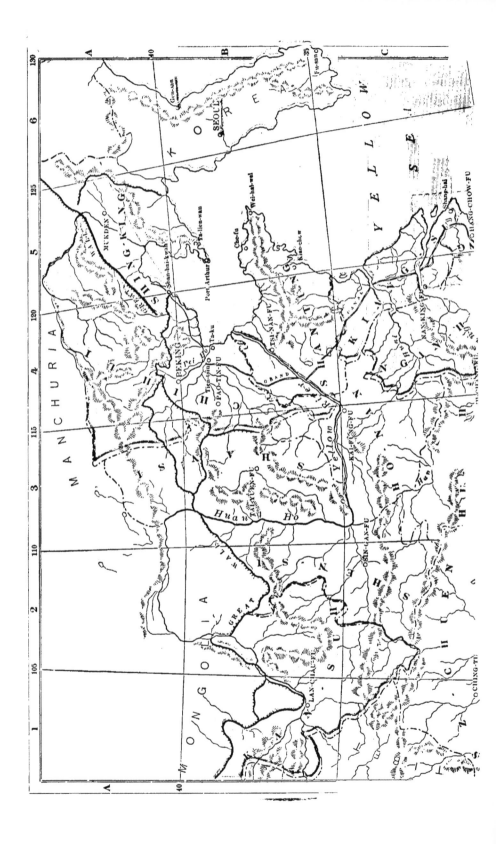

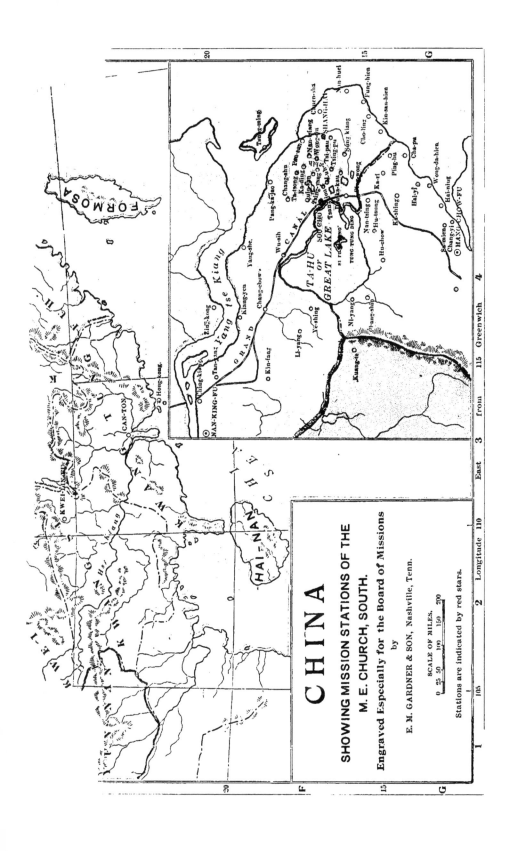

Doctor paid for that land at that time (I am sorry I cannot give you the exact figures) something like fifteen thousand dollars. To-day it is worth, at a very conservative estimate, one hundred and twenty-five thousand dollars. We have upon one corner of that land a block of five buildings for residences, which were built with part of the money that we received at the New Orleans collection in 1901. Now we have room enough there for twenty-two other buildings just like the ones we have. The cost of the buildings will be something like one hundred and fifteen or twenty thousand dollars. If we had that one hundred and fifteen or twenty thousand dollars, we would have at once an endowment of two hundred and fifty thousand dollars. That would bring us in an annual income of about seventeen thousand dollars now, and be constantly increasing, for the value of the property is still going up. It is a mere business proposition. The rent we get from the houses, which is about three thousand five hundred dollars a year, is largely used up in paying expenses and taxes. The more valuable the property, the heavier the taxes; but put the buildings on it, and it will carry itself and give us an endowment which, in connection with our tuition fees, will carry us along.

Now, I want to say just one word more. We have never, from the day our school first opened in Soochow, got one dollar from the Mission Board for our running expenses, not one. During the Boxer time, when I was afraid we would need help, I asked Dr. Lambuth to send us five hundred dollars. He sent it to us; but we did not use it. After the Boxer movement we sent it back.

Brethren, put the Soochow University on your hearts; it is your opportunity in the East; it is your opportunity in China to influence that great land and train the men who will be her leaders and who will bring China very near to God and establish his kingdom all through that old empire.

Will you think about it and pray about it? [Great applause.]

12

XIII.

KOREA: A GREAT RELIGIOUS AWAKENING.

We have had and are still having in Korea a genuine revival. Beginning four years ago in Wonsan, it has touched every important center in the land. The manifestations of God's working among the people have been similar to those which characterized the Wesleyan revival of a century and a half ago—conviction of sin coming upon whole bodies of people with such power as to make them forget everything except their great need of forgiveness and cleansing. God's Spirit has been working so directly that often even the human agent seems to be eliminated. In a service at which I was present the minister spoke only one sentence, and a wave of spiritual power took such hold upon the people that he could proceed no farther. From half-past eleven until six in the afternoon the meeting continued, led and directed by an unseen but real Presence. God alone knows the cleansing of hearts and change of lives that transpired in those awful and sacred hours. More significant, however, than the phenomena of these great meetings have been the evidences of permanent deepening of the spiritual life of the Church. There is great clearness as to the testimony of the inward witness, to answered prayer, to victory over temptation, and daily fellowship with God. The presence of the divine Spirit in the lives of the people is manifest by a consistency, a patience, and a love that are beyond mere human power to produce. Christians, too, have come to understand the difference between the reality and the pretense of religion, and their labors for others are not satisfied until there are evidences that new life has been received from above.

(180)

XIII.

KOREA: A GREAT RELIGIOUS AWAKENING.

REV. J. L. GERDINE, SEOUL, KOREA.

Mr. Chairman, Ladies and Gentlemen: Whatever fame Korea may have among the nations of the world, it rests not upon an ordinary basis. She has not breadth of area nor multiplied millions of population; she has no history of great achievements in war or statecraft; she has furnished to the world no masterpieces in literature or art; her inventions and discoveries have not largely influenced outside nations; yet we find many interested in this land and her people. Certain publications give prominence to happenings there quite disproportionate to the size and prominence of the country. Many of the travelers who go to the Far East make Korea the goal of their journey. A prominent platform speaker recently said to an audience of thousands that the very word "Korea" was a spell to quicken interest.

Why is this? For what reason does such a nation hold attention and interest from the public? The answer is found when you mention that those who are interested are chiefly Christian people, and the publications that note the happenings there are religious publications. Those who find interest in visiting this land are those whose chief concern is the progress of the kingdom of God. The word "Korea" quickens interest only with those whose hearts beat in sympathy with Jesus Christ in viewing the world for which he died. Korea is of interest to Christian people because of Korea's interest in the Christian's Christ.

Statesmen may say: "Korea has little weight among the nations; we pass her by; she is a little land and of little importance among the nations of the earth." Military leaders may say: "Korea is neither to be feared as a foe nor desired as an ally; therefore we have no concern with her." Commercial interests may

(181)

say: "Korea is a small field for us as compared with the larger and richer nations, and we will devote ourselves to the larger opportunities." The Church of Christ looks upon these people and says: "The Koreans are turning to God; they are accepting Jesus Christ as Saviour and Lord; they are brethren, and we must take an interest in them; we are interested in them because of the spiritual tie that binds together those who are one in Christ." We might say that but for the Christian Church in Korea there would be nothing there to consider; yet because of the history of the Church there, no other land has greater interest for Christian people anywhere. Korea has this unique distinction of claiming the attention of the Christian world solely from a religious view-point.

The subject assigned to me for to-day is "A Great Religious Awakening." The story of the establishment and progress of the Church in Korea reads like romance. Twenty-five years ago Korea and her people were unknown. No Protestant missionary had pressed foot on her soil. The people were spiritually dead, and knew not even the name of Jesus. Of those who first went with the message of salvation, all save one still live and labor there. They have seen one hundred and twenty thousand confess Christ as Lord and Saviour; they have seen two thousand churches established, where every Sabbath praise and prayers ascend to our God and Christ; they have seen certain cities where the percentage of churchgoers has already become greater than in most cities of Christian England or America; they have seen the attitude of a nation so changed that an official, not himself a Christian, could say: "There are now none of our people who are not favorable to Christianity." In the face of such facts we can only lift our eyes in humble adoration and cry: "Behold, what God has wrought!"

The success of our own mission has been proportionately great. In about twelve years, the length of time we have been in Korea, starting with a very small force, we now have one hundred and eighty Churches, with an enrollment of five thousand members and probationers, and perhaps five thousand more who have not been enrolled because not yet sufficiently instructed. The Church has grown sixfold in five years. The rate of increase has been more than thirty-three and one-third per cent each year. We have organized on an average more than a Church each week for the past two years; we have seen the people change in their attitude toward the Church, so that a most cordial welcome is extended to us in any part of the territory in which we labor; we are limited only by inadequate force and equipment. When we contemplate these facts, we can but stand in humility before God. Not only with reference to the growth of the Church can we call this a great religious awakening; but when you consider the character of our native Christians, it is wonderful indeed. This must be considered from various standpoints.

I want to say, in the first place, that we have there a loyal people. Becoming a Christian means much to the Korean. I believe I can say of them more truthfully than of any people I have met that they "seek first the kingdom of God." Only a few days ago I had a letter from my associates, telling of our District Conference having been in session in Wonsan, which is the most northerly station. There were more than three hundred enrolled at the District Conference. The Conference was held in the winter; snow was on the mountains; and yet four-fifths of these people had to walk from four to six days, paying their own expenses *en route* to the Conference and while they were there, in order that they might honor and serve the Church. When I look upon this splendid audience and see how you have come from the farthest confines of Methodism, as much as this means, I make bold to say it represents no more sacrifice on your part than it meant to those three hundred Koreans who tramped over the frozen ridges and mountain passes in order that they might attend the District Conference. [Applause.] That typifies the spirit of the people with reference to their Church relationship.

Again, the Church is liberal. We think that the character of our Christian Church will stand the test. From the very first these people have been commended for their effort toward self-support. The organized Church is not a drain upon mission funds. The Christians build their own houses of worship and contribute liberally to the support of the native ministers. These contributions are not made out of a surplus, but at a sacrifice. The people as a whole are poor, and every gift to the cause of the Church means a sacrifice of some necessity. At our Quarterly Conferences reports are made of the funds raised. At one Quarterly Conference I heard the leader of a group report a "fast collection." I asked him what that meant. He said they began a meeting at his church. The members agreed to lay aside all labor and business for the time and devote themselves to the work of soul-saving. A mighty blessing came, as it always does come under such conditions. Then the leader said to them: "We have had a great blessing, and we ought to be grateful. Now let us signify our gratitude. We are not working, and we do not need to eat much. [Koreans eat only two meals a day.] Let us live on one meal a day and give the price of the other meal to God each day for a week." Those people gladly did that, and so realized quite a sum. What do you think of such a spirit, you who think it hard if you cannot have three square meals a day?

The women raise funds in a way altogether unique. They have no access to the money till, but have control of the rice bag. After giving out the usual amount of rice for a meal, it is their custom to withdraw a small portion as a contribution to the Church. I know of no better way to characterize the giving of the Korean Christians than this act exemplifies. Every meal provided for the sustenance of life pays toll to the needs of the Church.

But more important, I believe, is the zeal of the Korean Christians. These large gatherings of which I have told you are not the only way of bringing the word to the people. The real evangelization is being done by the native workers themselves. The missionary's time is taken up, and more than occupied, in training those brought into the Church by these native agencies. Just to illustrate how this progress is made: I remember four years ago I came across from our station in Wonsan to Songdo, the first time that trip had been made by one of the missionaries, stopping at a place in about the heart of the Peninsula. I found there were no Christians there, and no one had been preaching the gospel among the people. In less than two years we had enrolled eleven hundred and fifty Christians and organized forty-eight Churches. This work had been done by native Christians, the missionaries merely leading and directing. [Applause.]

Loyalty, liberality, and zeal, important though they be, would not satisfy the ideal of the Church unless added thereto was spiritual life and power. We therefore consider of first importance the evidence of growing spirituality among our people. We have had and are still having in Korea a genuine revival. Beginning four years ago in Wonsan, it has touched every important center in the land. The manifestations of God's working among the

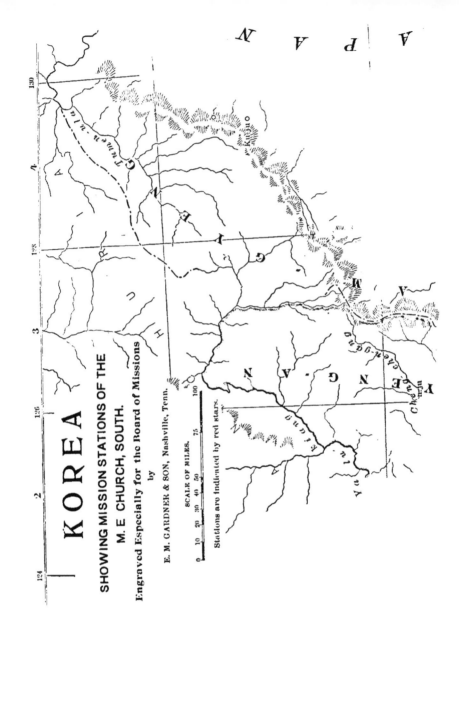

KOREA

SHOWING MISSION STATIONS OF THE
M. E. CHURCH, SOUTH.

Engraved Especially for the Board of Missions

by

E. M. GARDNER & SON, Nashville, Tenn.

SCALE OF MILES.

0   10   20   30   40   50   75   100

Stations are indicated by red stars.

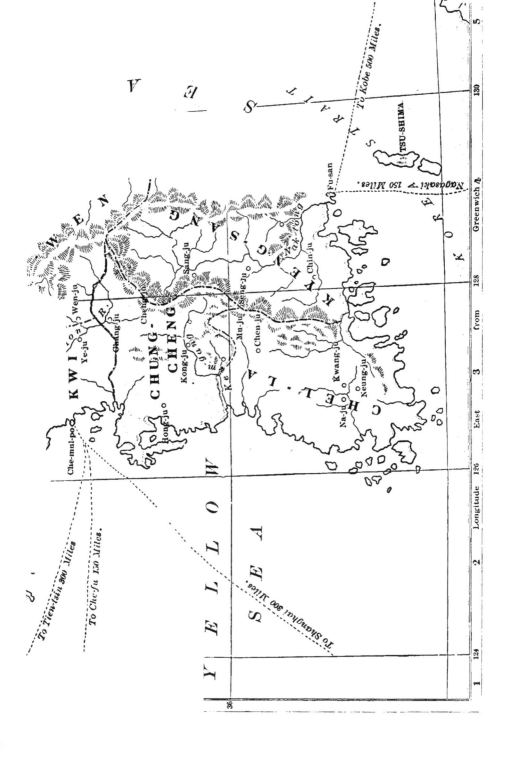

people have been similar to those which characterized the Wesleyan revival of a century and a half ago—conviction of sin coming upon whole bodies of people with such power as to make them forget everything except their great need of forgiveness and cleansing. God's Spirit has been working so directly that often even the human agent seems to be eliminated. In a service at which I was present the minister spoke only one sentence, and a wave of spiritual power took such hold upon the people that he could proceed no farther. From half-past eleven until six in the afternoon the meeting continued, led and directed by an unseen but real Presence. God alone knows the cleansing of hearts and change of lives that transpired in those awful and sacred hours. More significant, however, than the phenomena of these great meetings have been the evidences of permanent deepening of the spiritual life of the Church. There is great clearness as to the testimony of the inward witness, to answered prayer, to victory over temptation, and daily fellowship with God. The presence of the divine Spirit in the lives of the people is manifest by a consistency, a patience, and a love that are beyond mere human power to produce. Christians, too, have come to understand the difference between the reality and the pretense of religion, and their labors for others are not satisfied until there are evidences that new life has been received from above.

Having spoken of the growth of the Church and the character of those who compose it, we may have come to feel that Korea stands in no need. This, however, is taking a restricted view. We have no time to stop for congratulations on what has been accomplished; the great work is before us. Although there are one hundred and twenty thousand Christians in Korea, there are thirteen millions yet to be reached; although there are ten thousand connected with the Church, there are still two millions in the territory assigned to us who have not yet confessed Christ. Much has been done among those who are not Christians. They have come from the place of opposition and indifference to one of favorable attitude toward the gospel. The native Church, too, forms a force which, under proper guidance and instruction, can be used in reaching those who as yet have not accepted Christ. It is a situation full of hope, but also one involving tremendous sacrifice and labor.

Most significant, too, is the crisis that obtains at the present time. There is a crisis in the political situation. Within the past year Korea has lost her national independence, and an alien arm wields political control. Every day brings larger numbers of an alien race to live among these people who for centuries have had solitary seclusion. Without discussing the rights or wrongs of these political changes, permit me to say that the Christian Church stands as the sole bulwark in this time of political crisis. On the one hand, the Korean people are disposed to fling life away in a futile effort to resist foreign control. The Christian Church, with its teaching, stands directly against such a move. On the other hand, an alien power in control creates a tendency toward stamping out the very life and spirit of the people in subjection. The Christian Church resists this tendency. Christian character gives power to the individual which enables him to stand in the might of his own manhood against forces which otherwise would submerge him. I truly feel that the Christian Church, Korea's only friend, should have her full part in adjusting this trying political situation. [Applause.]

Again, there is a crisis in the educational life of the people. They have discovered the absolute incompleteness of their old system, and are clamorous for education along Western lines. This they will have. They appeal to the Church for aid. If the Church fails, it will come from some other source. The Church has the opportunity to hold control of the education of the picked youth of Korea. In this way, along with mental acquirement, they will receive a knowledge of Christian truth. Those who are to dominate the life and thought of the people may have their life and ideals molded by the Christian teachers and leaders, if we measure up to the present opportunity along educational lines. The Church should neglect nothing that will give her this mighty hold upon the future generation in Korea.

Then, too, there is a special crisis in the religious situation. Korea has been without a national religion. Buddhism has been under the ban for more than five hundred years, yet with the ascendency of the Japanese a concerted effort is being made to reestablish this as the national religion. There have been no temples in Korean cities and towns, yet to-day on the same hill with one of our churches in Songdo there stands a Buddhist temple and school. This is a challenge flung out to us who stand for the name of Christ. Shall it be Christ or Buddha for Korea?

The other crisis in the religious situation grows out of the success of our work. With the present force and equipment we have been unable to train and indoctrinate many of those who have come into our Churches. This is a real problem, and presents the strongest appeal of which I can conceive. Bishop Cranston, who recently spent some time in Korea, summed up the situation as follows: "Usually it has been the unfelt need of an unawakened people that has appealed to the Church of Christ; but now we hear the cry of millions who feel their need, and wait in tears before God and his Church for help. What shall become of us if, having excited their hopes, we only taunt their hunger with visions of bread beyond their reach?"

I have looked forward, my brethren, to this hour with both joy and fear. I look into your faces and remember that you represent the laity of the Church which has made me one of her representatives in Korea. I speak for a handful who labor there, and who look to you to supply what is needed in order to accomplish the task to which they have been set. They are taxed almost beyond human endurance, and ask that others be sent to share the ever-increasing burden of responsibility; they ask for equipment, that the work may be carried on to advantage. I have letters in my pocket telling me of the needs which we are depending upon you and upon the Church to satisfy. What shall be the message I carry back to these men whom you have sent to this land? I am glad to say that they are brave men who are laboring in Korea. I speak for ten thousand Christians connected with our Church, who pray for the mother Church as they pray for themselves. Many of them have as yet imperfect knowledge, and are asking to be taught the way more perfectly; they are asking that school privileges be provided, so that the coming generation may become a stronger and better generation than the present; they look in vain for better light unless we give it to them. I speak for the two million as yet unreached who live in the territory assigned to our Church. Other missions work elsewhere. We alone are charged with the responsibility for these. If we withhold the light and they perish in darkness, we shall have to give account for our neglect. They are ready to hear; they are open to our teachings; they eagerly await our coming. Shall they be disappointed?

I have given you Korea's message. What will your answer be

to this call? We have estimated that ten men and perhaps fifteen thousand dollars will be enough to enable us to minister to these people looking to us for the light. That will relieve the overtaxed missionaries; it will furnish teachers for the instruction in the Church and in schools for the youth; it will furnish leaders for pushing the work of evangelization among the two million as yet unreached. Please God, in a few weeks I go back to my labor. I count it not a matter for your sympathy, but a matter of joy. I go back to bear what message you may send to those who labor with me for these people; I go back to tell them of what your feelings toward them are, to tell them of what your attitude is with reference to pushing forward in Korea the work which we have begun; I go back, brethren, to those two million people who stand in their awful need and for whose evangelization our Church is responsible. The Southern Methodist Church has undertaken to give the gospel to that number of people. They sit there in need more tremendous than we can contemplate, every hope to which they have clung in the past having been shattered. And even the non-Christian people—how many times have I heard them say: "The last hope in which we have put our faith has been shattered, and we can only turn to God for help!" Here we have millions who realize their need, and wait in tears before God and his Church for help.

So I ask you again: What shall become of us if, having excited their hopes, we only taunt them with visions oi bread beyond their reach? What shall be the answer of the Church? I leave it with you in conclusion. The responsibility for meeting this crisis is upon us. Christ and a crushed people await your answer. [Great applause.]

XIV.

THE CHRISTIAN CONQUEST OF JAPAN.

If I were to take you to the city of Osaka, the Manchester of Japan, where capital is busy at work in industrial production, you would soon feel the necessity of bringing capital there under the control of the gospel of Jesus Christ. It is attracting large numbers to the city, away from their homes in the interior, largely women and children. You would find that they work twelve hours a day; you would find that they receive as their wage six or seven cents a day; you would find that they have no Sabbath rest; you would find that they are compelled to sleep thirty or forty in a room 18x18 feet in size; you would find these people enslaved by capital and subjected to all the temptations of the city. So the great problem in Japan, because the future Japan is to be one in which capital controls, is to Christianize capital; and I affirm that, inasmuch as capital has attracted people to the city in Japan and people to the city in America, capital must take care of these people; and inasmuch as capital has created city problems, it is responsible for the solution of city problems; and inasmuch as capital has produced the necessity for benevolence, capital must provide benevolence and meet the needs of the people it has attracted to the city.

(190)

XIV.

THE CHRISTIAN CONQUEST OF JAPAN.

DR. S. H. WAINRIGHT, ST. LOUIS, MO.

Mr. President, Ladies and Gentlemen:
I wish to speak of Japan as a distinct nation, and bring that country before your attention as perhaps the finest opportunity that the Church has to-day for Christian conquest.

The word sounded out in this generation as the watchword of our day has been "The Evangelization of the Whole World." I wish to modify that watchword slightly in order to bring it to bear upon Japan as a nation.

I think that we should not simply render the whole world Christian, but render the whole of life Christian. All life is one. We never have understood that so well as we do to-day, and the great call to the Church is to render all life Christian.

But the world of to-day, which is essentially a unit, breaks up in many forms; and it is the purpose of the Church not only to render the whole world Christian, but also to make every nation Christian, and to evangelize every family; to evangelize trade, industry, politics, art, literature, education; to render capital Christian, to render labor Christian, to render wealth Christian, and to render poverty Christian. In other words, our call is to evangelize the whole world, and to render the whole of the life of man Christian.

Now, if that is true, Japan affords the finest opportunity outside of the Christian nations for evangelistic work, because Japan is the most truly awakened of any Asiatic or non-Christian nation as regards politics, trade, industry, art, literature, and education and all those conditions that go to make up national life, and the most completely furnished in all those different forms which national life must possess. Japan is the most highly de-

veloped, the most politically developed nation outside of the range
of Christian nations.

Politically, it is more independent than any other Asiatic nation. In no other nation does the tide of common life flow more
freely than in Japan. It is more sensitive from circumference
to center than any of the older and non-Christian nations. Its
doors are open to a wider range of interests than any other
pagan nation. Its hospitality to strangers from the outside
world is more hearty, more intelligent, and more genuine than in
any other Asiatic nation. The mobility of the social life of the
nation is greater than that of Korea, China, India, or any other
nation outside of Christendom. There is a freer flow of population from place to place and from class to class. Men not only
move from the lower class to the higher classes, but also move
from the higher classes down to the lower classes. There is a
greater freedom in the movement of Japanese population toward
outside countries, back and forth, than is the case in any other
pagan nation. And the approach of Japan to the Christian world
is greater, is closer, than that of any other Asiatic nation. They
have entered more heartily into sympathy with our ideals of
national life than any other outside nation. And Christian nations have made greater concessions to Japan and have granted
more privileges to Japan and have accorded to Japan a higher
standing than has been the case with any other heathen nation
during Christian history.

If you should enter into the interior and study the organized
forms of national life in Japan, you would find it modern in
every respect. They have the most thoroughly organized system
of industry outside of the Christian nations. We heard to-day
that this city, whose hospitality we are enjoying, produces five
hundred different kinds of articles of commerce. That speaks
well for this city. You will find in Japan a greater number of
articles produced by her system of industry—a greater variety
in her industrial productions—than you will find anywhere else
outside of Christendom. You will find the channels of commerce greater and the facilities for trade greater than anywhere
else. You will find public opinion more effective and influencing
a larger number of people than anywhere else outside of Christendom. You will find freer forms of government, parliamentary

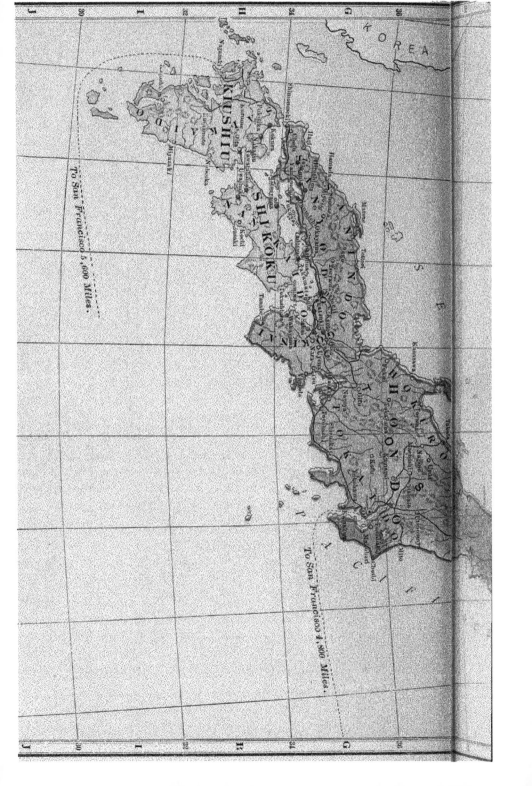

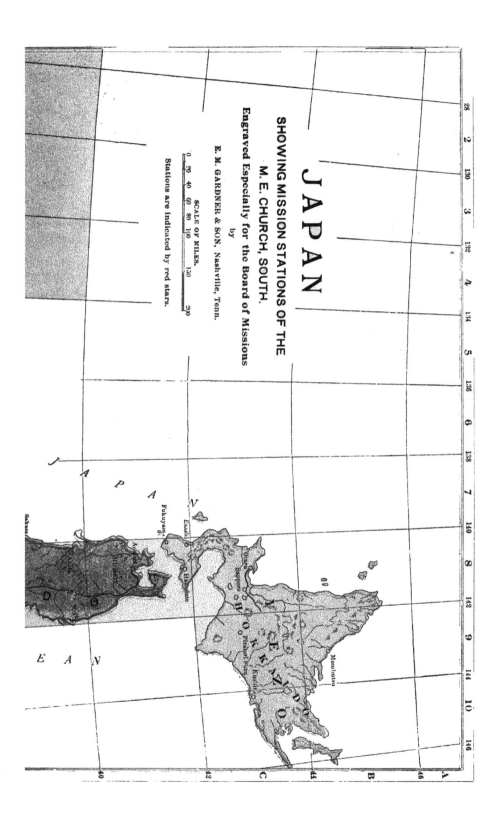

JAPAN

SHOWING MISSION STATIONS OF THE
M. E. CHURCH, SOUTH.

Engraved Especially for the Board of Missions

by

E. M. GARDNER & SON, Nashville, Tenn.

SCALE OF MILES.

0   20   40   60   80   100   120   200

Stations are indicated by red stars.

and constitutional government, than you will find anywhere else. And you will find, also, that Japan as a nation has broken away from her past more thoroughly than any other Asiatic nation. In every respect the changes that have been brought about in Japan have rendered Japan ripe for Christian conquest.

And if it is the business of the Church to save men and make Christian all of the relationships of men, Japan stands out as the greatest challenge, the most urgent challenge that we can find in the whole unevangelized world.

Of course the Church, in its primary and fundamental work, addresses itself to the human heart; and if we succeed in the Christian conquest of Japan, we must address our gospel to the heart, the national heart, in the secret chambers of which the destinies of men and of nations are forged. And if you bring the gospel to bear upon the heart of Japan, alongside of Confucianism and Buddhism, you can reach more effectively the goal for which we aim. We have reached more effectively the heart of the people than either of these traditional religions, because Buddhism and Confucianism are not clear with regard to the vital point in religion—that is, the relation between the soul, the individual soul, and God. It seems that Christianity is making that clear; that Christianity is winning triumphs over the heart of individuals in Japan.

But if you were to ask me to-day whether Japan as a nation is capable of progress, after study and observation in that empire for many years, I would be compelled to answer: "I do not know." And if you were to ask me if Japan is capable of assimilating Christian civilization, I would be compelled to answer: "I do not know." I do know that Japan has assimilated two civilizations: the civilization of India and the civilization of China. And I believe that Japan has sufficient national energy to assimilate Christian civilization; but that question is not yet settled in Japan.

But if you were to ask me, "Is Japan capable of the higher life? Is she capable of Christian service? Is she capable of devotion to Christ in evangelistic effort and in work with and for the Church?" I would be able to answer that question in the affirmative, and say that there is not the slightest bit of doubt about it. [Applause.] That question is settled in Japan as re-

13

gards the individual and as regards the Church. Japanese Christians as individuals and as a Church are capable of all that the spiritual life means.

But we are facing, in this age, conditions of great national importance, and I'll bring that close enough home to bring before your minds the difficulties we have in the enterprise of conquering Japan for Christ. Take capital, for instance—the last, almost the last, young giant that has sprung up in the world, and which must be brought into subserviency to Christ. It is the great force of the modern world. It is a new force in the situation in Japan.

If I were to take you to the city of Osaka, the Manchester of Japan, where capital is busy at work in industrial production, you would soon feel the necessity of bringing capital there under the control of the gospel of Jesus Christ. It is attracting large numbers to the city, away from their homes in the interior, largely women and children. You would find that they work twelve hours a day; you would find that they receive as their wage six or seven cents a day; you would find that they have no Sabbath rest; you would find that they are compelled to sleep thirty or forty in a room 18x18 feet in size; you would find these people enslaved by capital and subjected to all the temptations of the city.

So the great problem in Japan, because the future Japan is to be one in which capital controls, is to Christianize capital; and I affirm that, inasmuch as capital has attracted people to the city in Japan and people to the city in America, capital must take care of these people; and inasmuch as capital has created city problems, it is responsible for the solution of city problems; and inasmuch as capital has produced the necessity for benevolence, capital must provide benevolence and meet the needs of the people it has attracted to the city.

For example, take in the interior, where a man or a woman was cared for by kindred—God's natural surroundings, which he places about every individual life born into the world. When capital attracts that life away from the home, where domestic manufacturing has been carried on (and most of the beautiful things you get from Japan are manufactured in the home); when capital attracts those people away from the home into the city, where they have no homes and no kindred—then benevolence becomes a necessity. And inasmuch as capital has produced that necessity, capital is responsible for meeting the needs; and until capital is Christianized in the cities of Japan, there will be no hospitals, there will be no charity institutions of any sort, as there are none at present in the great cities there.

Not only is it necessary for us to Christianize capital and to follow those lines that have been opened up to us through capital in Japan, but we must do that in this country. And now that the laymen have united their forces with the forces already at work, the conquest of nations for Christ is on in earnest.

But there is one great agency that has not yet been consecrated and dedicated to the service of evangelizing the outside nations; and that is wealth. Can you single out to me any great gift that has been donated for foreign missionary work in our Church? The largest gift I have any knowledge of was a gift of $25,000.

But to-day, if we had the capital to provide for our institutions in Japan and to equip them, they would take first rank in the building up of a Christian young manhood and young womanhood in that country.

And what is it that has attracted the Japanese to the United States? It is our capital. They feel the economic pressure in their own country, and come here because our capital attracts them. I believe that, if it is in the order of God's providence that they should be attracted here, the Church should recognize it as the providence of God, and not shut the doors in their faces, but allow the Japanese to come in—under proper regulation, of course—and through that body of Japanese attracted to our nation reach the Japanese in their own nation.

The Laymen's Movement has this significance, if nothing else: that we must look to larger agencies for the reaching of nations than the mere preaching of the gospel through the ordained ministry in our great Christian conquest. When we think of it, that has been so with the conversion of the negro. The negro was not converted as a race by sending foreign missionaries to him; but, in the providence of God, he was brought into our midst, and there brought into contact with Christianity.

The broad intercourse between Japan, China, and Korea and

the United States is one of the greatest channels for assimilating Christian civilization on the part of these nations. I trust that this way will be opened up again, that the doors will not be closed, and that through the Japanese coming to this country and attending our universites and dwelling in our midst and then returning to their own country we may reach a larger number with the gospel than we can through the ministry.

I wish to mention, in conclusion, another fact with regard to Japan. Unlike any other Asiatic nation, and unlike any other non-Christian power, it has placed emphasis upon efficiency in all of its departments of national life. So impressed were some of the great statesmen of the West with the national efficiency displayed in the war with Russia that they advocated the doing away with party politics, that the nations in the West might have the efficiency displayed by Japan in the East. So great was her efficiency in her medical department that one of our great American doctors, a representative of the nations which have taught the Japanese the medical science, has brought before our government their efficiency in medical service during the war. They have laid so much emphasis upon efficiency in education that the British government has sent a commission to make a study of the Japanese national system, to report back to the government at home. And so great stress does Japan lay upon efficiency in commerce that she is spending more money to-day than the United States for the education of young men for business, imitating Germany in that respect, and providing education for commercial pursuits in her institutions, where thousands of young men who propose entering business life can receive a training. In these schools Japan lays so much stress upon efficiency that it is very difficult for one to secure a position as teacher. The standard set for all schools is a very high scale, and the school which does not measure up to that standard is placed under disability. So much stress, all the way through national life, is laid upon efficiency that, if the Church expects to impress its message upon Japan to-day, there is one thing that we must not overlook—the work of the Church must have the stamp of efficiency upon it.

If you take the history of our own college, our own school in Japan (the only school for boys representing our Church) and see how it has struggled up, in spite of its inefficiency, to a place of first rank in the Japanese Empire, you can realize what that institution might have accomplished if it had been amply equipped, and if it had been able to free itself from the disability placed upon it by the Japanese government because of its inefficiency, and if it had been able to take a place alongside the Japanese institutions in its curriculum and in its equipment. But that has not been the case; it has been a school that has worked its way up through poverty, and having no equipment practically except the character and the faith and the devotion of the men who constituted its faculty. When the Minister of Education went through the building and talked with the professors and saw our student body, he said: "I want to say frankly to you, as a minister of education for the empire of Japan, I admire this institution, and I congratulate you on the work you have done with your equipment." But, brethren, we cannot address ourselves as a Church to the Japanese people through the educational agencies we have there unless we equip our institutions and do first-class educational work in every respect.

Our college has stood for advanced work in every respect, and has tried to keep abreast of the age. It has combined this idea of scholarship with evangelical religion. And from time to time, under these limitations, we have had revivals of religion, and the college has become noted throughout the empire for its warmth of evangelical religion in its faculty and in its student body. And we believe that, if the Christian Church can have the efficiency in our institution that the other institutions of Japan have, it will be able to obtain recognition of the Japanese government and will occupy a place among Far Eastern nations.

But I want to stress this point: We must emphasize efficiency more in our missionary work. There are three aspects of missionary work—worship, teaching, and beneficence.

I think the missionary body makes a deep impression upon the Japanese people as regards worship; they are devout, and they lead the people to worship the one true God devoutly. Everywhere Christian worship makes a deep impression on national life.

The missionaries are beneficent; they are the go-betweens, standing between the nations in Europe and America and the Asiatic nations; and, consequently, missionaries have been peacemakers. They are the friends of the people, and the people have learned to appreciate the missionary as a friend and to look to him as their counselor and one who has deep sympathy with their aspirations and interests.

But the missionary body in Japan is not as efficient as it should be for teaching. When one of their own sages sits down before his Sacred Book and begins to teach it, there is one thing that Asiatics have always required of him—a thorough knowledge of that book. I believe that, if we equipped our missionaries all more thoroughly with a knowledge of the Bible, and with a knowledge of the religion they go to teach, they could present themselves to the Japanese as a body of thoroughly qualified teachers of the Sacred Book of the West; and that the general efficiency of the missionary body would be far greater than it is to-day.

The Laymen's Movement can stand back of this missionary movement, and make it more efficient; and it is largely with you whether or not it will be made more efficient. It depends upon you as to whether or not we shall be able to give the Japanese people more efficient institutions from now on. It is in your power to make our work more effective; for we are not addressing ourselves to the Japanese people as effectively as we should or as the rising standard in that country demands.

XV.

BRAZIL: A BUGLE CALL TO VICTORY.

And permit me, in this connection, to say that the Roman Catholic prejudice is not what you would expect it to be in Brazil. Largely, the people are in our favor. Nine-tenths of the educated people of Brazil are the friends of the Protestants. They have seen Romanism as Romanism is in a Roman Catholic country, and they have become tired of it. After being in Brazil some four or five years, I thought that the Brazilians were skeptical, and I at once rushed to the conclusion: "Why, the French lesson is to be repeated here in Brazil." We no longer have a Church of State; but the intelligent classes are driven from the Church into infidelity and into atheism. And permit me to say that Roman Catholicism is a thousand times better than skepticism. But I soon discovered that the men I thought skeptical were not skeptical at all, but had faith in God; but they had no faith in the work of the Church. And they watched the missionaries as we watch a spy. And the eyes of the thousands of people of Brazil are on us as the representatives of the cross in a way that they are fixed on no others in society.

(200)

XV.

BRAZIL: A BUGLE CALL TO VICTORY.

REV. E. A. TILLY, ASHLAND, VA.

Mr. Chairman, Ladies and Gentlemen: It is my pleasure to speak to you this afternoon on our South American neighbor, Brazil; and I wish to say to you frankly that the work of the Southern Methodist Church in Brazil is such that the missionaries can approve, and such that you can approve. From your missionary force in Brazil you never hear a despondent note. There is victory in every conversation, and we believe in the triumph of the gospel in the land of the Southern Cross.

Some twenty-one years ago it was my good pleasure to sail from Newport News, in company with the sainted Granbery, for Rio de Janeiro. Arriving in that city, I found we had some one hundred and eighty members. To-day in the republic of Brazil you have over six thousand members; you have an Annual Conference and you have a mission.

During all these years (and I believe that the Board of Missions will bear me out in this assertion) our reports have been excellent; the spirit of complaint has been banished from the hearts of our membership. We see difficulties, but we do not lose faith because of those difficulties; rather, we face the difficulties and with faith in God we conquer them.

With our small membership in the beginning, and with our increased membership to-day, the Church expects much of its working force in Brazil; and I say to you this afternoon, as Southern Methodists, you can always expect good reports from Brazil.

Our men and women who are laboring in Brazil are faithful in the discharge of their duties. They may make mistakes, but

(201)

they work in the fear of God, and they have the results to show for the work done.

For a few minutes permit me to call your attention to our college work at Juiz de Fora, the Granbery College. Will you Southern Methodists believe that you have a university in Brazil? Possibly in the Granbery College you have the largest enrollment in any of your foreign fields. I do not say positively that you have, but two weeks ago I received a letter from Dr. Tarboux, the President of Granbery College, in which he declares they have three hundred and five pupils in all the departments. We have our Preparatory school of three years; we have our College course of six years, modeled after the German system; we have a course of Pharmacy, three years; Dentistry, three years; we have our Theological course of three years; and we expect, in the providence of God, that the time is not far distant when we shall have a Medical school and a Law school, and our university will be complete.

We expect these things of the Board. If the Board does not give them to us, we will get them from the Church here or in Brazil. We are going ahead with the system we have begun. In this laymen's meeting, permit me to say, gentlemen, that you have a splendid opportunity to give us a Dentist. We have asked, year after year, for a Dentist in the Granbery, but he has not been forthcoming. We have asked for a Pharmacist, but he has not been forthcoming. You laymen to-day, if you could see how well your work has succeeded in Brazil, would give us a Dentist and a Pharmacist.

And, while I am on this line, I will say that in the city of Rio de Janeiro we have one of the best publishing houses of our Church. Yet, for years and years, we have been embarrassed. Some three thousand dollars has been hanging over our heads; and though we have had loyal agents and hard-working men, their whole life has been troubled because of these debts. I thank our Heavenly Father that at the expiration of this year the publishing house in Rio de Janeiro will not owe a dollar.

But, as a Laymen's Convention, I say to you to-day, we need the preacher who has been the agent of the publishing house for a number of years in the active affairs of evangelization. Give us a layman for that work in Rio. You have the ability; embarrass us not, as preachers of the gospel, with this secular work. I will not admit for a moment that the preacher is not capacitated to do this work as well as you are. We are capacitated, as our good Bishop said this morning, but "we have other fish to fry." We should be preaching the gospel to the people and not be looking after the business affairs of the Church; that is your business.

Let me say a word in regard to our educational work. (The ladies are not represented on this occasion, and so I know they will not hear what I have to say in regard to their work in Brazil.) Their mission fields speak for themselves. The women of our Church have splendid educational plants in Brazil. And, let me say to you as a representative of the Board of Missions, they are doing splendid work. Your school at Petropolis has over one hundred young women, the brightest, the fairest in Brazil. The work is excellent; just as good as you will get in any of our colleges in the United States, up to the freshman or sophomore year.

In the city of Rio de Janeiro you have three schools. You are doing excellent work in these three schools. You have more than two hundred children in attendance in the city. You have a magnificent college at Juiz de Fora, your own property. You have one hundred girls in that school. It is splendidly managed and noble work is being done. In the capital of the great State of Minas Geraes we have our Isabella Hendrix College, possibly the best school the women have in that vast republic. You are doing excellent work there. You have some one hundred pupils here. In Piracicaba you have your best school, with about two hundred pupils. In the city of Ribeirao Preto you have a magnificent girls' school. I do not know whether you women belong to a Woman's Laymen's Movement or not, but see to it that your Board of Missions has its own property in the city of Ribeirao Preto.

Run down to our independent mission in Rio Grande do Sul, and there you have a good Church, and the school doing fine educational work, under the control of the representative of the Woman's Board. Your work is excellent in that city. You have over two hundred pupils, and those pupils are being brought into the Church.

And let me say in this connection that the woman's work in Brazil has largely broken down the prejudice of Roman Catholics against our schools. Your women have exercised good judgment; they have made few mistakes; and the sensible Brazilian of to-day recognizes that his daughter can be sent to no better place to receive instruction than to one of our Protestant schools.

And permit me, in this connection, to say that the Roman Catholic prejudice is not what you would expect it to be in Brazil. Largely, the people are in our favor. Nine-tenths of the educated people of Brazil are the friends of the Protestants. They have seen Romanism as Romanism is in a Roman Catholic country, and they have become tired of it. After being in Brazil some four or five years, I thought that the Brazilians were skeptical, and I at once rushed to the conclusion: "Why, the French lesson is to be repeated here in Brazil."

We no longer have a Church of State; but the intelligent classes are driven from the Church into infidelity and into atheism. And permit me to say that Roman Catholicism is a thousand times better than skepticism. [Applause.] But I soon discovered that the men I thought skeptical were not skeptical at all, but had faith in God; but they had no faith in the work of the Church. And they watched the missionaries as we watch a spy. And the eyes of the thousands of people of Brazil are on us as the representatives of the cross in a way that they are fixed on no others in society.

I am glad that it is that way. I am glad that our lives, if we would have them what we would make them, have to be lived under the white light of such an examination. They look for faults; if they find no faults, they give themselves to Christ. In other words, the people do not study the Bible; but they do study the representatives of the cross. And what we are, that is what the people think can be done by the gospel of the Lord Jesus Christ.

I sometimes tremble. I sometimes feel a weakness and despair that it should be so. But many a time has the very thought that the eyes of the Brazilian are fixed on my life led me to do my duty in a way that it would never have been done had I been working in the United States, where the little things of

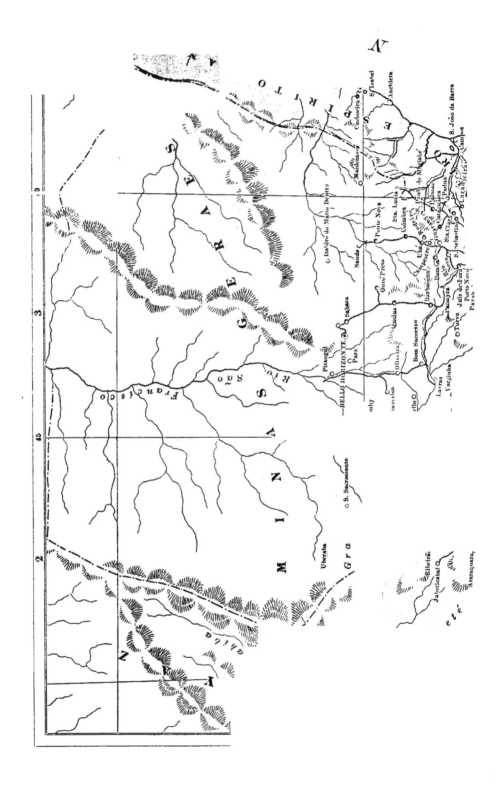

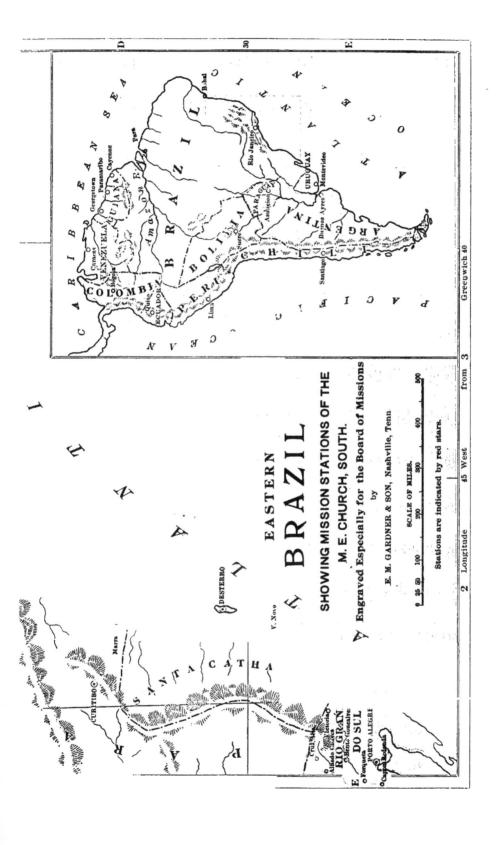

EASTERN

BRAZIL

SHOWING MISSION STATIONS OF THE
M. E. CHURCH, SOUTH.

Engraved Especially for the Board of Missions
by

E. M. GARDNER & SON, Nashville, Tenn.

SCALE OF MILES.

Stations are indicated by red stars.

life are passed over unnoticed. But it is not that way in a country like Brazil. Your every action is weighed. Your every word is listened to. And they form their ideas of the Christian religion by the life you lead. If it is a godly life, men have godly ideas. If the life maker is not up to the standard of the Christ of Christianity, people have wrong ideas of our religion. I regret that it is that way for the present. The time is not far distant when the people shall read their Bibles, and when they shall form their ideas of religion not from our lives, but from the true record as given in the Gospel.

Now, one word in regard to our publishing interests in the city of Rio. For years we have published our Christian papers. We have our *Sunday School Review,* we have our literature for the children in the Sabbath schools, our juvenile papers, and all that; but we want to reach out. We want to get up on a higher plane; we want to do more for the intelligent classes of Brazil; we wish to do more for our own people.

And I state here to-day that there has been a mention that other fields are so great that we, as a mission, cannot expect much from our Board. But O, you laymen are marshaling around the cross of Christ in this movement! Every missionary in the foreign field takes a new inspiration. He is ready for the fight. There is a new power upon us to-day, and we can enter the battle with more faith, with a greater hope, and our disposition is such that we can love the men and women we are working for as we have never loved them before. [Applause.]

Now, our publishing interests in Rio demand your attention. Think of it! in Brazil, with over twenty-two per cent of the people knowing how to read and write, with only one Church, and with a publishing plant that is not comparable to the others in that great republic, we should take the lead as Southern Methodists. We should have an excellent publishing plant in the city of Rio. We should publish our own literature. We should publish our own books. Year after year we have manuscripts to come in on us, and sometimes we send them to Nashville, but our Missionary Secretaries keep them for years. We haven't the means to publish them here. We rarely ever have a Brazilian on the ground to go over the manuscripts in this work.

In carrying the gospel to strangers you must carry it pure

and complete and perfect. We do not want mistakes in our literature in Brazil; for the Brazilian eye is open, and sometimes a little error, sometimes the wrong use of a word, brings a sneer of ridicule from the educated Brazilian, and that book is done for; it has no circulation. We want the books to be reviewed by Brazilian scholars. We want the printing done on our own presses and the proof-reading done not by our own representatives, but by educated Brazilians.

We wish to go to the people prepared thoroughly for the work that is before us; but our publishing plant certainly is not adequate for the work that God intended us to do. I throw this thought out for you laymen to think on. Now, isn't this a "bugle call to victory?"

I tell you, Brazil is ready to receive the gospel, and the only reason that the gospel is not received to-day in Brazil is that, as Protestant Christians, we have not done what we could have done, and what I believe, in the grace of God, we will do in the future. Not only the Southern Methodist Church, but other Churches—the Northern Presbyterian, the Southern Presbyterian, the Southern Baptist, the Protestant Episcopal—are already working in that land. But let me tell you that we are not quarreling with one another as Christians; but we are shoulder to shoulder, working together to plant the cross of Christ in the land of the Southern Cross, and we are going to do it. [Applause.]

You hear no uncertain sounds from our representatives of any of our Mission Boards in Brazil. We are hopeful; we are looking at the bright side of the picture. But do not think for a minute that we do not have our hardships, that we do not see the dark side. We do. But, on the other hand, there is so much more to hope for, and the pleasure is so much greater in doing what we have the power to do, in doing the work of Christ, that we think not of these things. We look at the bright side of the picture, and that is the way to do the work. [Great applause.]

XVI.

CUBA: ON THE FIRING LINE.

Cuba must be evangelized. This work is being pushed with might and main. She has turned from Romanism and stands on the threshold of materialism and general indifference, and challenges evangelical America. Such a challenge must fire the heart of every Christian. We offered to buy places in the ranks of the army that went over to battle for Cuba's political freedom. Shall we now fail to come to the front to do battle for the reason of the faith that is within us? Were there no other reason for organized, energetic, and immediate reënforcement of our forces in Cuba and throughout Latin America, all-sufficient would be the fact that these countries and Anglo-Saxon America are coming together at a rate of speed that is astounding. Reference to consular reports will convince any one of this fact—that we are perhaps facing the most serious problem we have yet known. Of the one hundred and fifty millions of people in the Western Hemisphere, sixty millions are Latin-American; of the twelve million square miles of American territory, nine millions are Latin-American. The center of population is moving South; emigration is changing from the West to the South. Its vast forests of timber lands and the fabulous wealth of its minerals are luring on the people of the North. The North in turn has attractions for the Latin Americans; they are coming to our borders faster than we can appreciate. As our people turn to these countries, frightful are the evidences that Christless, Sabbathless, immoral, rum-sodden Latin America may be the tomb of our boasted morality. There is something in the glamour of the unbridled vice of these countries that too often proves fatal to the sons of the North. Religious life-saving stations should be established immediately, all the way from the Rio Grande on the north to Tierra del Fuego on the south.

(208)

XVI.

CUBA: ON THE FIRING LINE.

REV. W. G. FLETCHER.

In the year 1898 the American people, convinced that Spain's cup of iniquity in the Western Hemisphere had been filled, caused their President to declare that Cuba was and of a right ought to be free and independent. This declaration was backed by the combined material and moral strength of the people unto whose ears had come Cuba's oft-repeated cry for freedom. From a reunited people the call for troops was answered. Sons of every State in the Union rushed to the front. Rapid and heavy were the strokes of the young giant of the West, and in less than a hundred days the mediæval shackles had been struck from the last of Spain's colonies in the New World.

For a century Cuba's path had been strewn with the corpses of both her own sons and the sons of other countries who had dared raise voice and strength against Spanish injustice. It is true that historians have not as yet classed Cuba's struggle for liberty with those of some other lands; but if voluntary personal sufferings and sacrifices mean anything, Cuba may justly claim for her patriots the admiration of the whole world. They sealed with death in a thousand private executions and public encounters their protest against the Spanish policy of plunder and barbarism, and saw in those shameless outrages the harbinger of a better day for the land they loved, calling to the world to witness the justice of their claim. The heroism of these unheralded martyrs is not to be despised by the sons of the men who echoed the cry: "Give me liberty or give me death!"

The breaking of the bonds of political oppression was merely the first step in the work of truly liberating that unhappy island. Its liberators faced possibly the most serious sanitary problem that man ever attempted to solve. The lowering of the Spanish flag marked the beginning of a terrific struggle with giants of filth, poverty, and disease. The work of sanitation, resuscitation, and rehabilitation was begun, aided by such acts of national and individual benevolence as have never been equaled. In order that the thousands of suffering ones might be fed, housed, and healed, shiploads of supplies were hurried south, and with lavish hand destitute Cuban and Spaniard were cared for without reference to political opinion. Within two years towns and cities of proverbial reputation for uncleanliness, where yellow fever had held high carnival for centuries, were converted into semitropical winter resorts. Prisons were not only cleared of their victims, who had waited years for trial, but were renovated and remodeled. Hospitals that had been the reverse of what such institutions are supposed to be were equipped with the best of modern materials and appliances. The public school system that had been a disgrace even to the Spanish carpetbagger government was reorganized, modernly equipped, and given an appropriation of four million dollars. Credit and commercial standing were restored, and the young republic entered upon a career of prosperity that was to astonish the world. The political conditions that shocked the world were nothing to be compared with the sanitary conditions that were found to prevail throughout the island; nor were these to be mentioned in the same breath with the moral and religious abandonment that was revealed. A faint idea is given by saying that it was a case of effete Romanism ministered by a priesthood utterly devoid of any standard of morality.

Many an American Roman Catholic has blushed for shame when brought face to face with some of even the minor evidences of the moral degradation of Cuba's priesthood. The very foundations of reverence had been swept away by the tide of the profligacy of the corrupt carpetbagger priesthood. The confessionals were dark with the blood of Cuban patriots. In the Cuban heart this so-called "Christianity" had been abolished; it had become a menace to society. A shocking per cent of the people were without names for the reason that exorbitant prices had been put upon matrimony, although the rite was declared a sacrament. The lot of the living was to support this parasite fastened upon them by law; upon the dying were attached the horrors of purgatory. No informed person will deny that for centuries Cuba was plundered by Rome. Every known means of extorting money was practiced. The altars of pretended blessing were turned into a means of destroying the foundation of society and government— the home. Children were denied a name, but were taxed in birth, taxed in life, and given purgatory as an inheritance in death.

Cuba became Protestant at heart long ago. Her thinking people said: "If this be the revelation of God to the world, we will reject it and take our chances; we will choose in favor of legitimate homes and educated children." This class turned to Renan, Voltaire, and others of the kind; the ignorant toiled on in slavish fear, but sullen protest. Cuba's protest was founded on and sustained by French infidelity. Is it not strange that evangelical America did not furnish this unhappy people the basis for their protest against the oppression and corruption of the Romish Church? On the contrary, we have seemed to be rather amused at the spasmodic efforts of these people in grasping for the Light. For a century we have let them move on toward the doom of a people who know not God, little thinking that in our unconcern we might be hewing out the sepulcher for the hope of the Western Hemisphere—evangelical Christianity.

Of the dozen Latin-American republics, not one is free. Their political freedom was only the first step toward that point. When the single-starred banner that Carlos Manuel de Cespedes flung to the breeze in 1868 had at last been recognized, not as a belligerents' banner, but as the emblem of a newborn nation, and Cuba's sons were shouting "Viva Cuba libre!" Cuba was not free, as a matter of fact. The soul of war was gone; her fight for independence had been won; it was certain she would never again feel the hand of Spanish oppression; but she was not free. She was still in the gall of bitterness and the bond of iniquity. The fight for her freedom was still to be made, not against flesh and blood, but against the powers and principalities of unrighteousness.

While the ravages of a most inhuman warfare were still wasting the land, before starvation had been checked, while pestilence walked at noonday and yellow fever was striking down its victims in the parks and streets, attention was being given to plans for the campaign that was to bring Cuba into real liberty—the liberty wherewith Christ makes free. Amid this danger and desolation the standard of Methodism was planted and our great Church called upon for men and means to sustain it. Less than ten years have passed, but Methodism is to-day established in its own quarters in each of the six provincial capitals and in all of the first- and second-class towns, and even in the villages and country districts of some provinces; she owns above two hundred thousand dollars' worth of property, a fair per cent of which was raised on the field; she has four day schools, in which are being trained hundreds of Cuba's brightest youths; she has three thousand members and more than a thousand candidates. The fact of signal success should be cause of renewed effort till the entire country is not only evangelized but thoroughly Christianized. There are the strongest of reasons why we should build in Havana a church and college in keeping with our needs and ability. That city has a population equal to that of Georgia's five largest cities combined; but the best we have been able to secure for the first and only Methodist church of this great Babylon is a hall upstairs. Our college should be equipped for the preparation of Cuban workers and the education of the ever-increasing number of American children of the capital city.

Cuba must be evangelized. This work is being pushed with might and main. She has turned from Romanism and stands on the threshold of materialism and general indifference, and challenges evangelical America. Such a challenge must fire the heart of every Christian. We offered to buy places in the ranks of the army that went over to battle for Cuba's political freedom. Shall we now fail to come to the front to do battle for the reason of the faith that is within us? Were there no other reason for organized, energetic, and immediate reënforcement of our forces in Cuba and throughout Latin America, all-sufficient would be the fact that these countries and Anglo-Saxon America are coming together at a rate of speed that is astounding. Reference to consular reports will convince any one of this fact—that we are perhaps facing the most serious problem we have yet known. Of the one hundred and fifty millions of people in the Western Hemisphere, sixty millions are Latin-American; of the twelve million square miles of American territory, nine millions are Latin-American. The center of population is moving South; emigration is changing from the West to the South. Its vast forests of timber lands and the fabulous wealth of its minerals are luring on the people of the North. The North in turn has attractions for the

Latin Americans; they are coming to our borders faster than we can appreciate. As our people turn to these countries, frightful are the evidences that Christless, Sabbathless, immoral, rum-sodden Latin America may be the tomb of our boasted morality. There is something in the glamour of the unbridled vice of these countries that too often proves fatal to the sons of the North. Religious life-saving stations should be established immediately, all the way from the Rio Grande on the north to Tierra del Fuego on the south.   .

A tottering wreck of what had once been a splendid business man stood one morning in Santiago de Cuba under a sign that read "Iglesia Metodista," and said with broken voice: "If this sign had hung here five years ago, I should not be to-day returning to the States on a charity ticket to die a pauper's death. This sign would have called up memories of home, mother, and righteousness. Why," continued the poor fellow, "does not the Church look after us fellows as do the beer concerns?" An alarming per cent of your sons are making moral shipwreck on the shores just to the south of you. To stay the tidal wave southward is utterly impossible; wealth, adventure, riches, and romance are calling. A clash of character is inevitable and near at hand. We have underestimated conditions in the South. We congratulate ourselves upon our stability, prosperity, and general worth as we think of the spring, summer, and fall revolutions that rend these Latin-American countries and discredit them in the eyes of the world. We say: "What a pity that they are not of our blood!" O slow of heart are we to read the fact that these disgraceful, destructive conditions have their origin in moral unrest and religious poverty and uncertainty!

Take notice that Latin America has invaded our borders and that one colony, though it numbers less than one thousand, is to-day dictating terms to the strongest city in one of our Southern States, saying: "If you allow your State to go for prohibition, we will ruin you financially." The Associated Press dispatches say that the representative citizens of that city have pledged themselves to sustain the immoral contention of this colony. If we cannot cope with this force within our own borders, where the best of influences prevail, what can be expected of us when we attempt to stem the current in a land seemingly devoid of moral conscience? The strange fact is that while Anglo-Saxon America feels itself so eminently superior to Latin America, yet she readily falls into its vices, is not only affected by its infidelity, skepticism, materialism, and general indifference to religion, but immediately begins to participate in its debauchery that destroys mind, soul, and body. We are wont to speculate and discuss at length the "yellow peril" and appear greatly agitated over affairs in the "chrysanthemum kingdom," with our backs to a cloud rising out of the south pregnant with tempests, on whose wings are riding the furies of moral destruction. The great question is: "Shall we save Latin America or be ruined by it?" It is but madness to say that our religious principles are too deeply rooted not to be able to withstand it. The absolute, unvarnished truth is that our people are not withstanding the pressure brought to bear, nor will they be able to maintain their integrity in these morally diseased countries unless reënforced by the very same and only safeguards that sustain them here. Our civilization itself is in danger of being wrecked on a sea that has flowed from an effete Romanism. A long, sad rôle of the victims, some of them the very flower of our civilization, show that our people are in great danger when subjected to the alluring temptations so abundant in those not far-distant Southern lands.

The ever-growing number of tourists so far forget themselves as to make a doer of righteousness in Cuba cry out: "From the American tourist, O Lord, deliver us!" Some of them are a blessing to the missions; but the great majority seem to think that the "narrow sea, like death, divides this heavenly land from ours," and, feeling relieved from all restraint, enter upon the most questionable conduct.

There is no time for a theoretical discussion of gospel work in Cuba and the other Latin-American countries. "But what can be done?" we are constantly asked. "Is it not difficult to persuade a people who have been reared under vitiated Romanism?" "Has not Rome compromised with the pagan rites and customs of these Latin countries, producing a condition of affairs harder to deal with than either paganism or Romanism?" The latter of these questions must be answered in the affirmative. But the opening wedge is to be found in the countries where sin has overreached itself. All the people will not be fooled or oppressed always. In guarded rooms Cuba's sons years ago began to hold privy councils over the political and religious state of affairs. The result was the rejection of Romanism and a declaration that led ultimately to their national independence. In this land at our very door, where baptized paganism fell of its own weight, is offered us a rare opportunity. There we may almost without let or hindrance evangelize and prepare workers for other fields of the kind.

The powers of the commercial world are being brought to bear to turn the trade of these countries from European ports to our own. A glance at the South American consular reports is sufficient to convince one that their efforts are meeting with success. Commerce to-day between Cuba and New York is a thousand times greater than between New York and some of our own Southern States. The answer to our former question, "How shall we evangelize Latin America?" may be found in the success of the commercial world there. Until recent years our commercial houses sent out shopworn goods, sent out by second-rate representatives, often men in search of health, who, after utter failure in competing with Europe's picked men who knew conditions and were prepared to meet them, came back crying: "Nothing can be done. Behold, the sons of Anak inhabit the land!" On the contrary, from the time that first-class goods, properly packed and shipped, were offered by first-class men, the trade began to grow by leaps and bounds.

A cheap or compromising gospel, doled out by shopworn preachers, will never command a hearing in Latin America. A "half loaf" missionary in Cuba is worse than none at all. To attempt to run a mission there with anything save the old-time religion, preached by such men as cannot possibly be spared from the home land, is a sinful waste of money. In the not very distant past a missionary was pictured as a gaunt, resigned, peculiarly attired, cadaverous-looking individual, standing under a palm tree on some wind-swept isle, handing out tracts to a mob of howling savages who would soon pick his unhappy bones and wear them for hair ornaments. This conception was followed by one equally erroneous to the effect that a halo around his head is always visible; that once he sets foot on foreign shore to declare the gospel to those who know it not, he has to give no further attention to his own spiritual welfare; that he is always in a shouting mood; that he is especially cared for by detailed angels and has a private wire on heaven. Now, the solemn fact is that so trying, vexing, and numerous are the problems that confront one, such and so heavy in every sense of the word are daily demands on him, that only the strongest physiques, the best-trained minds, and the bravest and most consecrated hearts should be sent out. Missionary posts are not health resorts.

If a man for any reason can be spared from the home land, don't send him to Cuba. The places and conditions that try men's souls in connection with the work are not all passed yet. The Cuban Mission is full of them, and a man works there under the same conditions and human limitations that he would here. To succeed he must be statesman, prophet, beast of burden, dove of peace, captain of industry, orator, and diplomat. He must have grace, grit, greenbacks, gall, and gumption. A sentimental "hope so" kind of being armed with some patent "get-good-quick-in-my-style" theory can only hope for dismal defeat. O that Cuba might be spared the scourge of "long-haired men and short-haired wom-en"—venders of religious quackeries! But given a worker who combines all the personal qualifications possible by nature and acquisition, and still there is one thing lacking—i. e., a stand for his wares, if you please. The wise commercial house sends out not only the best goods, intrusted to men of capability and con-science, but provides ample means for display and advantageous introduction. The best of goods displayed in a third-rate, smoky boarding house would stand little chance of winning favor. Any success would be at the expense of time and arduous labor on the part of the representative. Such a course would be manifestly the poorest possible business policy. The children of the busi-ness world are in their generation wiser than the children of light. They see to it that their goods are given a setting that is even more attractive than the goods themselves, because it pays; it saves time, it saves money. We may say all we like about the attractive power of the gospel—that it depends not on human con-ditions for success, that the gospel preached with power and dem-onstration of the Spirit will win its way—and still the half will not have been told of the wonders of redeeming love. But is it wise to withhold our means and leave the gospel to win its way against the odds we might remove by the stroke of a pen? Is it fair to the man who binds himself in exile to do your bidding to force him to wear himself out in dreary years of the hardest drudgery, overcoming difficulties that you could remove in an instant? If

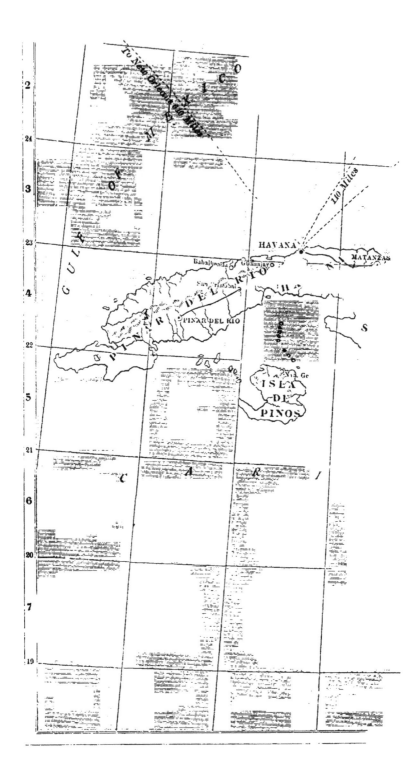

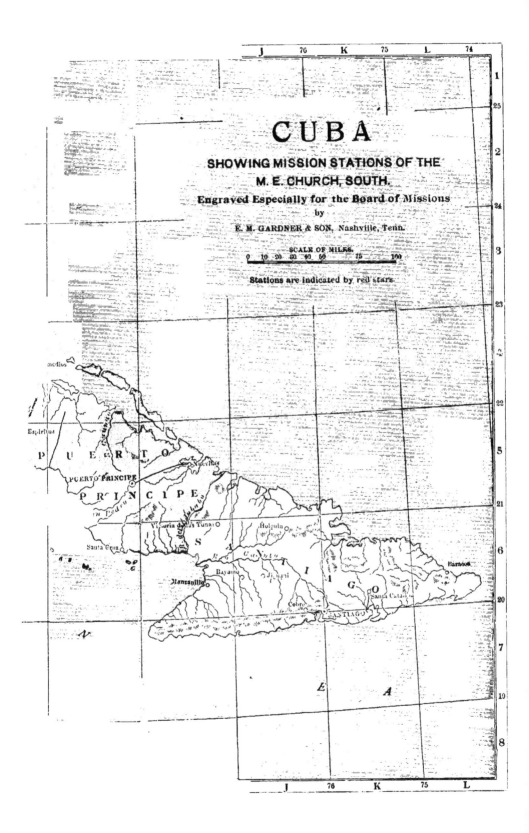

CUBA

SHOWING MISSION STATIONS OF THE
M. E. CHURCH, SOUTH.

Engraved Especially for the Board of Missions
by

E. M. GARDNER & SON, Nashville, Tenn.

SCALE OF MILES.
0 10 20 30 40 50   75   100

Stations are indicated by red stars.

a thousand dollars will do the work to-day that five thousand will one year hence, is it not wise to put in that five thousand to-day and let it do the work of twenty-five thousand ultimately? But the work will be done; it must be done; it is being done. Cuba will yet be free. Methodism is firmly rooted there. In the event of some catastrophe that would cut off all supplies of both men and money from the North, the work would go ahead.

But sometimes the question arises in the minds of the missionaries: "What will become of a Church that commands its men to make 'brick without straw' when the straw is piled high in the home land?" Our three thousand members are paying one hundred cents on the dollar of a heavy assessment for self-support and Church extension. The banner of Methodism flung to the breeze amid the death and desolation of '98 shall not be furled. This statement is backed by three thousand members, a thousand probationers, a host of sympathizers, and some missionaries as efficient and consecrated as ever crossed the seas. At the present outlay of men and money the island will be evangelized, but not Christianized, which is quite a different thing, calling for time, efficient work, and patience. We are winning out in old residences converted into chapels. Business men will readily see that success would crown our efforts with a great saving of time and money in more suitable quarters. The fact must be borne in mind that Roman skill in architecture has exhausted itself in the construction of churches in Latin America. We need to understand that with these people appearances mean everything. It is especially true of these countries that the better the appearances the more decided the success, the better the class of people we are able to reach. It is true "one man is as good as another;" but the higher we strike in mission work, the sooner are we able to evangelize a town, province, or nation.

Our response to the call in Cuba has been more generous than for other fields. We have spent a quarter of a million dollars there in less than ten years; but American beer concerns spent a million in only a few months after the war, and are satisfied with their returns. The question of the evangelization of all Latin America will be largely answered in Cuba. An intensive policy has been adopted.

Reports from one district last year showed an increase of nearly a hundred per cent in membership and an average contribution

of $17.10 per member. Three churches and a parsonage were
built with funds raised on the field. We come not to tell you
of an "open door" and of what could be done if we only had men
and means; we come with the stirring message that the whole
side of the house dropped out and we went in, and that our glorious gospel is repeating its record of liberation.

Cuba, though rich in romance, dark with four centuries of trag-
edy, and fraught with unbounded possibilities for good or evil,
is not unlike her score of sister republics. Christ has been laid
away in the tomb of paganism and the door piled high with the
stones of superstition and compromises. He has to be resurrect-
ed; he must come into a new heritage as Latin America proclaims
her living Lord. Thus shall the land of our fathers be saved from
an impending calamity; and instead of being ruined by those
countries, she will have saved them. There our Lord has lain for
centuries as surely buried as when he lay in the tomb of Joseph
of Arimathea. The citadels about his sepulcher must be taken;
the stones must be rolled away—not by angel hands. This honor
belongs to your sons; but as they go forth as modern crusaders,
not to wrench the empty tomb from infidels, but to liberate the
reburied Christ, Cuba Methodism is mustering her forces; and
when the assaults are being made and the walls stormed, above the
din and roar of battle a friendly note shall be heard; and as the
souls of the crusaders, struggling with the fury of despair against
the walls that encircled the empty tomb, were fired to almost
superhuman effort and immediate success by the sound of God-
frey's silver bugles ringing over the desert air, so shall your sons
be quickened by Cuban allies.

In that unfortunate island a thousand superstitions must be
buried, the hosts of darkness slain with the sword of the Spirit,
and in this work more than one man must lie down to sleep by
the summer seas that gird the unhappy isle. But already the star
of hope that shone above this plundered land through its long,
dark night of sorrow begins to dim because the Sun of Righteousness is rising with healing in his wings. The mountain peaks
are turning to burnished gold, the children in the valley of oppression are lifting their tear-stained faces as they hear the watch-
men on the towers calling them to rise and put on the garments
of righteousness and gird themselves about, that the day of their
deliverance has come.

XVII.

MEDICAL WORK IN THE ORIENT.

Where there are no licenses required to practice medicine, where superstition and gross ignorance combine to allow anything to be done which is dictated by the priest-physician and meddlesome midwife, where there is no such thing as a healthy public opinion, there are the very elements in which the charlatan can flourish and pursue his abominable and uefarious and deadly traffic. Here is far more than mere cruelty and immorality; it is touching the secret springs of a nation's life. If the wife and mother be degraded, love cannot flourish, and the home is blasted; if the home is blasted, the national unit of strength is destroyed, and there is moral decay. This is exactly the sight with which we are confronted in China and Korea to-day: The sick and injured of those lands are crushed like pack ice between two approaching icebergs. On the one side is disease, claiming from them their life; on the other, the less agonizing attempts at treatment. Their diagnosis of approaching death is none too certain; so it often happens that the closing hours or days are spent in terrible discomfort and pain, and the end is hastened by shameful neglect. Mentally contrast such scenes with those in the home lands when relatives and friends are passing from us. Here all is done in those closing hours which love and forethought can devise for the amelioration of pain and the quiet peacefulness of the sick one; there it is noise and din, wailing and mourning, cold and neglect, utter and hopeless darkness.

(220)

XVII.

MEDICAL WORK IN THE ORIENT.

DR. T. F. STALEY, BRISTOL, TENN.

 As a rule, physicians are not a success as public speakers, and I am no exception; but when the invitation was extended me to attend this Conference and say something of my impressions concerning my recent trip to the Orient in company with my good friend, Dr. Lambuth, I considered it my duty as well as my great pleasure to accept this opportunity to raise my voice in behalf of missions.

Emerson says: "The great crises of life are not marriages and deaths, but some afternoon at the turn of the road, when your life finds new thoughts and impulses; such crises occur as a man hears the strong crying of a great need unrealized before, and which he is conscious could be met by his own life service." It was thus that I felt when the call came to me to go to the Orient to inspect the hospitals and medical work there, with the hope of returning and more widely interesting the medical men of our Southland in this great work. I was impressed more and more on my recent visit, where I could view the situation face to face, that our nation is divinely guided for a divine purpose.

I have never feared that the American physician would fail to answer any questions at home or abroad which destiny or fate placed upon him, never doubted but that he would use his scientific knowledge more and more for the betterment of all mankind, and that the Orient—yes, the entire world—would come to know this class of men as one of the mightiest forces for good on all the globe.

We as a Christian nation have much to be proud of and much to be ashamed of; the Orient can teach us much we do not know, and America can give to them those things so essential to their betterment and uplifting as nations. I could not help but realize

(221)

on this trip of opportunity for me that, with all our money, our homes scattered all over this country, a free people with every luxury and enjoyment, we would come to realize that our highest purpose is the development of Christian character.

We have practically lost our opportunity to aid in winning Japan to Christianity by medical science. There is no longer need of medical missions in that empire. But must we fail to grasp the golden opportunity in China and Korea by failing to go hand in hand with the missionary, establishing hospitals for the care of the sick and medical schools for the education of the youth for such noble service in their home land? It is impossible for me to picture to you the great need of this important work. Now that the Japanese are in Korea, they will plant schools in every village, send out their physicians; and if we do not take advantage of our opportunities and properly build and equip, our Church will lose prestige, and we will have the same difficulties to face in Korea which we face in Japan to-day. If the Japanese take the lead in educational and medical work in Korea, it will be non-Christian; worse than that, it will be materialistic and agnostic.

One Sunday morning last spring I stood on a hill in Korea overlooking a city of seventy-five thousand people, where they know nothing of hygiene, nothing of surgery, nothing of asepsis, nothing of remedies and measures for the alleviation of pain, nothing of vaccination, nothing of anti-toxin—nothing but sin, weakness, sickness, uncleanliness—and I thought what a great privilege it would be to start a medical reformation in that great city. And then a few days later I stood in a city in China, and I saw under the touch of the knife, in the dispensary, at the bedside, the transforming forces brought about by medical missionaries and the masterful forces of Jesus Christ, as through sympathy and tenderness and unselfish devotion his life struck deep into the lives of those who knew him not. China has suffered from famine, pestilence, and disease. But this is not all; she has suffered and is suffering from the opium curse, which sends millions back to despair and deeper heathenism, has deprived helpless native workers of all means of support among poverty-stricken, starving millions, and has broken down one worker after another who has vainly starved himself or herself rather than go without the drug. But when we realize that on the same steamers on which we sail from San Francisco and Seattle and other Pacific ports, on the same steamers on which our missionaries are sent to the Orient, thousands and thousands of gallons of the white man's rum are being sent out there, we need not be surprised if we are asked: "Are there any Christians in America?" And I tell you, we will never be able to answer that question to the satisfaction of the Oriental mind until the majority of the God-loving and God-fearing men and women in America shall rise up and say to the world: "This damnable thing shall stop!" [Applause.] The opium curse is everywhere. The victims of the habit must have it at all hazards, and no crime will prevent their obtaining it. It is one of the most threatening evils of China, and indeed of all sections of the earth where it is gaining headway. In the Soochow Hospital I visited with Dr. Park a room used exclusively for the treatment of those addicted to this awful drug. These young men occasionally are awakened to the realization of what this habit means to them, and voluntarily, and often against the wishes of parents and friends, go and ask Dr. Park to treat them for the habit. In this room they are placed under guard; and after a while, under his scientific care and attention, they are freed from this terrible drug which is dethroning the reason and sapping the lifeblood out of the youth of China.

We have all heard of the footbinding in China until it no longer makes an impression on our minds; but if you could go and see one of the native women unbind her feet, as I did in the Soochow Hospital, and witness the frightful and unnatural deformity brought about by superstition, sin, and ignorance, you would rejoice at what Christianity and medical science are doing for the women of China. How true it is in the Orient that when we find the hospitals and dispensaries crowded with patients, then the chapels also are crowded, showing the intimate relationship between the two! Many hospitals and dispensaries are training colleges for theoretical and practical instruction in Western medicine; thus an opportunity is afforded of bringing the brightest natives into a sphere of influence for benefiting future generations. Medical education has been a spur to the higher education of women. It has given woman a higher ideal of life, for every one treated in a hospital learns something of cleanliness and care of the sick, and carries away a treasure of new ideas which cannot fail to bring comfort and health to cheerless homes. The character of the physician is always and everywhere honored in the East, and gives an easy and unsuspected admission to familiar intercourse with all classes and creeds. He who is a physician is pardoned for being a Christian, religious and national prejudices disappear before him, all hearts are opened, and he is welcomed as if he were carrying the dying the elixir of immortality. It is false economy which sends a fully trained and qualified American medical missionary to the field and does not see to it that he is provided with a hospital. If the medical man is to attract men and women from all parts of his district, it will be because he is able to deal with a vast mass of diseases; without a hospital he cannot successfully do this. America and Great Britain combined demand an army of five hundred thousand educated physiciaus to provide medical aid for their teeming multitudes; but Chicago can boast of more physicians than India and China together possess. America and Britain have one doctor to each eight hundred population; in non-Christian lands, one physician to every two and one-half million. Each doctor in China, if distributed over the empire to-day, would be surrounded by a population of four million people. There are five hundred thousand blind people walking through China to-day, seventy-five per cent of whom are blind from lack of simple remedial measures. The death rate is forty thousand daily. *If New York City had one physician to look after her sick and injured, teach preventable disease and hygienic living, she would have far better medical service than China has to-day.* Never before in the history of medicine has the Christian physician had at his command such immense resources. Are the benefits of these resources to be confined to about one hundred million people of America and Britain? Are the sufferings of two-thirds of the world's population to go untended? Is maternity to be a dreaded nightmare to our sisters in China and Korea, when the women of our own lands are tended with care and consideration? Are thousands to continue to lose their sight each year because there are no surgeons at hand to treat ophthalmia and remove cataracts?

The Chinese knew nothing until within the past few years of medical science, and awful havoc is being wrought all over the empire by a lack of such knowledge. For instance, in China their treatment of the insane: The poor lunatic is chained, his feet are fastened in the stocks, and he is beaten and half starved with the idea that if badly treated the devil will the sooner leave him; and then, as a last resort, when the friends have grown tired of giving even this sort of care to their relative, the lunatic is given his freedom in the desert, his hands are tied behind him, he is led out on the desert, and is never heard of again. They have no chloroform. If amputating a limb, they simply chop and saw it off without regard to the sufferer; to stop the flow of blood, the stump is dipped into boiling grease and cauterized. Not only is there cruelty in these dark places of the earth, but there is abundant evidence of what in civilized communities is indictable criminal malpractice. We know that abortion mongers are by no means infrequent in our great cities, yet here at least they have to pursue their craft secretly because of the pressure of a growingly healthy public opinion on the matter. Where there are no licenses required to practice medicine, where superstition and gross ignorance combine to allow anything to be done which is dictated by the priest-physician and meddlesome midwife, where there is no such thing as a healthy public opinion, there are the very elements in which the charlatan can flourish and pursue his abominable and nefarious and deadly traffic. Here is far more than mere cruelty and immorality; it is touching the secret springs of a nation's life. If the wife and mother be degraded, love cannot flourish, and the home is blasted; if the home is blasted, the national unit of strength is destroyed, and there is moral decay.

This is exactly the sight with which we are confronted in China and Korea to-day: The sick and injured of those lands are crushed like pack ice between two approaching icebergs. On the one side is disease, claiming from them their life; on the other, the less agonizing attempts at treatment. Their diagnosis of approaching death is none too certain; so it often happens that the closing hours or days are spent in terrible discomfort and pain, and the end is hastened by shameful neglect. Mentally contrast such scenes with those in the home lands when relatives and friends are passing from us. Here all is done in those closing hours which love and forethought can devise for the amelioration of pain and the quiet peacefulness of the sick one; there it is noise and din, wailing and mourning, cold and neglect, utter and hopeless darkness.

Dr. Young J. Allen, of Shanghai, invited me to dine with him while there. He took me into his study after dinner, and told

15

me a great deal of the work of China, past and present, and he spoke with authority, for he had lived there forty-nine years, and had held most important positions with the Chinese government. He credits medical men with doing more for China than any other class. I bade him good-by May 7, standing in the shade of his porch, his silver locks glistening and his face radiant with the smile of a life well spent. When I reached San Francisco, the news had preceded us announcing his death. Young J. Allen left as a legacy to his Chinese fellow-men that there is no life so quiet and obscure that it does not give a chance for splendid, civilizing, ennobling, and uplifting endeavor, and the living of a life whose essence is the essence of Christ's own Christianity. To young medical students I want to say that, from past personal experience, you will talk and think many times as you approach your senior year of a most serious proposition: "Where am I going to locate?" You will be told that something like five thousand to seven thousand medical men are graduated from our schools every year, that we already have one doctor to eight hundred of the population in America; and if you want to place your own life where it will count most, if you want to be a genuine benefactor to the human race, if you believe in uplifting humanity, if you believe in a common human brotherhood, I want you to consider prayerfully and soberly the appeal going up for well-equipped medical men in the Orient.

> "For life is the mirror of king and slave,
>   'Tis just what we are and do;
> Then give to the world the best you have,
>   And the best will come back to you."

Who knows better than the doctors the results of a city robbed of its medical science and all it stands for? Who but the doctors can teach scientific hygiene and proper care of the sick and afflicted of those lands? When our medical men learn the full force of their obligations to the non-Christian lands, when they realize it (and they will realize it if they but look the proposition square in the face and get the facts), then by their aid we will be enabled to free the Orient from its ignorance, superstition, sin, and suffering.

One of our writers pictures to us the sounding of a bell upon the arrival of accident cases in European hospitals. Let us imagine that we hear the sound of that bell reverberating around the world this afternoon. Did you hear it just now? It was from China that the sound came: a poor Chinaman has fallen and injured himself; a crowd gather round; they gaze and laugh at his sufferings, and when they have had enough move off and leave him to die. Exaggeration, you say? No, a sober truth; there is no Red Cross man there to take him to a hospital, no ambulance to carry him, no hospital to which to take him. If he cannot move, his fellow-countrymen will not help him; he will lie there and die. The bell is ringing in Korea now: a boy has broken his leg; a string will be tied tightly around the fractured limb until at last gangrene sets in, and a foreign doctor is sent for to amputate in order to save his life. The sound of the bell in India is wafted to us across the plains and mountains of Asia: it tells of a woman in the hour of nature's sorest trial. When the doctor suggests that an operation may save her life, the husband replies: "Better let her die; it is only a wife; it is easy enough to get another." Now it is booming and tolling in Africa, for a child is in convulsions. What is to be done? A red-hot iron is pressed to the skull till a hole is burned down to the brain to let the demons out. Why not? It is only a girl; let her die. The bell sounds clearer and clearer now: it is ringing in a city in America. Some poor fellow has had his arm wrenched off by machinery. What is going to be done? In an instant the telephone notifies the hospital. A few moments later, and an automobile ambulance and surgeon arrive; tenderly and carefully he is placed on a soft couch and wheeled into the automobile; in a few moments the hospital is reached, he is wheeled on to an electric elevator, and hastened to the operating room. There the house surgeon sees him, a nurse is there to carefully tend him; if an operation is performed, it will be done under anæsthesia. It rings again in the home land, and this time a child is sick. If it is a poor child, our splendid children's hospitals are open for its reception; if it is the child of rich parents, the nursery will be made bright, relatives and friends will bring flowers and toys and fruits, a trained nurse will be there to relieve every discomfort, and a physician stands there doing his noble best for the little life which hovers on the border land of life and death. And all for a child in America. It rings once more a loud and urgent summons: a sister is in the pangs of motherhood. Thank

God! there are gentle voices, hushed footsteps, the skill and **care** of doctor and nurse are immediately and as a simple right bestowed on her and on the little life for whose sake she is in sore distress.

Members of the medical profession, members of the **Laymen's** Missionary Movement, why this difference if we believe in a common human brotherhood?

IV.

MOBILIZING THE FORCES.

XVIII. THE EDUCATIONAL MOVEMENT IN MISSIONS.

XIX. Protestant Literature in Spanish.

XX. The Work of the Conference Lay Leader.

XXI. The Work of the District Lay Leader.

XXII. Work of a Lay Leader in the Congregation.

(229)

Men enough? Yes! There are to-day enough ordained men in the ministry of the United States alone to furnish from their ranks the army of missionaries needed to evangelize the world in twenty-five years. And this, too, without impairing the efficiency of the Church in holding Christian America for Christ. In this country there are 154,320 ordained preachers. The population of the United States is 85,568,159. This gives us one ordained man to every 554 persons. It is estimated by those who have most closely studied this question that 50,000 ordained missionaries will be sufficient, taking into account the activities of the native Church, to evangelize the world in twenty-five years. There are now 16,000 missionaries on the field. This means that we need 34,000 recruits. Take this 34,000 men from our 154,320 ordained preachers, and we have 120,320 left for the work of the home land, or one ordained preacher for every 711 souls. This would be an ample force if the Church possessed the true missionary spirit and the men were rightly distributed. We hear a good deal about the dearth of young men entering the ministry. The real problem, however, is not one of ministerial supply, but it is a question of quality and distribution. The fact is, Churches and preachers in this country are too thick to thrive. All over the land Churches are multiplied where one Church would meet all the religious needs of the people. Alas, how often are we found contending for a name, a doctrine, a polity, or a history! And that, too, in this day of opportunity to spread the gospel over all the earth. Christian men of business experience will not long stand for this extravagant and unchristian policy. In the face of our abundant supply and the great need for workers in heathen lands and the ever-enlarging opportunity for Christian conquest in our time, is it not strange that the great need of the Church is still for men to man the fields?

(230)

XVIII.

THE EDUCATIONAL MOVEMENT IN MISSIONS.

REV. ED F. COOK, NASHVILLE TENN.

I AM invited to speak to you concerning "The Modern Educational Movement in Missions." This privilege I hail with delight because of your peculiar interest in the fundamentals of missionary success.

This is indeed one of the great movements of our time: great (1) because it is so actively and potentially engaged in the making of the missionary Church which shall speedily evangelize the world; (2) because it deals with that human agency in the kingdom susceptible of the largest development, and therefore capable of the greatest achievements—namely, the young people of the Church of to-day; (3) because education is indispensable to advancement. Being an educational movement, it lies necessarily at the very foundation of the future missionary progress and success of the Church.

Philosophy of the Movement.

The philosophy of this movement lies, first, in the fact that the Church is not ready for her missionary opportunity.

This is a day of wonderful opportunity for the extension of the kingdom of Christ, for the doors of the heathen world are now wide open. A generation ago they were scarcely ajar; two generations ago they were tightly shut, and apparently impenetrable. How changed to-day! Yet, with the doors flung wide and the heart of heathendom laid bare to the missionary, with his message of salvation to a lost and ruined world, the Church is unprepared to enter and adequately possess the land.

Not only are the doors of opportunity wide open, but all the facilities of modern progress are at the command of the Church

(231)

for carrying forward Christ's kingdom. The wonders wrought by steam and electricity have not only brought the remote nations of the earth together and held them, as it were, at our very door, but these agencies are enabling us to penetrate the interior of the continents that have been so long unevangelized. By the building of railways, by the establishment of telegraph lines and the laying of ocean cables the work of evangelizing the people has been facilitated in all lands. When Young J. Allen went to China, he was more than six months in making the journey. After untold hardship, sacrifice, and peril he reached China's shores, only to face distances, difficulties, and dangers. More than a year passed before a message could reach the home Church and an equal time before he heard from loved ones at home. But to-day, so remarkable are the facilities of travel and communication, that three or four weeks of comfortable travel suffice to reach the remotest field entered by our Church, and the doings of the mission fields to-day are told in to-morrow morning's papers. In the face of such facilities the Church is planning only small things, and has scarcely begun to employ these agencies in any adequate sense.

Not only is this true, but we have come to the world at a time when the nations of the earth are in transition. They are turning from the social and religious systems of the past. The currents of national thought and life are changing. Through the touch of Western civilization, through commercial contact with Christian nations, through the growing influence of the missionary and Christian literature, the leaders and student classes are coming slowly to discredit their ancient religious systems. Distrustful of their old religions and turning away from the dark past, the nations are feeling about if haply they may find God. To adequately enlarge our force and equipment in heathen lands, in this day of transition, is to channel these new currents for the kingdom of Christ. Otherwise, infidelity and materialism will mark the new life of the nations. And yet the Church has not put one-fourth the force in the field demanded by the situation.

The laymen of America are awaking to their missionary responsibility at a time when the physical agencies for extending the kingdom are ample. There are men enough and there is money enough in the Christian Church of America to-day to evangelize the world in one generation without impairing the interests of the Church at home, if God could but command the lives of men and control money enough to finance this world-wide enterprise. [Applause.]

Men enough? Yes! There are to-day enough ordained men in the ministry of the United States alone to furnish from their ranks the army of missionaries needed to evangelize the world in twenty-five years. And this, too, without impairing the efficiency of the Church in holding Christian America for Christ. In this country there are 154,320 ordained preachers. The population of the United States is 85,568,159. This gives us one ordained man to every 554 persons. It is estimated by those who have most closely studied this question that 50,000 ordained missionaries will be sufficient, taking into account the activities of the native Church, to evangelize the world in twenty-five years. There are now 16,-000 missionaries on the field. This means that we need 34,000 recruits. Take this 34,000 men from our 154,320 ordained preachers, and we have 120,320 left for the work of the home land, or one ordained preacher for every 711 souls. This would be an ample force if the Church possessed the true missionary spirit and the men were rightly distributed. We hear a good deal about the dearth of young men entering the ministry. The real problem, however, is not one of ministerial supply, but it is a question of quality and distribution. The fact is, Churches and preachers in this country are too thick to thrive. All over the land Churches are multiplied where one Church would meet all the religious needs of the people. Alas, how often are we found contending for a name, a doctrine, a polity, or a history! And that, too, in this day of opportunity to spread the gospel over all the earth. Christian men of business experience will not long stand for this extravagant and unchristian policy. In the face of our abundant supply and the great need for workers in heathen lands, and the ever-enlarging opportunity for Christian conquest in our time, is it not strange that the great need of the Church is still for men to man the fields?

Money enough? Yes! And millions to spare, if the Church would but recognize God's claim upon the wealth of the Church to-day. We are the richest people on the globe. The estimated wealth of the Church in America to-day is $25,000,000,000. Of this amount, $257,500,000 is contributed for Church purposes. This is, however, only one ninety-seventh of the amount due if we recognize the justness of God's claim upon the Jewish Church when he demanded a tithe. Suppose we had learned the kindergarten lesson that God taught the infant race when he began to train a people to receive the loftier doctrine of the "Lordship of Jesus and the stewardship of men." Having begun the training of the Jew by requiring one-tenth, he surely expects the Christian Church to go beyond this primary lesson in Christian giving. If we had followed God's plan, he would have to-day an annual income of $2,500,000,000 for the work of the kingdom. How ample this seems when compared with the $257,500,000 now contributed by the United States for all Church and benevolent enterprises at home and abroad! Of this $257,500,000, only $7,500,000 is invested in the foreign mission enterprise—$250,000,000 for the benefit of the 85,568,159 people in the United States and $7,500,000 for the benefit of the 900,000,000 unevangelized people of the world. More than thirty-three times as much in Christian America as in all the heathen world! Does this look like a just division of even that which we offer God?

It is estimated that $80,000,000 a year for twenty-five years is sufficient money to accomplish the evangelization of the world. The missionary offering of Christendom is $20,000,000—$60,000,000 short of the mark. The question is, are we able to do better? Is it possible to make an offering adequate to the enterprise? If we admit that the tithe was just and expedient under the old dispensation, we must certainly admit that it is a just and expedient minimum mark for Christian liberality in this day. This admitted, we find that we are easily able, out of that which should be in God's hands for investment, to devote $80,000,000 a year to the work of missions and have left for the home Church and benevolent enterprises the enormous sum of $2,420,000,000 per year.

Nothing is plainer than this: If the Church stood on the high doctrine of Christian stewardship as taught in the New Testament, and was consecrated in heart and purpose to the work of winning the world for Christ, we could in one generation, with abundance to spare, finance this tremendous enterprise and land the nations of the earth within the kingdom of our Lord Jesus Christ. [Applause.] And yet the constant cry of the Church is for money enough to finance the movement that looks to the salvation of all people.

The questions you face as representative Christian business men are these: How shall we bring the Church fully to enter the open doors, wisely to utilize the agencies of progress, and with a strong hand to channel the new currents in heathen lands for Jesus Christ? How shall we secure a sufficient supply of men to adequately man the work? How shall we spring the Church to such liberality as will safely finance the whole gigantic enterprise?

The only answer to such questions is: Educate, educate, educate. A systematic and thorough campaign of education in the great gospel and facts of missions is the only means by which we can bring the Church to see her opportunity and responsibility. By this means alone can we bring strong young men and women to volunteer for the work. By such a process alone can the Church be brought to lay at God's command money enough to carry out his missionary plan for the world.

The philosophy of this movement is further seen in the fact that the basis of all interest is information. The foundation of every conviction is knowledge. Information must, therefore, precede interest, and knowledge must come before a deep and abiding conviction.

Now, I submit that the dominant purpose of the great Church of the living God in Christian America in this hour is not to take this world for Jesus Christ in a generation, because the Church is lacking the advantage of adequate instruction concerning the gospel of missions as taught in the divine Book and is ignorant of the facts of the modern missionary enterprise.

Our difficulty has been that we have relied too largely upon agitation in the preparation of the Church for her missionary responsibility. Agitation is good, but insufficient. Agitation can only create an atmosphere in which to educate. As good and helpful as they are, the occasional missionary sermon or missionary address or missionary editorial can no more educate a Church in the gospel and facts of missions than an occasional literary or scientific lecture can give to a boy a university training.

Education implies a process more technical and more careful; it suggests the text-book and the teacher, the class and the class hour, the preparation and the recitation, and all else that enters into a great campaign of education among a magnificent constituency that is to be made ready for life and life's responsibilities.

So I present to you, as the remedy for our lack of preparation, our lack of interest, our lack of conviction, and our lack of liberality, a Church-wide and thorough campaign of missionary education. Short of this, our great Church can never be brought up to the full measure of her opportunity and responsibility in this great work of bringing the world to Christ.

It is with fervent zeal, therefore, that I stand before this magnificent company of Southern Methodist laymen and plead for sympathy and coöperation in this great educational campaign that looks to the preparation of our Methodism for her rightful place in the forefront of Immanuel's army now advancing to the conquest of all nations. [Applause.]

THE FIELD.

The field of this educational movement in missions is naturally and logically the great young life of the Church of to-day. The movement's efforts are directed toward the whole Church through the young people's societies, the Sunday school, and the schools and colleges of the land. By reaching this magnificent constituency, with broad and thorough plans of missionary education, the Church of to-morrow may be made ready for its divinely appointed responsibility. My brethren, if ever the Church is to be thoroughly missionary in faith and obedience, if ever the Church is to be more liberal, its training must begin now.

If this campaign is vigorously pushed, we shall live to see our Church fully prepared to handle with faith and efficiency her share of the work of winning the world for Christ.

MATERIALS.

I wish to say a word to you concerning the character of the materials for this campaign. The movement, entering this great field which I have indicated, is committed to the making of the best possible missionary literature, a literature best adapted to the purposes for which the movement stands—namely, the education of the whole Church in the gospel and facts of missions. No pains are spared in the accomplishment of this end. The best men in the world, regardless of cost, are secured for the preparation of this literature. Each year new text-books on home and foreign missions are issued for the study classes and for general circulation through the Church. This, however, is but a small part of the output.

The publication of literature for the Mission Boards is increasingly becoming an important phase of the movement's activities. To April 1 there were sold, through the Mission Boards and other agencies, 242,712 mission study text-books, 12,396 books of methods, 170,151 volumes of libraries, 18,319 charts, 35,749 maps, 106,-216 pamphlets, and nearly 2,000,000 pieces of smaller literature. As a direct result of the movement, twenty-six Secretaries under the direction of nineteen Home and Foreign Mission Boards are now giving their whole time to missionary education in their denominations.

The plan of campaign comprehends not only the mission study class in the young people's societies and in the schools and colleges of the land, but a wise and practical scheme of missionary education in the Sunday school, extending from object lesson teaching in the primary grades to a postgraduate course for teachers.

THE RESULTS.

The results have outrun our expectations. One hundred and seventy-five thousand young people in the United States and Canada have been enrolled in mission study classes in the current course. At least ten millions of the fifteen millions of Sunday school pupils have been reached by the missionary lessons in the Sunday school literature, and nearly all the denominational colleges where the Student Volunteer Movement has organized for mission study have been brought in closer touch with the Mission Boards.

In our own Church the records for this year will show: Ten thousand young men and women enrolled in mission study classes, more than thirty thousand Junior Leaguers engaged in the study of missions, mission study introduced into nearly all the schools and colleges of the Church, and nearly five hundred thousand Sunday school pupils using the special missionary lessons now regularly published in our Sunday school literature. A generation of such missionary education will surely bring in a new era of missionary interest in the home Church, and therefore immensely larger activities and results abroad. [Applause.]

In the two minutes left to me, may not I say to you that there is every providential indication of the rapid and great success of the Laymen's Missionary Movement, which you are here to represent? For a generation God has been preparing for this great

Movement. The pulpits of this country have been publishing the great commission with growing faith and vigor; the good women have been organized and diligent in prayer and study; the Student Volunteer Movement has been placing the cause of missions upon the hearts of the choice young men and women in the colleges and universities of the land, and training them for service; for six years the Young People's Missionary Movement has been waging a vigorous campaign of missionary education in the United States and Canada. By these means the Church is being prepared to respond with enthusiasm to the aggressive leadership of her laymen. If they will but lay hold and press this campaign of missionary education, ere long the whole Church will be ready to enter vigorously the work and finish up the task of evangelizing the world. She only waits for the leadership and means of strong and successful business men. When such men put their brains and money into it, the missionary enterprise will command the attention of all laymen of the Church. Then we may expect to see the whole Church aroused as never before and such an advance along all lines of missionary activity as has never yet been made.

As you bring your judgment and experience to the missionary work of the Church, I beg that you remember that our chief responsibility now is to *educate,* to push all the lines of agitation and education, all the time and everywhere, until the *whole Church* shall be brought to see that God means that we shall take the whole wide world for Christ in our time. [Applause.]

As I face this great company of representative Southern Methodist laymen and catch the heart beat of your enthusiasm my faith and expectation reach full tide. I see everywhere the signs of speedy victory. With vast educational agencies at work in the Church, with all the facilities of modern progress at your command, with all the world accessible for conquest, surely you will lead our great Church forward to victory in the name of the Lord. The command is from God; the missionary meaning of his providence is plain; his pledge of divine presence and help is unfailing.

> "To doubt would be disloyalty,
> To falter would be sin."

[Applause.]

XIX.

PROTESTANT LITERATURE IN SPANISH.

In his "Gleanings of the Past" the late Mr. Gladstone speaks very highly of the natural gifts and literary ability of José Blanco White, a Spanish priest who, early last century, went to England and joined the Anglican Communion. His father being a Spaniard and his mother an Irish lady, he knew perfectly both languages. In 1825 Blanco translated Paley's "Evidences of Christianity," and sent his manuscript to Spain to be printed. The vessel was lost near the coast of France, but among portions of the cargo that were rescued out of the waters there was a box of books, and in it a tin can containing Blanco's translation. This was printed in London, but in the course of time also went out of print. In 1893 the second edition of this splendid work was published in Nashville, and since then over one thousand copies have been sold. In this country it is considered an antiquated treatise; but not so among the Latin race. In Mexico, for instance, conditions are now very similar to those that prevailed in England in the seventeenth century.

(240)

PROTESTANT LITERATURE IN SPANISH.

P. A. RODRIGUEZ.

THE work of translating and publishing Protestant literature in Spanish, under the auspices of the Board of Missions and the Publishing House of the Methodist Episcopal Church, South, began in the fall of 1888, and has continued without interruption.

In 1891 Volume I. of Mr. Wesley's "Sermons" was published. So great had been the demand for the Wesleyan Standards that in less than six months the edition of five hundred copies was exhausted. In the following year Volume II. was printed. These "Sermons" are now in the third edition. Over one thousand sets have been sold, and are in use by the preachers and theological students of the Methodist Episcopal Churches in Cuba, Puerto Rico, Mexico, and South America; also by the British Wesleyans in Spain.

Paley's Natural Theology.—When, in 1821, Mexico gained her independence and became a republic, there was a strong reaction not only against the Church and the clergy that had sided with Spain, but also against religion. Fortunately the chief leaders of the Revolution were native priests, most of whom endeavored in several ways to stay the tide of unbelief that threatened to sweep over the whole country. Among other books published at that time was Paley's "Natural Theology." It was translated in London in 1824 by Lorenzo J. Villanueva, Secretary of the Mexican Embassy. The President of the new republic of Mexico, Ramos Arispe, ordered the said translation to be used as a textbook in the public schools. But in the course of time all religious teaching ceased in the public institutions, and the book disappeared. For years it was out of print. In 1892 a reprint of it

16   (241)

was published by Barbee & Smith, and the book sold very well. It is now in the third edition.

In his "Gleanings of the Past" the late Mr. Gladstone speaks very highly of the natural gifts and literary ability of José Blanco White, a Spanish priest who, early last century, went to England and joined the Anglican Communion. His father being a Spaniard and his mother an Irish lady, he knew perfectly both languages. In 1825 Blanco translated Paley's "Evidences of Christianity," and sent his manuscript to Spain to be printed. The vessel was lost near the coast of France, but among portions of the cargo that were rescued out of the waters there was a box of books, and in it a tin can containing Blanco's translation. This was printed in London, but in the course of time also went out of print. In 1893 the second edition of this splendid work was published in Nashville, and since then over one thousand copies have been sold. In this country it is considered an antiquated treatise; but not so among the Latin race.

The Man of Galilee.—All over Mexico and Cuba—and I fear the same is true of all Spanish-speaking countries—the traveler finds in almost every bookstore translations of French skeptical works, chiefly those of Voltaire and Rénan. To counteract this evil influence as far as possible, a splendid treatise on the divinity of our Lord was translated and published in 1894. "The Man of Galilee," by the late Bishop A. G. Haygood, has proved a boon to many minds. It has sold, and is selling, better than any other book we have printed.

History of the Christian Church.—The ever-increasing number of candidates for the ministry of the Evangelical Churches in Spanish America demands the preparation of text-books, and the call is greater and louder every year. With the consent of the late Bishop John F. Hurst, of the Methodist Episcopal Church, his "History of the Christian Church" was translated and published in the year 1900. Although an expensive book, it has sold very well, and is now in its third edition.

The Spanish Reformers.—Charles V., and afterwards Philip II., took with them respectively to Germany and to England some of the leading ecclesiastics of Spain. These priests and monks not only became acquainted with the German and English reformers, but also lived among them for months, and some of them for years. They accepted the teachings of the Reformation, and wrote books, which were printed chiefly in Geneva. A Spanish convert by the name of Julianillo, small of stature but of great cunning and fortitude, introduced these books in barrels, carrying them across the mountains on the backs of mules. After a time the Inquisition burned at the public *autos da fé* both writings and most of the writers. However, the Spanish Reformers had taken the precaution of sending copies of their books and manuscripts to all the universities and public libraries of Europe.

During the first quarter of last century Professor Edward Boëhmer, of the University of Strassburg, found a copy of one of these books in the library of Munich. His royal employer, William the Great, relieved him of his duties at the university, and requested him to devote his time to search for these books. In the course of several years he found no less than twenty volumes. The largest of them is a fine translation of Calvin's "Christian Institutes;" another is a "History of the Inquisition" by an eyewitness; others are on theology and controversial matters, and one is on the "Origins or Sources of the Spanish Language." They all are written in the Spanish of the golden era.

An English man of letters, Benjamin Wiffen, and a Spanish nobleman, Luis Osoz y Río, about the middle of last century, published reprints of said twenty volumes, and introduced them into Spain. Again the Church managed to destroy nearly the whole edition. A few complete sets were saved by placing them under the protection of the British and Foreign Bible Society, and are now in London. By order of the Secretaries of said Society the agent in Madrid, in 1901, presented the Board of Missions of the M. E. Church, South, with a complete set.

Works of Constantino Ponce de la Fuente.—In 1902 we reprinted these two volumes, which contain "Six Sermons on the First Psalm," the "Confession of a Sinner," and a "Doctrinal Summary," with an Exposition of Christ's Sermon on the Mount. The "Confession of a Sinner" is a prayer from the inmost soul to the Son of God, who had been given to man by the eternal Father to be his Saviour and Judge. Going orderly through the Ten Commandments and the Creed, the suppliant sees every form of self-righteousness desert him, and finds his sole consolation through faith in the forgiveness of sins through the merits of Jesus Christ.

Works of Juan Perez.—The following year, 1903, a third volume of the Spanish Reformers was reprinted. In it the author contrasts the old (biblical) doctrine of God with the (comparatively) new doctrine of men, making·copious and apt use of Holy Scriptures. For the third time these books have entered Spain, and it seems that they have escaped destruction; for we have sold nearly two hundred copies of each.

Systematic Theology.—For many years a Manual of Christian Theology for the students in the theological schools in Spanish America has been greatly needed. In June, 1905, a translation of "Personal Salvation: Studies in Christian Doctrine," by Dean W. F. Tillett, of the Theological Faculty in Vanderbilt University, was translated, and five hundred copies were printed. Of these, only twenty-two remain in stock. A second edition is being carefully prepared for the press.

Skilled Labor for the Master.—In 1906 this fine work on Pastoral Theology, by Bishop Eugene R. Hendrix, was translated and published.

Last year translations of "Christus Auctor," by Bishop W. A. Candler, and of "The Kingdom in the Cradle," by Bishop James Atkins, were published. The former translation was made by Prof. Servando I. Esquivel, of Chihuahua, Mexico, and the latter by Rev. S. A. Blanco, a missionary of the British Wesleyan Church, stationed at Algiers, Africa.

Sunday School Literature.—For the past sixteen years the *Senior Quarterly*, the International Sunday School Lessons, has been published in Spanish; and now we are also editing the *Junior Lessons*. According to the last report of the Secretary of the Sunday School Association of the Republic of Mexico, there are in that country about eleven thousand children who regularly attend the Sunday schools of different Churches. We have 3,600 subscribers to the *Senior Quarterly* and 3,465 to the *Junior Lessons*.

By the establishing of the Inquisition, Pope Pius V. and Philip II., with the help of Domingo de Guzmán and of Ignacio de Loyola, brought about the counter Reformation, and succeeded in keeping Spain and her American possessions in the darkness and superstition of the Middle Ages for no less than four hundred years; but the dawn of a glorious era, the century of missions, has come, and, under the influence of the gospel, better things are in store for my race.

GROUP OF CONFERENCE LAY LEADERS.

Begin at top, and read from left to right

T. B. KING, C. M. PHILLIPS, A. D. REYNOLDS, EPPS G KNIGHT, JUDGE A. G. NORRELL, W. W. CARRE, R. F. BURDEN, L. M. PENNINGTON. JUDGE W. ERSKINE WILLIAMS, P. W. FURRY.

XX.

THE WORK OF THE CONFERENCE LAY LEADER.

The appeal for men of courage, of knowledge, and of action by religious bodies of the world is almost if not quite pathetic, because of the leaden ears upon which they have been falling, even among those who call themselves the elect. Commerce is also calling in clarion tones for the truest, bravest, and best, and the response is more universally heeded, the reason being that the captains of industry are everywhere greatly honored and the wizards of finance are being lionized by their fellows. When we consider the relative importance of the kingdom of Christ with that of the kingdom of this world, it seems to me that we should blush with shame that the opportunities in the Church are not made even more attractive than those that the world has to offer. In this great Laymen's Movement we must have men, and the best at that, if we succeed. In order that the services may be volunteered rather than forced, we ourselves should become enthusiastic, and should by earnest support make the conditions more congenial. We must make the official duties and the entire ongoings of the Church the greatest achievements belonging to the labors of this life. We feel quite confident that the time is at hand when we should address ourselves studiously and prayerfully to the manning of the ship of Zion rather than to the remodeling of her creeds or to the reconstruction of her polity. I do not mean to underestimate the value of forms, ceremonies, and doctrines in their effect upon the propagation of a great truth, yet I contend that now is not the time for the expenditure of energy and talent in this direction when our fathers have wrought so wisely and comprehensively. Since man, then, is the crying need of the hour, it is very important that no mistake be made in selecting leaders in our Annual Conferences as well as others connected with this Laymen's Movement.

(246)

THE WORK OF THE CONFERENCE LAY LEADER.

THOMAS B. KING, MEMPHIS.

Mr. Chairman and Brethren: We have been listening with profound interest to the distinguished men who have presented the needs of the foreign fields as they have studied them, both theoretically and practically. We heartily enter into the spirit of this occasion and join the distinguished visitors and returned missionaries in their zeal and earnestness concerning the great work we are here to consider. It might appear that what I have to say, after these thrilling speeches, would be somewhat tame; but I assure you it is none the less important, because it is very essential that we become thoroughly aroused in our home Churches before much lasting good and definite results can be accomplished.

The question which presents itself at this moment is: "What are we going to do with the facts that we have gathered and the inspiration that we have received when we return to our homes?" Personally, I have great confidence in the laymen of our great Church, and I believe they will respond with a heartiness that shall not only awaken the indifferent among our fellow-members at home, but will make glad the hearts of the millions of souls committed to the Southern Methodist Church in the great Missionary Movement among the various bodies that have banded themselves together in Christian service. The doctrine of the Southern Methodist Church is broad enough and her polity comprehensive enough to perform her part in evangelizing the whole world before the twentieth century is gone. As important as these doctrines and this polity are, they are not self-propagating nor self-operative. Probably too much stress has been put of late upon the catholicity of the doctrines adopted and of the complete-

(247)

ness of the machinery constructed by the followers of our Lord
and Christ among those called Methodists. Even statistics giving the number of members and the valuation of the property
may operate to mislead with respect to power and efficiency.
There is danger of producing a self-satisfied condition even among
the leaders and of extending the effect farther among the masses,
so as to defeat the purposes to which we are committed by these
facts. To be sure, we may rejoice without sin in whatever increase in numbers and improvement in machinery a careful stock-
taking will disclose, provided it stimulates us to thankfulness and
brings about an increased endeavor.

We as a Church have a history that excites pardonable pride;
but what might have been done with all the splendid opportunities that we have allowed to pass unheeded may some day take
the wind out of our kites when we stand before the final Judge.
Brethren, we must be reassured that the most superbly constructed machinery and the best-contrived formulas will never, in
themselves, comply with the commandment: "Go teach all nations." It is not enough even to say that these have received
divine approval and that they have age as a guarantee for the
future. Had this been true, there would have been no need for
the Master to have called the twelve apostles and committed to
them the duties of propagating the gospel until all the world
should know of its power to save. Nor would there have been
any necessity for the appointment of the deacons to take charge
of the business of the Church when murmurings had become common among the people because of evidences of partiality in the
daily administration. Man plays the supreme rôle, therefore, in
the enforcement of all known law, and especially is this true with
reference to the divine command. Divinity and materialism
strangely blend in us, so that we can take things spiritual and
express them in everyday vernacular, thus making heaven and
earth work in harmony with the one supreme law of love and good
will. This shows the reason why the divine purposes and plans
are committed to and depend upon human agencies. A true conception of such honor and responsibility should fill us with a holy
impulse and quicken us into an outlay of every faculty of body,
mind, and spirit in the accomplishment of the great work for
which we have been called together at this time.

The appeal for men of courage, of knowledge, and of action

by religious bodies of the world is almost if not quite pathetic, because of the leaden ears upon which they have been falling, even among those who call themselves the elect. Commerce is also calling in clarion tones for the truest, bravest, and best, and the response is more universally heeded, the reason being that the captains of industry are everywhere greatly honored and the wizards of finance are being lionized by their fellows. When we consider the relative importance of the kingdom of Christ with that of the kingdom of this world, it seems to me that we should blush with shame that the opportunities in the Church are not made even more attractive than those that the world has to offer. In this great Laymen's Movement we must have men, and the best at that, if we succeed. In order that the services may be volunteered rather than forced, we ourselves should become enthusiastic, and should by earnest support make the conditions more congenial. We must make the official duties and the entire ongoings of the Church the greatest achievements belonging to the labors of this life. We feel quite confident that the time is at hand when we should address ourselves studiously and prayerfully to the manning of the ship of Zion rather than to the remodeling of her creeds or to the reconstruction of her polity. I do not mean to underestimate the value of forms, ceremonies, and doctrines in their effect upon the propagation of a great truth, yet I contend that now is not the time for the expenditure of energy and talent in this direction when our fathers have wrought so wisely and comprehensively. Since man, then, is the crying need of the hour, it is very important that no mistake be made in selecting leaders in our Annual Conferences as well as all others connected with this Laymen's Movement.

1. I consider that the first step to be taken should be an appeal for divine guidance. In this the preachers should join with the laymen in their everyday work, and especially at the sessions of the Annual Conferences. At these Conferences there should be public prayers offered and discussions engaged in with reference to qualifications and requirements of the leader and at the same time the ascertainment of the willingness on the part of all present to coöperate in the movement by preaching and talking and working in their respective charges and Churches when they return home.

2. The leader should have a definite religious experience. I do

not mean an experience that is found only underneath the rubbish of one or more years' accumulation growing out of a zigzag life, but one that has the freshness of the now and the glow and vigor of the present upon it. I am not unmindful of the fact that this is a trite saying, still it is a qualification that is as essential to good discipleship and leadership as when Christ said to his apostles: "Whom say ye that I am?" There must be a knowledge in the heart of Christ as the Divine One, not revealed by flesh and blood nor by any of the natural forces. A no more valuable asset could the leader possess than this in the performance of religious services. The fact is, the relating of living experience is about the most effective way of impressing a great truth. I believe that our great doctors of divinity are now claiming that the best theology to have is that of the heart and not of the head. A man without this is like a reed shaken by every wind of doctrine; but with it he is as steady as the oak amid the blasts of the storm.

This deep hold on God will anchor the ship far better and hold it much steadier than even the prefixed title to a name, though it may have been rightly won in other lines of human endeavor. In other words, no man should be selected for the responsible place of Conference leader in this great religious movement whose chief qualification is that of Judge or General or Honorable So and So. They may even have decided influence in the realms in which they have succeeded, but the methods they would seek to employ in this new field might not be conducive to real success. The question is: "Can 'the leopard change his spots, and the Ethiopian his skin?'" We should not despise nor reject a man because he has won distinction in other lines of human endeavor, but we insist that this should not be the chief prerequisite ror the work we have specially in hand and which we are to-day considering.

3. The Conference leaders should love men in the broadest, deepest, and widest sense. This includes an intelligent conception of man and his greatest needs and a supreme willingness to labor and to make necessary sacrifices in order that these two might be brought face to face. In doing this he may have to lift men up and steady their steps while he is teaching them the way of eternal life. He may have to go through the "Samaria" of some preconceived prejudices or he may have to lay aside some of the ways of self-indulgence that so easily beset and hinder him in his Christian usefulness. This love for men must have a clear and

unmistakable and unselfish ring about it. What effect enlisting
in this great struggle will have upon his business or political pros-
peet or professional successes should be of secondary consideration if considered at all. God's work and man's needs should be
the supreme motive prompting him to offer himself to the Church
for such a responsible place.

4. He should love the Church, the Methodist Church, the warm
and genial branch known as the Southern Methodist Church. Not
that he should be ever claiming a divine monopoly upon all the
means of grace known for the redemption of man. Such an assumption would be an abomination to every benighted heathen
and a stumbling-block of offense to intelligent people. He should,
however, know the doctrine and polity so that he could intelli-
gently and, you might say, with pardonable pride tell of the faith
that is in him whenever the occasion required. This knowledge
must be of a kind that comes from the study of both the history
and the everyday movements of his Church. While it is well
enough to know what our fathers said and did under varying conditions in the past, yet it is far better to "attend upon the ordi-
nances and support the institutions" of his Church as they now
exist. This means that he should attend each service as far as
practicable held at his own church, and should attend every official meeting of his Church from Church Conferences up to the
General Conference. He may not always receive an election to
these higher bodies, but that should not keep him from attending
occasionally, so that the entire machinery of his own Church will
be familiar to him. He should be faithful to the call of his own
pastor, and at the same time be willing to help the brethren in
other sections of the Conference of which he has oversight; he
should ever keep in mind the fact that he is a layman, and therefore should not attempt to assume the function that belongs exclusively to the regular ordained minister; he should, however, be
willing to preach lay sermons and exhort people to live righteous-
ly and to loyally support the Church in all its branches; he should
keep in close touch with the laymen or leaders in every presiding
elder's district by calling them in conference at least twice or three
times a year and by the frequent use of the mail; he should encourage the district laymen in organizing their districts, so that
religious service of some sort will be held in every church each
Sunday within the bounds of the Conference. To attempt, of

course, to fully outline the work as it affects each Church would be to understand the conditions prevailing in each, which would require greater time than is allowed here. "Sanctified" common sense must govern all these matters.

5. A Conference leader should diligently strive to secure the attendance of each lay representative to every Annual Conference. This includes those elected by the District Conferences and those who are members of the standing boards. This can be done by letter, by personal appeal, and by arranging for a special meeting for the laymen at the Annual Conferences, where all are expected to take some part. He can facilitate this much-desired end greatly by stirring up the pure minds of the preachers by way of remembrance, so that they will be more enthusiastic in their efforts to get the laymen to attend and discharge their duties at the Annual Conferences.

6. He should crown these with the splendid virtue of being a missionary in theory and in fact. He need not go into foreign lands nor personally lead the heathen to the foot of the cross in order to be a full-orbed missionary. Preaching to the unsaved at home by precept and example and a scriptural division of his money with the regularly constituted authorities of the Church who have in charge the mission fields will entitle him to the honor of being a missionary. We can all in a measure fulfill the marching orders: "Go into all the world." I pray God that we may bend every energy to do this.

XXI.

THE WORK OF THE DISTRICT LAY LEADER.

I will close by giving you a practical application of such a vision by a small country Church in Arkansas, with less than two hundred members. After struggling along in a half-hearted way for two years, paying from three hundred dollars to six hundred dollars for all items of Church support, it suddenly assumed obligations of much larger proportions both for home and foreign work, and the Church at once became very much alive, and like a magnet drew to it men and women who formerly were extremely indifferent. The scriptural observance of tithing, systematically and proportionately, made it possible to steadily take on more territory until at present one home missionary is employed, reaching through the pulpit and Sunday school not less than five hundred souls. A deaconess was secured to assist the pastor in charge, and hence the charity and help department of the Church through her labors and influence has resulted in incalculable good, especially in the work among young men in night classes, as well as Bible study. The home field has not localized the Church members, but to the contrary special emphasis is given to foreign missions through Sunday school missionary programmes, special illustrated lectures, and not less than one thousand dollars per year is contributed for the foreign work. A kindergarten school in Kobe, Japan, was largely built and maintained by the local Church. The pastor of this small Church receives his regular salary of one hundred and twenty-five dollars per month. This Church is doing only what it ought to do, and shows what any Church can do when the latent forces are brought into action. My lay brethren, and especially those upon whom have been placed the responsibilities of the work of district leaders, will you not pray for a vision and use the means at hand to spur the Churches in your district to greater activity along the lines outlined in the declaration of our Laymen's Missionary Movement?

(254)

THE WORK OF THE DISTRICT LAY LEADER.

A. TRIESCHMANN, CROSSETT, ARK.

In the development of our Laymen's Missionary Movement I consider the district lay leader's position one of vital importance. Upon him depends largely the ultimate success or failure of this Movement in his particular territory. It would be an unnatural result if the inspiration and sentiment of the layman in his district exceeded that of the leader, as his title, "Lay Leader," carries with it the suggestion of what is expected of him. Hence the importance of choosing wisely and prayerfully the man for this office. He must have a world-wide vision and feel that Christ's command to teach and preach the gospel to every nation means not only ordained preachers, but every follower of Christ. His faith must be strong enough, so that he is willing to back it up with service and gold. If you want to "set things afire," fire up with coals from off the altar first. Enthusiasm must be manifest in all that we attempt, but good judgment and practical methods also have an important part.

Let us consider very briefly a few pros and cons: Don't try to work independent of the leaders above you. The Conference lay leader and the presiding elder of the district should be called upon frequently for consultation and advice. A district meeting should be held at least once a year, and the most convenient time in my opinion is at the District Conference, where a whole day can be profitably spent in planning and discussing the work of the laymen. The leaders should have a carefully prepared record of all the pastors and lay leaders of his district in order to be able to communicate with these as often as necessary, and should make a special effort to conduct a laymen's meeting in every charge and make a personal appeal, as well as through the lay leaders, to the men of the Church to enlist in the "emergency brigade" of ten thousand, and thereby make it possible for our missionaries at home and abroad to carry on an aggressive warfare against sin and heathenism and aid in the fulfilling of the prophecy to evangelize the world in this generation.

The district leader has the opportunity, through suggestions at least, to help the local Church to attain a higher efficiency in Church finance; and how much need there is of reform in this department of worship! The average Church has ceased to consider seriously its financial obligations in the development of the Church in its broader meaning. The pastor is handicapped on account of debts and indifference, and the Church ceases to be a means of grace in consequence of its selfish membership. The pastor has no business to worry with petty collections, and this should by all means be delegated to the men of the Church, who, as a rule, are good business men, and their businesslike methods should be put in operation in the Church, and thereby increase the efficiency and opportunity for good tenfold. It will require faithful pleading and judicious action on the part of the leader, but success is certain if we are in earnest. Possibly the leader needs to begin the campaign of education with himself, and the very best source of instruction is found in the Scripture. A very good help in disseminating information is the free use of printer's ink. It is the secret of many a successful business career, and can be made to serve the same purpose if judiciously used by our lay and district leaders.

The greatest need I see in the Church to-day from the standpoint of a district lay leader is to talk along the lines of systematic and proportionate giving. I do not know of anything that is so needful in the Church to-day as that. Some of the best helps dwelling specially on these subjects may be secured from the following addresses, inclosing with each order twenty-five cents for a sample lot: "Laymen," 310 Ashland Boulevard, Chicago; Charles A. Cook, Bloomfield, N. J.; E. L. Miller, Peru, Ind.; and Smith & Lamar, Nashville, Tenn. Systematic and frequent distribution of such literature by a few of the leaders of the Church will accomplish marvelous results. The Church to which I belong, with a membership of less than two hundred, now

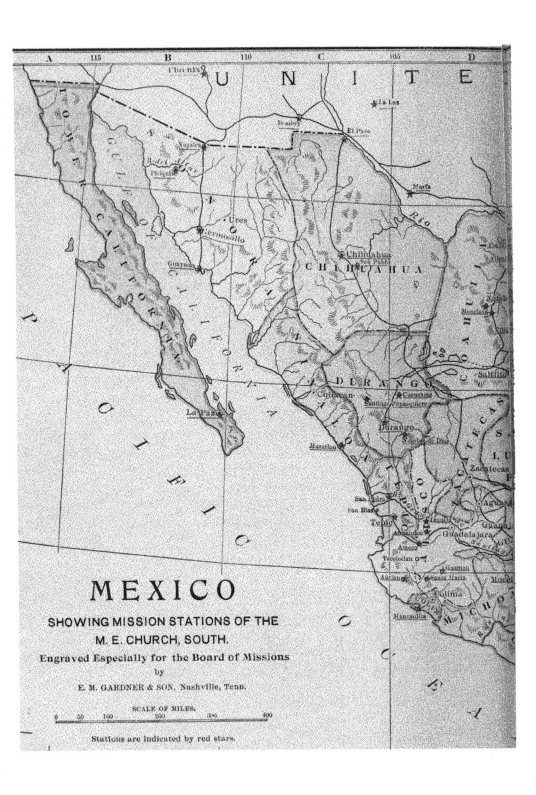

MEXICO

SHOWING MISSION STATIONS OF THE
M. E. CHURCH, SOUTH.

Engraved Especially for the Board of Missions
by
E. M. GARDNER & SON, Nashville, Tenn.

SCALE OF MILES.
0   50   100   200   300   400

Stations are indicated by red stars.

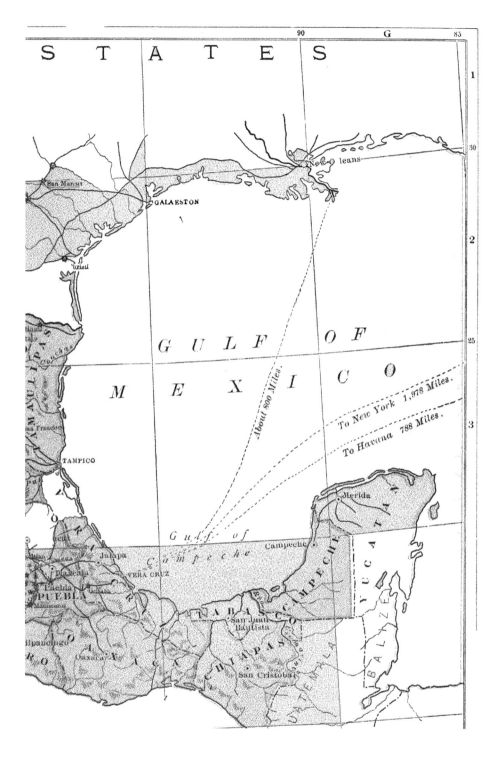

raises in the aggregate seven thousand dollars annually, whereas it raised seven hundred dollars formerly before the subject of systematic and proportionate giving was agitated.

But giving, so to speak, has become a lost art. We do not fully appreciate or understand what is meant by giving. I have been noticing on this board [indicating chart hung above the platform] Paul's method of Church finance, which I think should be universally adopted. [1 Cor. xvi. 2.] Some of you become greatly exercised when some one breaks the Sabbath in your community. Ask yourself the question down deep in your heart if you have ever broken the Sabbath by not bringing to the Church as God has prospered you during that week. If that plan were followed by every Christian, it would solve most of the questions we have been discussing here to-day. There's no question about it, if the Southern Methodist Church would give in proportion to income, we would not have to limit our offerings to three million dollars for missionary work; we could raise it to ten million dollars. I have enough confidence in the members of the Methodist Episcopal Church, South (and I haven't been a member of that Church very long), to believe that we have more than ten thousand men that will go down for one hundred dollars each not only once, but every year as long as they are living. What would that mean? If we had ten thousand men (and I believe we can raise it to twenty thousand) who would instruct this Missionary Board to just "call on us, just make a draft if you want to, for one-fifth, one-fourth, or one-third of the amount at any time you need it," wouldn't these missionaries go home with hearts lightened? Just to think, one million, two million, three million at their command for this work!

Yesterday I heard a great deal of demonstration on the part of this audience as the pictures were put on the canvas and as these great statements were made by these great men. I could not cheer. It made my head hang blushingly to think these men were giving up their lives while this great work was suffering for the lack of money, and while we as a Church were giving less than two cents per day not for missions, but to cover every item in our financial budget of the Church. Now, I did not see anything to cheer about, with that staring us in the face, as we waste that many times over every day. You know we don't give willingly! Why, I saw men get up yesterday very nervously; they were

17

afraid we were going to put that one-million-dollar proposition through.

Now, we talk a great deal about educating people to missions before we get them to give. Now, I'll tell you a secret: The best way you can educate a man on missions is to first get him to give his money for missions. Pardon this personal reference: I never was much enthused over missions until about four months ago. A pastor stated to me: "We have a school at Kobe, Japan, that is to be discontinued if we don't raise four or five hundred dollars." Well, I thought that was too bad, and something told me to just tell that burdened pastor that I would provide the amount, and to wire that missionary that the money had been raised and to go on. Ever since that I've been interested in missions. If we'll get a paying people, we'll get a praying people and we'll get a pious people. We have certainly lost sight of the scriptural teachings along the lines of giving; and as a district lay leader I know of no other work that we can do so profitably and that will be so helpful as to try to inspire others by example and instruction on this great subject of systematic and proportionate giving. The most that a district leader can hope to do in bringing his district to a high standard of perfection in the development of men in our Churches is to inspire them, and by precept and example try to present a vision of the world-wide needs. With such a vision the development of the latent resources of our laymen will accomplish wonders.

I will close by giving you a practical application of such a vision by a small country Church in Arkansas, with less than two hundred members. After struggling along in a half-hearted way for two years, paying from three hundred dollars to six hundred dollars for all items of Church support, it suddenly assumed obligations of much larger proportions both for home and foreign work, and the Church at once became very much alive, and like a magnet drew to it men and women who formerly were extremely indifferent. The scriptural observance of tithing, systematically and proportionately, made it possible to steadily take on more territory until at present one home missionary is employed, reaching through the pulpit and Sunday school not less than five hundred souls. A deaconess was secured to assist the pastor in charge, and hence the charity and help department of the Church through her labors and influence has resulted in incalculable good, especially in the work among young men in night classes, as well as Bible study. The home field has not localized the Church members, but to the contrary special emphasis is given to foreign missions through Sunday school missionary programmes, special illustrated lectures, and not less than one thousand dollars per year is contributed for the foreign work. A kindergarten school in Kobe, Japan, was largely built and maintained by the local Church. The pastor of this small Church receives his regular salary of one hundred and twenty-five dollars per month. This Church is doing only what it ought to do, and shows what any Church can do when the latent forces are brought into action.

My lay brethren, and especially those upon whom have been placed the responsibilities of the work of district leaders, will you not pray for a vision and use the means at hand to spur the Churches in your district to greater activity along the lines outlined in the declaration of our Laymen's Missionary Movement?

XXII.

WORK OF A LAY LEADER IN THE CONGREGATION.

In the diamond fields of the world, before an ounce of quartz has been raised to the surface vast expenditures of money have been made and extensive preparations entered into; and as the shaft sinks deeper and deeper into the rugged mountain side, and as the ore from day to day is elevated and spread before the skilled eyes of the expert, and finally, as the rich vein is lifted and he discovers it to be fine—yea, he says, "Now we have a diamond in the rough"—then, and not until then, does the dexterous hand of the skilled polisher and setter begin; and for days and weeks and months, and sometimes for years, does he work in fashioning the precious stone to become a fit occupant for the king's crown. Within the breasts of the rich and poor, the high and the low, the well-dressed and the rugged and rough-clad laymen who do not yet realize their duties nor their responsibilities pulsate hearts all aglow with warmth and love to God. They are diamonds in the rough, but yet diamonds for all that. If we devote so much time to a soulless thing which shines only by reflection, and which gives pleasure only to the eye, is it not worth far more of our time to bring out these qualities that they may adorn the crown of the King of Glory and shine on through endless eternity?

(262)

XXII.

WORK OF A LAY LEADER IN THE CONGREGATION.

MR. L. M. PENNINGTON, EATONTON, GA.

Mr. Chairman, Ladies and Gentlemen: I have been chosen to speak to you on this the third day of our Convention, my superiors, my peers, and my fellow-laborers, on the subject of "The Third Wheel of the Laymen's Missionary Movement; or, The Work of the Lay Leader in the Church." I lay down the follow-ing general propositions:

1. That work is of noble birth and holy parentage.

2. That the lay leader is of a high calling.

3. That the Church is of divine origin.

We have no respect for any man, regardless of what his finan-cial ability, educational qualifications, or social standing are, who loiters around idling away the precious time intrusted to his care.

The great God who created all things and set this old ball to rolling set the pace and example by laboring industriously for six days, and presented the result of his skill and handiwork, which has elicited for ages past and which will elicit for ages to come the admiration of all his creatures.

Our Saviour worked at the carpenter's bench, and doubtless as the finely finished work passed his skilled hands and his trained and observant eyes he thought of the finish, the symmetry, the beauty and development of a well-rounded Christian character. Away back yonder when the world was in its infancy and sin had obtained its first victory God stated in no uncertain terms that man should eat only as a result of his labors. The Saviour said on one occasion: "My Father worketh hitherto, and I work." By precept, by example, and by command from the two highest possi-ble authorities comes the word that work is honorable, high-toned, and necessary for a Christian character.

(263)

The lay leader is a man chosen from the rank and file· not to do ordinary work, but to do extraordinary work, and to do it in such a way that all will imitate it and do it themselves as easily and as pleasantly and more profitably than the ordinary work was previously done. The successful leaders in all ages have been men— laymen, if you please—men frequently of obscurity from man's point of view, but of prominence with God. The Church, the bride of Christ, was founded at the close of a ten days' prayer feast by one hundred and twenty despised Galileans, who had been filled with the Holy Ghost; and when we can trace our genealogy back to a Holy Ghost prayer meeting, it has the right blood and the right pedigree. So putting together the divinity of the Church, the nobleness of work, and the high calling of its lay leaders, we find that of necessity to be successful the "work of the lay leader in the Church" must, is, and should be of a high type.

The idea has prevailed for a long time that the leaders in Church work must do all the work themselves. In no other warfare would such a theory or idea be permitted to find a setting. The leader in the Church occupies exactly the same relative position that the leader in any other work does. It is distinctly his province to go over the ground, survey the situation, lay out the work, and by precept, by admonition, and the instilling of confidence in the work undertaken to get "all at it and always at it." The lay leader in the Church should so arrange his affairs as to render material aid to his pastor in all things which he undertakes for the good of the Church.

Leaders have varied and different qualifications. The lay leader, Moses, was a stammerer, and it became necessary to engage the services of the fluent-tongued Aaron to repeat the commands to his followers; but the world of literature is richer for his having wielded a stalwart pen.

St. Paul, the great giant who had sat so low at the feet of Gamaliel, who had stood so high in the Jewish Sanhedrin, thrilled the world with his eloquence and proclaimed the glad tidings to many nations. Joshua, the military genius, finished the work undertaken by Moses, and yet he had no more sense than to obey God. (O God, do give us just enough sense to know thy will and enough consecration to do it.) Stephen could face the furious multitude and say and do and die for Christ's sake. Thus in the early formation of the Church we find fluency of speech and pen,

the cold-blooded determination to obey (which is better than sacrifice), and the ability through the influence of the operation of
the Holy Spirit to die for right and righteousness. And we find
also that the laymen were leaders as much as the apostles, and on
down for centuries the laymen did a great many things that the
ministers are now doing. But we see signs of relief for the over-
worked clergy. The laymen are re-realizing their duties and responsibilities and are hastening to take them up again.

We have to-day in our Churches men whose eloquence is capti-
vating, whose logic is convincing, whose writings are highly
prized masterpieces; we have those whose incomes are enormous,
whose purses and bank accounts are bursting with fatness; and,
alas! we have those whose ideas and views are contracted and
whose lack of knowledge is pitiable; and all of these the lay leader
undertakes to bring out into lives of usefulness, to secure the
consecration of voice, of pen, and of money, all of which rank
equal in value in the accomplishment of the evangelization of the
world in this generation.

In the diamond fields of the world, before an ounce of quartz
has been raised to the surface vast expenditures of money have
been made and extensive preparations entered into; and as the
shaft sinks deeper and deeper into the rugged mountain side, and
as the ore from day to day is elevated and spread before the skilled
eyes of the expert, and finally, as the rich vein is lifted and he
discovers it to be fine—yea, he says, "Now we have a diamond in
the rough"—then, and not until then, does the dexterous hand
of the skilled polisher and setter begin; and for days and weeks
and months, and sometimes for years, does he work in fashioning
the precious stone to become a fit occupant for the king's crown.
Within the breasts of the rich and poor, the high and the low, the
well-dressed and the rugged and rough-clad laymen who do not
yet realize their duties nor their responsibilities pulsate hearts
all aglow with warmth and love to God. They are diamonds
in the rough, but yet diamonds for all that. If we devote so much
time to a soulless thing which shines only by reflection, and which
gives pleasure only to the eye, is it not worth far more of our
time to bring out these qualities that they may adorn the crown
of the King of Glory and shine on through endless eternity?

How may they be reached? Not by abuse, not by scorn, nor
by harsh criticism; but, sirs, by heart-to-heart conversations, by

instilling of interest in the Church and its various operations at home and abroad, by breaking down the barriers of ignorance, indifference, and unconcern. A campaign of education on these lines has been going on steadily for nearly a century, and blessed indeed are we who' live in this the twentieth century of Christian enlightenment and civilization.

The work of the lay leader should be to organize in each Church the young men and young women into study classes, that they may know the Bible, the mission fields, the rules and regulations of the Church, and learn to know how to pray, how to study, how to work, and how to give for the evangelization of the world. They will soon take our places, and should be prepared for the responsible duties of life. We prepare our children to occupy places of responsibility and honor here, and so frequently fail to prepare them for following in "His steps."

The lay leader should work to the end of seeing that every fixed charge on the Church is paid in full and more, and whenever a Church or circuit begins to lag have his able corps of assistants push it to the front again. And I am more persuaded every day that one of the best ways for a Church to always pay these fixed charges is to form the "living link" and come into close "vital touch" with a special missionary from each charge which is paying nine hundred dollars or more for a pastor's salary. We can do it; will we do it? My fellow-associates, the old gospel chariot has for a long time been dragging on its axles. As I see around me those highest in authority in our Church circles and those who have returned temporarily from active service in the foreign mission fields, and as I observe the silvery setting above their temples, which indicates much prayer, much thought, and much labor, and as I see the deep furrows down their faces, indicating the paths of the burning tears over the indifferences, the failures, the shortcomings of the people of this Christian land of ours as regards the condition of the heathen—as the shining sun behind the clouds, I think I see the smile of pleasure as the old battle-scarred veterans think of and hear the steady tread and "forward march" and listen to the battle cry of the relay, the relief party, the laymen of the Church hitching on to move the world to Christ.

Now, my fellow-associates, whether by election, selection, or of your own volition you have undertaken the leadership of your people, remember that your duties to them and your responsibilities to God are greatly increased, but that in consequence thereof neither their duties nor their responsibilities are in any way diminished; and do not forget that your work, if done, must be done by each individual member; and if you do not know your duty and your place, go home, get down your old Bible, and read Christ's farewell sermon, recorded in the fourteenth chapter of John's Gospel; and when you have read verse 26, ask God to show you your duties, to teach you his will, and to give you his filling of the Holy Spirit.   And then, too, my brethren, when all is done, in the words of the Lord Bishop of Thetford, remember this: "If that bit of work which you have undertaken is for the love of God (and it must be that) and for the glory of God, then it cannot fail. There is no such thing as failure in real Christian work.   We may make mistakes, but it cannot fail, for it is God's work; and if it is done for God, when we have done our best, he will take it and make use of it, perhaps so that we can see it; if not, we shall see it in the light of the world to come.   He will take us as we are and our work as it is, and in the time to come perhaps make use of our very mistakes and build upon the work which we began in humble faith and quiet hope the very work we wanted to do, but were too clumsy.   There has never yet been a work for Him that failed."

APPENDIX.

APPENDIX.

PAPERS AND RESOLUTIONS.

The papers and resolutions printed below are those not included in the chapter on "Purposes and Plans:"

Exhibit "A."

Resolved, That Dr. James H. Carlisle, of Spartanburg, S. C., one of the most consecrated and gifted laymen of Southern Methodism, who, on account of his feebleness and age, was unable to attend this Convention, but who still wields a ready pen, be requested to write at once an article on some phase of the Laymen's Missionary Movement, and that it be published along with other addresses in the pamphlet to be issued by this Convention.

As this great Southern layman is in his eighty-fifth year, this article will be in the nature of a farewell message to his brethren, and it will not fail to be productive of the best results.

It is to be much regretted that Dr. Carlisle was not physically able at this time to comply with this request.

Exhibit "B."

Whereas missions and Church Extension are parts of the same great department of Church effort; and whereas the laymen of the Church are interested in whatever contributes to the spread of the Kingdom; and whereas the last General Conference committed the Church to the building of a representative house of worship in Washington, D. C.; therefore be it

Resolved: 1. That we hereby give our indorsement to this proposition and assure the committee intrusted with this task of our willingness to coöperate with them in this important work.

2. That we rejoice at the growth of sentiment in favor of an increased Loan Fund capital for our Board of Church Extension, and trust that our people generally will observe Loan Fund Day, May 10, 1908, as proposed by the Board of Church Extension.

Exhibit "C."

For Exhibit "C," on the subject of systematic giving, urging a tenth as a minimum, etc., see chapter on "Purposes and Plans."

Exhibit "D."

To Our Fathers and Brethren.

Numbers of laymen in the Church are standing idle in the market place, and often we are thus standing idle all the day long; and if we were asked, "Why?" the answer would often be: "No man hath hired us."

We laymen want some definite work. We want something to do. It is the desire of our heart to do some useful labor in the cause of Jesus our Master. We want to be helpful in his kingdom, and helpful to our pastors and preachers. We believe in a division of the work. Looking to this end, we recommend that this paper be the memorial of the Laymen's Missionary Movement of the Methodist Episcopal Church, South, to the next General Conference of our Church so to change existing law, in some appropriate way, that the laymen of each charge, under the supervision of the pastor, shall have intrusted to them the collection of the Conference claims and assessments. Such a service, if asked from us, and such a duty, if placed in our hands, we will accept as a loving service for our Church and a sacred duty which we owe to our God.

Exhibit "E."

Resolved, That the Laymen's Movement of the Methodist Episcopal Church, South, have a button badge, and that the designing and selecting of such badge be hereby referred to the incoming Executive Committee with power to act.

Exhibit "F."

For Exhibit "F" see chapter on "Purposes and Plans."

Exhibit "G."

Resolved, That we, the laymen of the Methodist Episcopal Church, South, representing the Laymen's Missionary Movement, in Conference assembled at Chattanooga, Tenn., this 23d day of April, 1908, believe the time has now come when our Church should build and equip hospitals to care for the sick and infirm in such of the leading cities and such other places of our Southern Methodism as seem most needful.

Resolved, That our General Board of Missions, having already been given authority in this matter, be requested to proceed at once to carry out a policy for the Methodist Episcopal Church, South.

Exhibit "H."

Resolved, That it is the sense of this Conference that it would be well for the Methodist Episcopal Church, South, to have a great assembly ground on the order of Northfield, Mass., for the gathering together of our forces at stated times, and that such grounds should be so located and so improved as to make them suitable for the various Conferences of our Church when desirable to hold them there, and for Bible institutes and such other organizations for the help of the preachers and laymen and the general upbuilding of the Church and her forces as may be decided upon in our onward movement for the evangelization of the world.

Resolved, That a committee be appointed consisting of John R. Pepper, John P. Pettijohn, Gen. Julian S. Carr, N. M. Burger, R. S. Schoolfield, R. B. Davenport, A. D. Reynolds, with the request to take this matter in hand and take such steps as they may think best, with the approval of and under the direction of the Executive Committee.

Exhibit "I."

Exhibit "I," containing the resolution on the Emergency Corps, will be found in the chapter on "Purposes and Plans."

Exhibit "J."

Whereas the Sunday school is the teaching and training service of the Church; and whereas it affords the best and most opportune channel through which all educational matter covering every phase of the great mission of the Church can be disseminated; therefore be it

Resolved, That we recommend the appointment of a Missionary Committee in every Sunday school of our Church for the purpose of distributing missionary literature to every member of the Church and the teaching systematically of missions in the Church.

Exhibit "K."

We rejoice in the rapid development and splendid success of the Methodist Training School at Nashville, and recognize it as one of the most important institutions of the Church. Since it is owned and conducted by the Board of Missions for the purpose of giving thorough and practical training to our missionary candidates for the home and foreign fields, and consequently occupies a strategic position in the Church and has in it untold possibilities for good to our missionary cause, we therefore give it our unqualified indorsement and pledge it our hearty support.

Exhibit "L."

Resolution on Home Mission Department will be found in chapter on "Purposes and Plans."

Exhibit "M."

Whereas we appreciate the importance and far-reaching results of the work of the Methodist Episcopal Church, South, in the cities of our home land; and whereas Methodism is weak in New Orleans, La, the greatest city in the far South; and whereas we realize our obligation to aid and help strengthen our Church in that great city, and realizing this Conference would be a great uplift to our work there; therefore be it

Resolved, That we recommend to the Executive Committee the city of New Orleans, La., as the place for holding the next Conference of this Laymen's Missionary Movement.

18

On Raising Extension Fund.

In view of the fact that we must make provision for the administration of the Laymen's Missionary Movement in our Church for the next two years, in order that the work may be aggressively prosecuted; therefore be it

Resolved, That we raise now $15,000 in order to carry on this work as it should be done.

Some of the items to be provided for are as follows:

1. The employment of a General Secretary, a layman of excellent ability both on the platform and in the office.

2. A stenographer to aid him in the great volume of work that will undoubtedly come to his hand.

3. The creation and sending out of a large body of literature, pamphlet, booklet, and otherwise, so necessary to the education of the great army of laymen in our Church.

4. Postage and other necessary office expenses, which will also amount to considerable.

5. Traveling expenses, as it will be absolutely necessary for the General Secretary to be in the field a great deal. The amount to be raised here will be payable quarterly in advance for the next two years, provided any subscriber does not wish to pay all the amount at one time.

We believe this splendid body of laymen assembled here, all of whom are active, enterprising business men in their own communities, will appreciate the necessity for this fund for the administering of the work so necessary to be done, and will gladly give us the amount required.

We recommend that the election of a General Secretary be left to the Executive Committee when a suitable man can be found.

Recommending Church Conferences.

Recognizing the importance of the rank and file of the Church being fully and early informed as to the aims and plans of work adopted by this Laymen's Missionary Movement; therefore be it

Resolved, That, as the best method for disseminating this information, we recommend to the pastor and key man of each Church that a Church Conference be held as early as possible in every Church, before which shall be brought for indorsement the plan and work of this great Movement.

MEDICAL MISSIONARY SOCIETY.

The following announcement was made by Dr. Lambuth:

I take great pleasure in announcing that, after two meetings of the medical men who are delegates and in attendance upon this Laymen's Missionary Conference, a Medical Missionary Society of the Methodist

Episcopal Church, South, working under the auspices of the Board of Missions and in coöperation with that Board, has been organized. [Applause.]

This society has for its purpose the study of missions, with special reference to the study of medical missions, and also the dissemination of literature upon the subject of medical missions, and desires to swing into line the eight or ten thousand medical men in our Church and get them behind our medical missionary work. [Applause.]

They have elected Dr. T. F. Staley the first President of this society [applause], Dr. J. L. Scales, of Louisiana, Vice President [applause], Dr. George Trawick, of Nashville, Secretary [applause], and are ready to go to work. [Applause.]

They simply make this request of you: that you will turn the names of all the medical men who are members of the Methodist Episcopal Church, South, at once into Dr. George Trawick's hands, Nashville, Tenn., by correspondence, that he himself may get into immediate correspondence with these medical men.

During the session of the Conference at Chattanooga, April 21-23, a meeting of the delegates who were medical practitioners was called; and after a discussion of the needs and of the field of work, it was decided to adopt the following preamble and resolutions, with the understanding that this organization is a coordinate department of the Laymen's Missionary Movement:

Whereas medical missions has been a pioneer in opening the way for the gospel; and whereas we understand that the Board of Missions is in need of more men and equipment to carry on this work; and whereas there are in the Methodist Episcopal Church, South, some eight or ten thousand medical men; therefore be it

Resolved: 1. That the time has come for the formation of a Medical Missionary Society, which shall work under the auspices of and in coöperation with the Board of Missions in furthering this great work.

2. That a committee of three be appointed, which, in addition to the Senior Secretary of the Board of Missions as an ex officio member, shall be given authority to draft and adopt a basis of organization and to act with the Secretaries of the Board in carrying out the purposes of the Society.

The committee was appointed, the basis adopted at a subsequent meeting, and the following were elected officers and Executive Committee of the Society: T. F. Staley, M.D., Bristol, Tenn., President; J. L. Scales, M.D., Alden Bridge, La., Vice President; George C. Trawick, M.D., Nashville, Tenn., Secretary; W. R. Lambuth, M.D., Secretary Board of Missions, Nashville, Tenn.

Inasmuch as this organization has the hearty indorsement of the Executive Committee of the Laymen's Missionary Movement, it is requested that every physician in the Church send his name and address at once to Dr. George C. Trawick, 208 Sixth Avenue North, Nashville, Tenn., for enrollment in the Medical Missionary Society, one of the most inspiring movements in the history of our Church.

CHARTER MEMBERS.

Dr. W. R. Lambuth, Nashville, Tenn.; Dr. George R. West, Chattanooga, Tenn.; Dr. George C. Trawick, Nashville, Tenn.; Dr. John L. Scales, Alden Bridge, La.; Dr. B. L. Branch, Collierville, Tenn.; Dr. A. G. Henderson, Imboden, Ark.; Dr. John Johnson, Sidney, Ark.; Dr. L. E. Moore, Searcy, Ark.; Dr. C. B. Van Arsdall, Harrodsburg, Ky.; Dr. F. H. Gardner, Fabius, Ala.; Dr. J. W. Tankard, Lilian, Va.; Dr. J. R. Brown, Malta Bend, Mo.; Dr. T. F. Staley, Bristol, Va.-Tenn.

CONSTITUTION.

1. The name of this organization shall be the Medical Missionary Society of the Methodist Episcopal Church, South.

2. The purpose of this organization shall be to enlist the ten thousand medical and dental practitioners of our Church in the study of missions in general and of medical missionary work in particular; to get them in touch with our medical missionaries in the foreign field; and to coöperate with the General Board of Missions in supporting these medical missionaries, in building mission hospitals in which the sick and suffering may be ministered to, and in maintaining such medical missionary work under the Board both at home and abroad as shall directly contribute to the evangelization of the world.

3. This Medical Missionary Society shall work under the auspices of and in coöperation with the Board of Missions of the Methodist Episcopal Church, South, and shall not be considered a separate and independent organization, but shall be a part of our Laymen's Missionary Movement and shall direct its energies and contributions through the regularly constituted channels of the Church.

4. Any member of the Methodist Episcopal Church, South, who is a graduate of a regular medical or dental college may, upon application through the Secretary of the Society, by a majority vote of the Executive Committee and by payment of the registration fee, be enrolled as a member. All medical missionaries of our Church shall be made honorary members of this Society upon presentation of their names by any member.

5. The officers of this Society shall be a President, a Vice President, and a Secretary. The Senior Secretary of the Board of Missions shall be *ex officio* a member of this Society, and the Treasurer of the Board of Missions shall receive and transmit all funds, keeping a separate account of the same on his books and rendering an annual statement of receipts and disbursements.

6. The registration fee in this Medical Missionary Society shall be two dollars, payable annually to the Treasurer of the Board of Missions of

the Methodist Episcopal Church, South, 810 Broadway, Nashville, Tenn., on or before the first of January of each year. The registration or membership fee shall be applied to the expense of correspondence and to the preparation and circulation of such literature on medical missions as shall promote the interest of the work.

7. The organ of the Medical Missionary Society shall be the monthly periodical, *Go Forward,* published by the Board of Missions, which, in consideration of the payment of the annual fee of two dollars, shall be sent free of charge to each member.

8. The members of the Society shall be encouraged to join the Emergency Corps of ten thousand men, to whom the emergency needs in the ongoing of our mission work at home and abroad may be presented either for contribution or for personal service, both contribution and service being voluntary, and left in every case to the ability and convenience of the individual member of the Emergency Corps at the time the call is made.

9. There shall be a meeting every two years of the Medical Missionary Society at the same time and place of holding the Conference of the Laymen's Missionary Movement, at which time the Secretary of the Society shall present a report of the membership, of the literature circulated, the work done, and the needs and outlook of our medical missionary work.

THANKS EXTENDED.

The following paper was offered at the closing session by the Executive Committee, and adopted with applause by a rising vote:

We hereby extend our most sincere thanks to the people of Chattanooga for the unstinted kindness and hospitality extended to us during our stay and for the innumerable special courtesies; and to the association of citizens known as "The Chattanoogans," who have so splendidly entertained our distinguished guest, the British Ambassador, we would express our sincere thanks.

We also desire to record our high appreciation of the part that Mayor Crabtree has taken in and for this body.

But very especially do we wish to thank the Local Committee for their untiring efforts and for their most generous and comprehensive arrangements on behalf of the Conference.

To the press of the city for uniform and constant kindness in the use of their columns we heartily accord just praise.

The railroads have given us reduced rates and otherwise helped toward the success of the meeting. For their courtesies and coöperation we acknowledge ourselves indebted.

We ask that these expressions be adopted by a rising vote.

MISSIONARY EXHIBIT.

The Missionary Exhibit, arranged under the supervision of Mr. J. E. McCulloch, Superintendent of the Training School, was one of the telling features of the Conference. It occupied the Sunday school room of Centenary Church, and was visited and enjoyed by large numbers of people. It was indeed an exhibit of missionary work. It contained a museum of curios from foreign lands, charts and statistical tables in colors, samples of literature and methods in all departments of missionary activity, pictures of buildings, of groups of natives, of workers, together with appliances for teaching missions in the Sunday school. This exhibit was the product of much thought and toil, and was itself a school of missions.

LITERATURE.

A vast amount and great variety of literature was displayed, both for free distribution and for sale. The patronage of both kinds was liberal, and there were many inquiries for the best literature for given conditions, showing a spirit of investigation and a determination to acquaint the uninformed with the great cause of missions. This literature as well as the exhibit was emphasized by liberal and skillful advertising.

MOVING PICTURES.

One of the most attractive features of the Conference was the lectures given by Dr. Lambuth each afternoon with moving pictures from mission fields. They were not only object lessons of immediate value to those present, but also as an illustration of the possibilities of the stereopticon as a means of missionary education. The scenes were illustrative of mission work and of the habits and customs of heathen peoples. The speaker's personal relation to many of the persons and scenes and his own recital of his memories and experiences on the field gave a thrilling touch of realism that brought forth frequent applause.

Dr. W. F. McMurry was on the programme for a speech on the "Problem of the Downtown Church." He very generously surrendered his time to others, with the promise that the manuscript would be furnished for publication in this volume. Owing to the sickness of his assistant and the pressure of duties in the office, he was unable to furnish us the address in time. Our first regret was that this vital home mission theme should not have been discussed on the platform by one so able to illumine it; and our second is that we cannot print it in this volume.

REAL AND POSSIBLE GIFTS OF THE M. E. CHURCH, SOUTH, TO FOREIGN MISSIONS.

What we give to Foreign Missions annually, $736,000.

If each Sunday school scholar in our Church gave one cent a week, it would amount to $586,226.

Five cents per week from each Church member would be $4,486,214 annually.

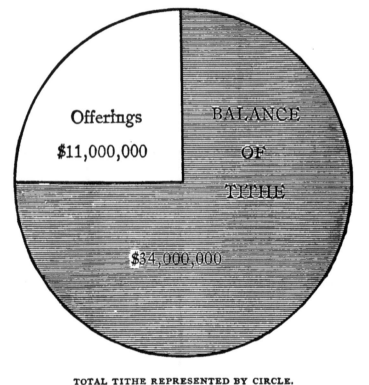

JUST THE TENTH.

Annual Income of Membership of M. E. Church, South, at 75 Cents a Day Each, $450,000,000.

Offerings $11,000,000

BALANCE OF TITHE

$34,000,000

TOTAL TITHE REPRESENTED BY CIRCLE.

WHAT A TENTH WOULD MEAN.

The income of the average citizen is at least 75 cents a day. Ten years ago it was 55 cents. For Church members who are mostly adults and also above the average it would be higher. The above is on the very conservative basis of 75 cents a day income for each Church member.

(280)

Field of one missionary of the M. E. Church, South, 150,000.

Field of worker of M. E. Church, South, in the United States.

800.

We have one worker for about every 800 in the United States; in heathenism, 1 to 150,000.

On each one of the 40,000,000 heathen for whom we are responsible we spend 1½ cts. annually.

1½ cts.

On each one of the 8,000,000 in the United States to whom we minister we expend each year $1.26.

Comparison of per capita distribution of funds at home and abroad.

MISSIONARY FORCE AND FIELD OF THE M. E. CHURCH, SOUTH.

FORCE.

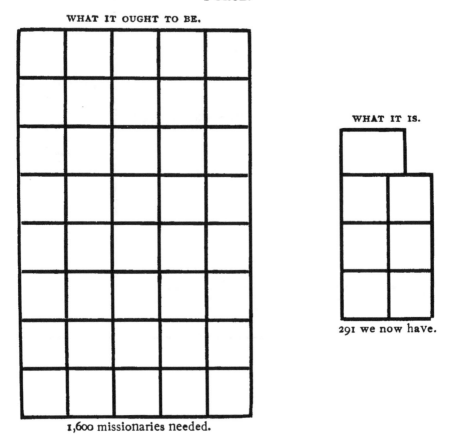

WHAT IT OUGHT TO BE.

WHAT IT IS.

291 we now have.

1,600 missionaries needed.

FIELD.

7,000,000 we are now reaching in foreign lands.

40,000,000 for whom we are now responsible in foreign fields.

NEED AND SUPPLY AT HOME AND ABROAD.

8,000,000 people in the United States on whom we expend $10,000,000.

40,000,000 people in heathen lands on whom we expend $750,000.

It is estimated that the M. E. Church, South, ministers to 8,000,000 in the United States and is responsible for the evangelization of 40,000,000 in heathen lands. These squares indicate the relative way in which we are meeting this responsibility.

What we aim to raise annually.

$3,000,000.

What we raise annually.

$750,000.

INCREASE OF RECEIPTS FOR FOREIGN MISSIONS
IN THE UNITED STATES.

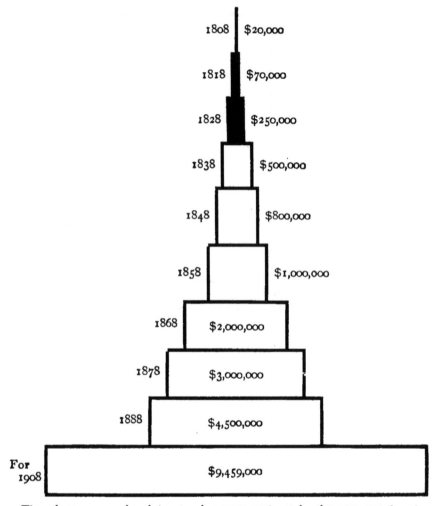

1808 $20,000

1818 $70,000

1828 $250,000

1838 $500,000

1848 $800,000

1858 $1,000,000

1868 $2,000,000

1878 $3,000,000

1888 $4,500,000

For
1908 $9,459,000

The above can only claim to show approximately the average for the decade beginning with the date on the left. Only round numbers are given. The last block indicates the income for the year 1907, and shows the total increase for two decades in yearly contributions.

(284)

RELATIVE NEEDS OF MEDICAL
MISSIONS.

To every 2,500,000 people in heathen lands, one
medical missionary; to same number in
United States, 4,000 physicians.

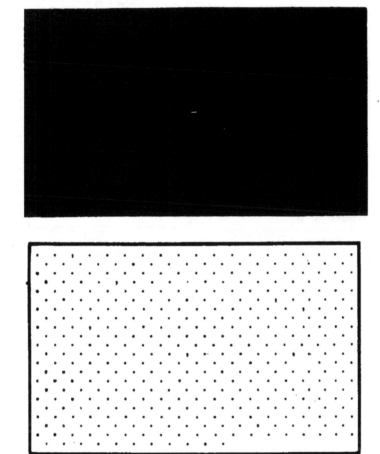

EACH DOT REPRESENTS 10 PHYSICIANS.

That there is need for all talents and abilities on the foreign field is illustrated by the need for physicians and medical missionaries there. While there are 4,000 physicians to minister to 2,500,000 people in the United States, there is but one available to the same number of heathen whose needs are greater in proportion to their ignorance of the right principles of living and caring for themselves. There are openings for all God-given talents on the field.

STATISTICS OF FOREIGN MISSIONS OF THE PARENT BOARD, M. E. CHURCH, SOUTH, 1907–08.

	Missionaries	Wives of Missionaries	Native Traveling Preachers	Local Preachers	Members, Including Local Preachers	Increase	Sunday Schools	S. S. Officers and Teach'rs	Scholars	Epworth Leagues	E. L. Members	Societies or Organized Churches	Churches Entirely Self-Supporting	Boarding Schools	Teachers	Pupils	Day Schools	Teachers	Pupils
China	23	23	24	25	2,190	307	53	177	2,573	32	892	27	8	4	46	533	12	20	293
Korea	14	9	..	..	1,988	761	83	111	1,770	..	..	181	89	2	8	246	3	8	82
Japan	23	13	14	24	1,776	203	62	247	5,401	14	379	24	..	3	37	1,278	7	11	584
Brazil	17	16	14	11	5,368	307	73	236	2,884	43	1,830	44	5	1	1	291	1	..	....
Mexico	19	18	45	62	6,815	410	136	464	5,157	37	1,377	108	3	2	20	466	1	2	60
Cuba	14	10	11	20	2,847	482	44	176	2,847	17	675	37	....	4	19	345	3	..	45
Total	110	89	111	145	20,990	2,270	401	1,401	20,632	143	5,153	425	108	16	110	3,159	26	41	1,014

	School Buildings	Value	Hospitals and Dispensaries	Value	Patients Treated	Collected for All Purposes	Church Buildings	Value	Parsonages	Value	Total Value of Mission Property.
China	12	$201,807	1	$14,792 00	20,901	$ 4,319 75	23	$ 17,900 00	14	$22,926 00	$257,425 00
Korea	1	4,500	2	1,500	1,852	2,380 26	5	8,000 00	7	35,000 00	49,000 00
Japan	15	81,500	..	....	....	3,927 34	13	20,130 00	6	2,287 50	103,767 50
Brazil	2	98,000	1	6,000 00	....	11,854 24	31	163,190 00	9	41,000 00	289,990 00
Mexico	2	90,000	..	....	29,653	6,505 88	74	162,772 00	34	79,785 00	348,557 00
Cuba	4	57,000	..	....	....	11,924 85	28	106,025 00	14	2,175 00	204,723 71
Total	36	$527,807	4	$22,292 00	52,406	$40,912 42	178	$478,017 00	84	$207,123 50	$1,253,463 21

Receipts for foreign missions on regular collections, $400,864.08; received from all sources, $540,523.50. Increase in regular collections, $14,535.89; increase in total collections, $21,307.17.

STATISTICS OF THE WOMAN'S FOREIGN MISSIONARY SOCIETY OF THE M. E. CHURCH, SOUTH, 1907–08.

	Missionaries.	Native and Foreign Helpers.	Total Teachers.	Boarding Schools.	Pupils in Boarding Schools.	Day Schools.	Pupils in Day Schools.	Total Pupils.
China	24	40	64	8	420	10	390	810
Korea	11	10	21	4	100	5	150	250
Brazil	22	50	72	6	130	6	631	761
Mexico	19	97	116	7	1,300	9	1,000	2,300
Cuba	6	12	18	2	322	....	....	322
Indian Mission	....	6	12	1	75	....	....	75
Total	82	215	303	28	2,347	30	2,171	4,518

	Bible Women.	Bible Schools.	Scholarships.	Hospitals.	Buildings Owned by Woman's Board.	Buildings Rented by Woman's Board.	Value of Property Owned by Woman's Board.
China	106	3	211	1	13	10	$110,000
Korea	35	2	105	1	5	5	20,000
Brazil	13	....	31	....	5	6	120,000
Mexico	19	2	96	....	6	9	160,000
Cuba	1	....	25	....	1	1	27,500
Indian Mission	....	....	4	....	1	....	10,000
Scarritt Bible and Training School	....	....	....	....	....	....	100,000
Total	174	7	472	2	30	31	$547,500

Collections during past year, $226,192.88.   Increase in collections, $51,000.   Membership, 84,995.   Increase in membership during past year, 448.

SUMMARY OF STATISTICS OF FOREIGN MIS-
SIONS, M. E. CHURCH, SOUTH, 1901-08.

	1901.	1908.	Increase.	Decrease.
Missionaries (including wives of missionaries)...................	194	281	87	....
Teachers and helpers	138	371	233	....
Bible women....................	71	174	103	....
Day schools.....................	76	56	....	20
Pupils in day schools............	2,099	3,185	1,086	....
Boarding schools.................	24	44	20	....
Pupils in boarding schools........	1,196	5,506	4,210	....
Hospitals and dispensaries........	6	4	....	2
Patients treated.................	13,132	52,406	39,274	....
Total value of mission property...	$897,807	$1,800,963	$903,156	....

INCREASE OF MEMBERS IN MISSION
FIELDS, 1906-07.

Total for all Protestant missions............................. 137,714

For every day in the year..................................... 377

Or an increase of members amounting to..................... 9%

Total for all American Protestant missions.................... 66,147

A ratio of increase of.. 11%

At 9% our increase at home would be....................... 150,000

At 11% our increase at home would be..................... . 180,000

In Korea our gain last year was............................. 62%

At 62% our gain at home would be......................... 1,029,200

The gain in Korea for each missionary in our Church was..... 54

At that rate at home we would gain......................... 378,000

(288)

ANNUAL CONFERENCE LEADERS.

CONFERENCE.	LAY LEADER.	ADDRESS.
Alabama	Judge A. E. Barnett	Opelika, Ala.
Arkansas	P. W. Furry	Van Buren, Ark.
Baltimore	F. B. Thomas	Roanoke, Va.
Columbia	J. J. Lamb	Coquille, Oregon.
Denver	—	—.
East Columbia	—	—.
Florida	T. J. Watkins	Orlando, Fla.
German Mission	—	—.
Holston	Maj. A. D. Reynolds	Bristol, Tenn.
Kentucky	J. L. Gaugh	Wilmore, Ky.
Little Rock	Judge J. S. Steel	Lockesburg, Ark.
Los Angeles	—	—.
Louisiana	W. W. Carré	New Orleans, La.
Louisville	C. M. Phillips	Louisville, Ky.
Memphis	T. B. King	Memphis, Tenn.
Mississippi	Judge A. G. Norrell	Florence, Miss.
Missouri	Judge B. J. Casteel	St. Joseph, Mo.
Montana	—	—.
New Mexico	Judge D. G. Grantham	Carlsbad, N. Mex.
North Alabama	Dr. S. C. Tatum	Center, Ala.
North Carolina	Gen. J. S. Carr	Durham, N. C.
North Georgia	L. M. Pennington	Eatonton, Ga.
North Mississippi	Judge F. A. Critz	West Point, Miss.
North Texas	E. G. Knight	Dallas, Tex.
Northwest Texas	Judge W. E. Williams	Fort Worth, Tex.
Oklahoma	Dr. A. E. Bonnell	Muskogee, Okla.
Pacific	—	—.
St. Louis	Dr. J. W. Vaughan	St. Louis, Mo.
South Carolina	J. B. Carlisle	Spartanburg, S. C.
South Georgia	R. F. Burden	Macon, Ga.
Southwest Missouri	—	—.
Tennessee	Prof. Wm. Hughes	Spring Hill, Tenn.
Texas	R. D. Hart	Texarkana, Tex.
Virginia	J. P. Pettyjohn	Lynchburg, Va.
West Texas	R. H. Wester	San Antonio, Tex.
Western N. Carolina	C. H. Ireland	Greensboro, N. C.
Western Virginia	Mr. M. W. Thomas	Ashland, Ky.
White River	F. M. Daniel	Mammoth Spr's, Ark.

19

(289)

COMMITTEES OF THE CONFERENCE.

COMMITTEE ON PERMANENT ORGANIZATION.

W. W. Carré, Louisiana, *Chairman.*

A. Trieschmann, Arkansas;
W. M. Sloan, Missouri;
J. L. Dantzler, Mississippi;
O. A. Park, Georgia;
Judge Newman;
J. R. Deason, Tennessee;
J. D. Whitcomb, Texas;

Judge O'Rear, Kentucky;
L. B. Blaylock, Texas;
T. S. DeArman, Oklahoma;
T. J. Watkins, Florida;
Chairman and Secretary *ex officio* members.

COMMITTEE ON RESOLUTIONS AND BUSINESS.

W. G. M. Thomas, Chattanooga, Tenn., *Chairman.*

E. F. Sheffey, Virginia;
W. Erskine Williams, Texas;
R. F. Burden, Georgia;
George McNapier, Georgia;

W. M. Tatum, Mississippi;
C. M. Phillips, Kentucky;
Satterfield, Oklahoma;
W. B. Stubbs, Georgia.

LOCAL COMMITTEES.

COMMITTEE OF ARRANGEMENTS.

J. L. Foust, *Chairman.*

Creed F. Bates,
J. N. Trigg,
B. F. Fritts,
T. O. Trotter,

W. E. Brock,
J. H. Thomas,
J. A. Hargraves,
W. A. Schoolfield,

Peter Engers,
C. R. Wallace,
R. F. Calloway,
W. H. Frazier.

GENERAL RECEPTION COMMITTEE.

Charles W. Rankin, *Chairman.*

L. A. Webster,
Earl M. Alexander,
Hugh Burger,
Charles Clinton,
Howard D. Crowe,
Walter Fisher,
Carl Groner,
William H. Marsh,
Robert Parsons,
Charles Simmons,
Frank Stone,
Thomas H. Weatherford,
A. S. Oakman,
Lee Barnes,

Mike Cureton,
Rudd Loder,
Clifford Longley,
Robert Woodberry,
Harry E. Chapman,
T. E. Patterson,
H. F. Wenning,
Orville Beasley,
Elmer Cornes,
Clarence Graves,
Forrest Groover,
Roy Kirven,
Will Light,
Charles Sparks,

T. T. Rankin,
Robert M. Bennett,
James R. Cash,
Ralph Garmany,
Edgar Jones,
William S. Latimore,
Lewis F. Turner,
Ralph Wardlow,
Lyle W. West,
Neil Thomas,
S. B. Cook,
J. E. Ramsey,
Lavins M. Thomas.

SPEAKERS' RECEPTION COMMITTEE.

J. Milton Browne, *Chairman.*

Mayor W. R. Crabtree,	Judge M. M. Allison,
S. G. Gilbreath,	Creed F. Bates,
E. B. Craig,	W. H. Weatherford,
Frank H. Atlee,	C. W. Beise,
C. W. K. Meacham,	R. F. Calloway,
Rev. R. A. Kelly,	W. I. Young.

COMMITTEE ON MUSIC.

W. J. Smith, *Chairman;*
Rev. John C. Orr, *Director.*

J. S. McLearen,	R. F. Calloway,
H. F. Wenning,	T. O. Eldredge,
H. B. Wood,	S. H. Seymour.

PRESS COMMITTEE.

J. A. Burrow, *Chairman.*
A. M. Trawick.

EXHIBIT COMMITTEE.

J. E. McCulloch, *Chairman.*

Mrs. J. B. Cobb,	W. E. Towson.

COMMITTEE ON LITERATURE AND MISSIONARY EDUCATION.

Ed F. Cook, *Chairman.*

COMMITTEE ON HOTELS.

Charles W. Rankin, *Chairman.*

S. B. Cook,	J. E. Ramsey.

COMMITTEE ON HOMES.

Lavins M. Thomas, *Chairman.*

T. E. Patterson,	H. E. Chapman.

RECEPTION COMMITTEE.

Charles W. Rankin, *Chairman.*

Lavins M. Thomas,	T. E. Patterson,
S. B. Cook,	H. E. Chapman,
J. E. Ramsey.	

COMMITTEE ON USHERS.

J. H. Thomas, *Chairman.*

W. E. Brock,	J. E. Ramsey.

INTERDENOMINATIONAL COMMITTEE.

John R. Pitner, *Chairman;*
T. E. Patterson, *Vice President.*

John S. Martin,	Rev. J. A. Baylor.

BIBLIOGRAPHY.

Foreign Missions.

The Foreign Missionary. Arthur J. Brown, D.D...............$1 50
The Call of Korea. Underwood................................. 75
The New Horoscope of Missions. Dennis...................... 1 00
The Missionary and His Critics. Barton...................... 1 00
The Awakening of China. Martin............................. 3 50
In the Valley of the Nile. Watson........................... 1 00
The Missionary and His Critics. J. L. Barton................ 1 00
The Missionary Interpretation of History. Stevenson............. 75
The Bible a Missionary Book. Dr. R. F. Horton................ 1 00
God's Missionary Plan for the World. Bishop Bashford.......... 75
John G. Paton. Cloth..................................... 1 50
Pastor Hsi. Mrs. Howard Taylor.............................. 1 00
Missions in the Sunday School. Miss Hixon.................... 50
A Century of Protestant Missions in China. (Historical volume of
　　the Centenary Conference in Shanghai)...................... 2 50
With Tommy Tompkins in Korea. Underwood.................... 1 25
The Vanguard. J. S. Gale.................................... 1 35
The Lady of the Decoration. F. Little........................ 90
Sunrise in the Sunrise Kingdom. DeForest.................... 50
Griffith John. The Story of Fifty Years in China. R. W. Thomp-
　　son 2 00
East of Suez. Penfield...................................... 2 00
New Forces in Old China. A. J. Brown...................... 1 50
The Bible in Brazil. H. C. Tucker. Net..................... 1 25
A New Era in Old Mexico. G. B. Winton...................... 1 00
The Romance of Missionary Heroism. John C. Lambert.......... 1 50
Islam: A Challenge to Faith. S. M. Zwemer.................... 1 00
Strategic Points in the World's Conquest. John R. Mott.......... 85
Protestant Missions: Their Rise and Early Progress. Dr. Thomp-
　　son. Cloth, 50 cents; paper............................... 35
Life of Laura Askew Haygood. O. E. Brown.................... 1 00
The Evangelization of the World in This Generation. John R. Mott 1 00
The Why and How of Missions. Arthur J. Brown. Cloth, 50
　　cents; paper... 35
Modern Missions in the Far East. Lawrence. Revell & Co........ 1 50
Christianity in Modern Japan. E. W. Clement.................. 1 00
The Evolution of New China. Eaton & Mains.................. 1 50
American Diplomacy in the Far East. John W. Foster........... 3 20

MEDICAL MISSIONS.

The Healing of the Nations. Dr. J. Rutter Williamson, member of
the British Medical Association. 12mo. 95 pages. Price, paper,
25 cents; cloth..$0 40
The Medical Mission: Its Place, Power, and Appeal. W. J. Wan-
less, M.D. 12mo. 96 pages. Price, paper................... 10
Medical Missions: Their Place and Power. John Lowe. 12mo.
Cloth. Price 1 50
John Kenneth Mackenzie, M.D., Medical Missionary to China. Mrs.
Mary I. Bryson. 12mo. Cloth............................. 1 50

HOME MISSIONS.

The Present South. Murphy..................................... 1 50
Christianity's Storm Center. Stelzle.......................... 1 00
Christianity and the Social Crisis. Rauschenbusch.............. 1 25
The Open Church for the Unchurched. McCulloch................ 1 00
The Challenge of the City. Josiah Strong. Paper, 35 cents; cloth. 50
The Incoming Millions. Grose. Cloth, 50 cents; paper........... 30
Workable Plans for Wide-Awake Churches. Reisner. Net....... 1 50
Aliens or Americans? Grose. Net............................. 50
The Good Neighbor. Richmond. Net........................... 60
The Church and the Changing Order. Matthews. Net........... 1 50
The Bitter Cry of the Children. Spargo. Net.................. 1 50
Poverty. Hunter 1 50
The Negro the Southerner's Problem. Net 1 25
Migrating Nations: America's Opportunity. Pamphlet. Bishop E.
R. Hendrix.. 1c
The Call of the West. Pamphlet. Bishop James Atkins........... 1c
Order these books of Smith & Lamar, Nashville, Tenn.

INDEX.

INDEX.

Accidents and what is done, 229.

Advance accelerating, 43.

Adventurer and trader, 95.

Agriculture, 115.

Allen, Y. J., quoted, 227.

Ambassador Bryce, Introduction of, 86.

America a laboratory, 126.

America divinely guided, 223.

American evil in China, 169.

America's place in the world's influence, 57.

Amputation in China, 227.

Apostles Asiatics, 78.

Appendix, 273.

Asia first had our gospel, 78.

Asia, industrial changes in, 123.

Assembly Grounds, 272.

Awakening of the Orient, 58.

Badge for Laymen's Movement, 272.

Battle of Mukden, 31.

Battles about Chattanooga, 27.

Begging to be taught, 175.

Bell, sounding for accident, 229.

Bibliography, 292.

Blind people in China, 226.

Boards splendidly organized, 40.

Boston and China, 46.

Bound as a slave to give the price, 69.

Boy and Shinto drum, 151.

Boys and girls in city, 122.

Bricks without straw, 217.

Broken-hearted people, 140.

Bryce, Ambassador, 86.

Buddhism in Japan, 137.

Business methods, 216.

Call to Laymen, x.

Campaign of education, 6.

Campaign of education needed, 237.

Capen, S. B., address, 35.

Captain of life, 105.

Carlisle, James H., 271.

Catholicism Protestantized, 136.

Center of civilization, 55.

Center of the world's news, 160.

Charter members of Medical Missionary Society, 276.

Charts and Statistics, 280-285.

Chattanooga Conference characterized, 3.

China and America, 169.

China, a new mind, 161.

China anti-foreign, 161.

China awake, 160.

China awakening, 37.

China not warlike, 171.

China's cry, 45.

China's need, 173.

China's strength, 170.

China's weakness, 172.

Chinese bravery, 141.

Christ entombed, 218.

"Christus Auctor" in Spanish, 246.

Church buildings a necessity, 216.

Church Conferences, 274.

Churches in the city, 120.

Church extension, 271.

Church the greatest thing, 73.

Cities dominant, 117.

Cities multiplying gifts to missions, 66.

Civilization not enough, 141.

Coleridge, 30.

Collections in full, 266.

Colleges and missions, 40, 173.

Commerce and Latin America, 215.

Commerce and missions, 56.

Committees, 290.

Comparative number of workers at home and abroad, 46, 281, 282.

Comparison of Methodists and Presbyterians, 15.
Conditions of Church membership strict in Korea, 163.
Conference Lay Leader, 249.
Confession, our missionary, xvi.
Confucianism failing, 139.
Constitution of Medical Missionary Societies, 276.
Contrast of races, 96.
Conviction rests on knowledge, 237.
Coöperation needed, 58.
Corruption by prosperity, 146.
Cost of reaching each person, 65.
Crabtree, Mayor, 27.
Crisis in Korea, 186.
Critical period, 97.
Cry of the hungry, 187.
Cuba, 209.
Cuba set free, 209.

Danger to our own sons in Cuba, 213.
Dawn in the Arctic, 32.
Declaration card, 48.
Definite work for laymen, 272.
Definition Laymen's Movement, viii.
Dewey, the agent of Providence, 160.
Diplomat and missionary, 39.
Diplomats of United States, 42.
Disease and death a terror, 227.
District Lay Leader, 255.
District meeting yearly, 255.
Dr. Goucher in India, 67.
Domestic missions, 19.
Doom of pagan faiths, 135.
Drift of population to cities, 122.
Duty of every Christian, 87.
Dynamite, social, 120.

Educational Crisis in Korea, 186.
Educational movement in missions, 233.
Educational policy and methods, 21.
Education in missions, 6.

Egypt in process of change, 158.
Emergency corps, 17.
Emergency men, 6.
Emerson, crisis in life, 223.
England and America as missionary nations, 58.
England and America without Christianity, 88.
English taught in Japan, 51.
Equipment a necessity, 216.
Estimates of the Chattanooga Conference, 7.
Examination in Western learning, 37.
Exhibit, Missionary, 278.
Expense Fund, 274.

Far East no longer, 142.
Fast collection, 183.
Few laborers, 46.
Financial ability, 236.
Financial panic, 145.
Field of missionary education, 228.
Food demand limited, 116.
Food supply, 115.
Foot-binding in China, 225.
Force not needed, 96.
Foreign and home field compared, 45.
Foreigners in cities, 119.
Forward, the call to go, 131.
Foundation-laying, 43.
Freedom from sin, 213.

Giving as a means of education, 258.
Gospel and flag, 160.
Gospel not Anglo-Saxon, 78.
Governments and uncivilized, 95.
Government sympathy, 40.
Governments weak to uplift, 76.
Growth of Chattanooga, 27.
Growth of the Church in Korea, 182.

Hardy, Alpheus, 50.
Hay, John, influence of, 58.

Haystack prayer meeting, 35.
Heathen, not savage, 141.
Heathen unprovided for, 61.
Hendrix, Bishop, introduction, 86.
Heroic age, 107. ·
High civilization of China, 171.
Hiroshima Girls' School, 153.
Historical Statement, vii.
Hoisting Magnet, 31.
Home and foreign field compared, 45.
Home Department, 19.
Home missions, responsibility for, 80.
Homes in the city, 121.
Home work helped, 47.
Hospitals essential, 226, 272.
Human agency demanded, 250.
Hungry souls taunted, 187.

Ideal of the Church, 74.
Immigration, 119.
Imperfections of the Church, 77.
Income from a tenth, 236, 280.
Increase of income for missions, 284.
Increase of wealth, 124.
India restless, 158.
Indifference of the many, 44.
Industrial changes in Asia, 123.
Industrial revolution, 121.
Influence of Cuba on us, 212.
Influence of Latin America, 214.
Influence of missions on nations, 42.
Information begets interest, 237.
Insane and their treatment, 226.
Intelligent plan, 5.
Intemperance, 94.
Interdenominational committees, 48.
Intolerance of truth, 132.
Introduction of Mr. Bryce, 86.
Invasion from the South, 213.
Investigation by fifty men, 49.
Investment that pays, 68.

Jackson at New Orleans, 143.
Jacob Riis quoted, 47.

Japan eager, 46.
Japan in Korea, 224.
Japan learning, 138.
Jenny Lind, 106.
John Hay's influence, 58.

Key men, 48.
Korea, 181.
Korean Christians, 164.
Korean liberality, 183.
Korea's crisis, 186.

Laborers at home and abroad, 46.
Laborers few in Korea, 187.
Latin America, 211.
Lay Leader in congregation, 263.
Lay Leader of Annual Conference, 249.
Laymen in home missions, 80.
Laymen's Missionary Movement in England, 60.
Laymen's Movement defined, viii.
Leaders, list of, 289.
Leader's qualifications, 251.
Liberality of Koreans, 183.
Liberality, too broad, 132.
List of books, 292.
Literature circulated, 239.
Loyalty of Koreans, 183.
Lunatics in China, 226.
Luxury weakens, 125.

Machinery, its effects, 114.
"Man of Galilee" in Spanish, 244.
Massachusetts and China, 46.
Materials for missionary education, 238.
McMurry, W. F., 278.
Mechanical wealth, 116.
Medical missionaries, 46, 285.
Medical Missionary Society, 6, 274.
Medical missionary welcomed, 226.
Medical work in the Orient, 223.
Methodism and evangelization, 144.
Methodist Training School, 273.
Method of missionary education, 22.
Michael Angelo, 31.

Million dollars asked, 13.
Missionaries few, 46.
Missionaries needed to evangelize the world in this generation, 60.
Missionary and diplomat, 39.
Missionary Conference, xvi.
Missionary Exhibit, 278.
Missionary, false idea, 215.
Missionary force, 282.
Money is abundant, 49.
Money needed, 79, 176.
Monroe Doctrine, 38.
Mountain sections, 28.
Moving pictures, 278.
Mukden, battle of, 31.

Napoleon and Alexander, 30.
Need and how met, 281.
Need and supply, 283.
Need of missionaries, 46.
Need of more laborers in Korea, 187.
Need of strong missionaries, 216.
Need of the nations, 140.
Need realized in China, 173.
Need, where greatest, 44.
Neesima, Joseph, 50.
New England with only two physicians, 46.
New mind in China, 161.
New Orleans recommended for next meeting place, 273.
Newspapers in China, 160.
New York and China compared, 226.
New York and Cuba, 215.
Niagara and commerce, 26.
Niagara of wasted power, 30.
Northern Presbyterians quoted, 14.
Number enrolled in Mission Study, 239.
Number heathen compared to number at home, 62.

Old religions dying, 98.
One meal a day, 184.
One physician in New York, 226.

Opium and officeholders, 39.
Opium curse, 224.
Opportunity, the, 41.
Oppression in Cuba, 210.
Organization Laymen's Movement, 48.
Organization, Plan of, 50.
Origin of Laymen's Missionary Movement, 36.

Pagan Religions doomed, 135.
Paley's "Natural Theology" in Spanish, 243.
Papers and Resolutions, 271.
Paradise regained will be a city, 127.
Pastor and finances, 256.
Personnel of the Chattanooga Conference, 4.
Peter's sense of obligation, 105.
Philosophy of missionary education, 233.
Physicians few, 46.
Plan, intelligent, 5.
Plan of organization, 20.
Plan of the Movement, 47.
Playing at missions, 49.
Policy of missionary education, 21.
Political crisis in Korea, 186.
Postage stamp a week, 36.
Postage stamp, reading a, 104.
Power of the Church, 75.
Preachers as business men, 79.
Preachers compared to population, 61.
Preachers to spare, 58.
Preaching in Catholic churches, 131.
Presbyterians, Northern, quoted, 14.
Priestly immorality in Cuba, 210.
Problem of downtown church, 278.
Problem of missions, 124.
Problems of the city, 119.
Progress, why slow, 91.
Prohibition resolution, 19.
Protection of the weak, 96.
Protestantized Romanism, 136.
Protestant literature in Spanish, 243.

Publications circulated, 239.
Purpose of Laymen's Missionary Movement, 21.
Purposes and plans, 13.

Qualifications of leaders, 251, 264.
Queen Victoria, 108.

Reading a postage stamp, 104.
Religious crisis in Korea, 186.
Religious experience of Leader, 250.
Resolutions, 271.
Response to address of welcome, 29.
Responsibility, sense of, 103.
Results of mission study, 239.
Revival in Korea, 185.
Revolution in the air, 158.
Rice toll for Christ, 184.
Rich men and missions, 50.
Riis, Jacob, quoted, 47.
Romanism degenerate, 135.
Romanism in Cuba, 210.
Romanism Protestantized, 136.
Rum of the white man, 225.

Sale of a temple, 137.
Saloon in power, 118.
Secretary Taft on missionaries, 35.
Selfishness of withholding the gospel, 134.
Shanghai, the center of the world's news, 160.
Share of heathen for American Churches, 62.
Share of unevangelized for M. E. Church, South, 64.
Skeptical literature in Mexico and Cuba, 244.
Social dynamite, 120.
Soldiers furnished by States in Civil War, 63.
Something doing in the world, 156.
Soochow University, 174.
Southern Methodist missionaries commended, 152.
Southern Presbyterians quoted, 15.

South needed by the nation, 35.
Spanish literature, 243.
Spanish oppression in Cuba, 210.
Spanish reformers, 244.
Spanish treatment of American natives, 92.
Speculation fails, 133.
Spirit of the Chattanooga Conference, 3.
Staley, T. F., 223.
Statesmanship and missions, 56.
Statistical results of missions, 35.
Statistics of Foreign Missions, 286-288.
Stir in the East, 82.
Stir in the world, 157.
Story of Chattanooga quoted, 9.
Strength of Christ, 102.
Strict conditions of Church membership in Korea, 163.
Struggles of Cuba, 209.
Success abroad, 37.
Success at home, 39.
Success measured, 89.
Sunday School Missionary Committee, 273.
Surface imperfections of the Church, 77.
Systematic giving, 256.

Taft, Secretary, 35.
Taj Mahal, 164.
Taunting the hungry, 187.
Team work, 49.
Tenth a financial basis, 16.
Tenth, what it would mean, 280.
Testimonies concerning the Chattanooga Conference, 7.
Text-books of missions sold, 239.
Thanks extended to Chattanooga, citizens, and others, 277.
Thetford, Bishop of, quoted, 267.
Thinking in millions, 105.
Tides of the Spirit, 101.
Tithe the kindergarten of stewardship, 236.
Tithe urged, 16.

Tithing and its results, 258.
Toll of rice, 184.
Trader and adventurer, 95.
Trade with Romish countries, 215.
Training the young, 266.
Transition in heathen lands, 234.
Travel and communication, 234.
Tribute to American missionaries, 90.
Truth in personal form, 73.
Truth intolerant, 132.
Turkey, "The Sick Man," 158.
Turning to the West, 82.
Two sons given to missions, 145.
Type of missionary needed, 215.
United States a world power, 41.
Uprising of men, 66.

Village stage of civilization, 122.

War is on, 17.
War with Japan, 151.
Washington City Church, 271.

Wealth of American Church, 235.
Wealth of the city, 117.
Wealth of United States in 1940, 125.
Welcome, 27.
Western learning, 37, 174.
White, Jose Blanco, 244.
White races dominant, 97.
Why the Laymen's Missionary Movement? 37.
Woman degraded, 45.
Women and medical missions, 225.
Work and its dignity, 263.
World a neighborhood, 159.
World campaign for missions, 55.
World shrinking, 41.
World's news center, 160.

Yellow peril, 141.
Young people a new constituency, 40.
Yun Chi Ho, 154.